Božo Skoko

UNDERSTANDING CROATIA
A Collection of Essays on Croatian Identity

Zagreb, 2018

Božo Skoko

UNDERSTANDING CROATIA
A Collection of Essays on Croatian
Identity

Zagreb, 2018

UNDERSTANDING CROATIA – A Collection of Essays on Croatian Identity
by Božo Skoko

Revised and updated edition.
Originally published in Croatian under the title *Kakvi su Hrvati?* (What Are the Croats Like?) by Fokus in 2016.

Translator
Michael Durgo

Editor
Andrea Durgo

Reviewers
Robin Harris, PhD
Vladimir Peter Goss, PhD

Cover image
Zvonimir Hrupec, Studio 2M, Zagreb

Contents

Foreword												vii

PART I To Be a Croat									1
What Are the Croats Like?									3
If You Don't Behave, a Croat Will Come Get You				15
The Destroyers of Yugoslavia								26
Builders of Europe – Captives of the Past					36
Do Croatian Politicians Love Their Country?					48
Woes with Statehood Day									57
How Does One Become a Croat?							67
The Sellers and Buyers of Freedom							77
Unknown Croatian Greats									94

PART II Croatia and Europe							103
The Battle of Siget and the *Cravate*						105
Part of Western Europe or a Post-Communist Neighbor		113
What Are the Real Capabilities of Croatian Diplomacy?		124
Croatian Variety of Cultural Cringe							138
Why the Danes Are Happy and the Croats Are Not			145
What Did Croatia Bring to the European Union as a
Dowry?													156
Croats Teaching Europe about Islam						167

PART III Croatia and Its Balkan Neighbors			173
Two Truths about the Wars								175
Dreading the Prospect of Regional Cooperation				186
Croats Have Too Many Complexes and Serbs Too Few		192
Who Does Nikola Tesla Belong To?						200
Nation with Two States									210
Međugorje as a World-Famous Brand						218

PART IV Croats and Church							227
The Croats Celebrate the Patron Saint of Ireland and
Ignore the Patron Saint of Croatia						229
The Greatest Dalmatian									235
The Centuries-Long Alliance between the Vatican and
the Croats												243
Pope John Paul II's Promotion of Croatia					251

A Catholic Country Led by Atheists   260

PART V Homeland and Diaspora   269
Unrealized Dream of the Croatian Diaspora   271
Between Assimilation and Return to the Homeland   277
Why They See Croatia as a Promised Land   287

PART VI Made in Croatia   299
Sea and Water   301
Do Croats Have Wine?   310
Why Brand Croatia? How to Brand Croatia?   319
The Fragility of Croatia's Tourist Brand   330
Innovative and Creative Croatia   343
Croatian Sports Gene   359

About the Author   373

Foreword

When introducing a book, the first question is who and what it addresses. As this book has been written in English, it, obviously, addresses the English speaking community, i. e. "The World." There are about 10 million Croats around that world, five millions of them outside their mother country – in the U.S., Canada, Chile, Argentina, Australia, South Africa, Western Europe. They should also be co-beneficiaries of this book.

What we just said has underlined the split nature of Croats ever since they settled between the 6th and the 8th century in the land they inhabit today. This split is the major stumbling block of Croatian history, including the present-day predicament. Overcoming it has always been a major achievement, and the moments when it happened were the most fruitful periods of Croatian history. How did this come about?

One's life is determined by one's surroundings, the eternal space – our natural ecology. The appearance of human beings within a landscape endows it with spirit. Together, spirit and matter, nature and culture, constitute our total ecology. The land the Croats settled in consists of three major regions – the plain, the mountains, the coast – which appear very different. Yet they have much in common. They are built from small, poorly connected and sparsely populated units. Dependence on local resources breeds rural, closed way of life. The village, the fort, and a rural community (the "župa") are the basic units of territorial organization, the city as practiced in Roman times truly comes back only within the last two hundred years. The rural culture of a petty nobleman or freeman is an important component of the Croatian national psyche. Such a milieu may breed mediocrity, but it can also very creatively respond to a well preserved tradition. When a happy balance is struck between the city and the countryside, we have the culture of the Renaissance Dubrovnik villas and mansions, or of those of the Zagorje region between the 16th and the 19th century; the architecture of the Secession and Moderna, or Croatian naïve art. But imposed urbanization is a crime over Croatian total ecology, and Croatia has rarely been a land of the metropolis.

Having arrived as a rural, prehistoric, nation from beyond the Carpathians, the Croats faced the remains of a Roman urban civilization. They retained their Slavic tongue and within three centuries of their conversion to Christianity (around 800) made important steps toward absorbing the old urban order. The duality inherent in retaining elements of the old Slavic faith and culture, and the Latin urban tradition, the native versus foreign, as wonderfully revealed by Radoslav Katičić, has been a constant feature of Croatian history. It is as prominent today as ever. An uncritical acceptance of foreign trash is a suicidal act and, within a contemporary context, a crime even against the broader European community.

With a wonderful sensitivity and skill Božo Skoko guides us through the historical vicissitudes of the dualist historical experience suggesting ways of realizing who we are and how to communicate our character and achievements, our triumphs and failures, our ups and downs. Thus the book is not just an exposé for the benefit of others, but a wise guide to self-realization for ourselves. Not knowing who we are, how can we ever navigate through the vicissitudes of history?

This self-knowledge is of utmost importance in the current, artificially induced duality within the Croatian national body – homeland and diaspora. The Liberation War was one of the brilliant moments of Croatian history, a proof of what a nation can achieve when it unites together. When the war was over, the unity collapsed. Skoko is very aware that if Croatia is ever to become safe, prosperous, and happy, the Croats around the world must unite again. For this the homeland must not treat groups within the diaspora as potential extensions of this or that party or policy interest, but a single body dedicated to the well-being of the whole. The Croatian diaspora is not a monolith block. For example, in the US, it is 90% the offspring of those who had been leaving ever since the end of the 18th century, well-integrated and respected by their communities, a tremendous block of political, social and commercial power. 9% are children of political émigrés after WWII, by now also fully integrated but not infrequently, as victims of totalitarian persecutions, bringing a special zeal to community activities. And finally, 1%, those who had been leaving over the last half a century, top scientists, humanists, experts, businesspeople, looking for more satisfactory careers in freedom and democracy. They are at home among their peers by knowledge and social standing, able to access many a seat of power, and provide leadership for the entire community. Exactly on that basis the diaspora fought alongside the Croats at home during the Liberation War, and in that sign we were victorious. This harmony must be reestablished. Skoko's exceptional book is definitely also a step in that direction. Thus the essays form a single poignant narrative about Croatia's potential and map with authority the road to realizing that potential. A must-read for all friends of Croatia.

Vladimir Peter Goss

PART I

To Be a Croat

What Are the Croats Like?

The Croatian national character

On the eve of Croatia's entry into the European Union I received an email from a Japanese colleague in which he kindly asked me to provide an answer to the following set of questions: What are the Croats like, what are the main traits of the Croatian mentality, what values do the Croats subscribe to and what differentiates Croats from other European peoples? I have to admit that I perceived the esteemed Japanese scholar's request as a daunting task, especially in light of the fact that his field of study is the character and identity of nations. To be sure, satisfying his curiosity would not have presented an exacting chore had I been able to draw on scholarly papers and studies pertaining to his query. Unfortunately, there's an alarming dearth of studies and research in Croatia dealing with this seemingly simple but in reality very complex issue. Complicating things further was my acute awareness of my countrymen's proclivity to quickly express annoyance at other Croats and go to great lengths to stifle any desire to give credit where it is due, especially if the would-be recipient of praise is a fellow Croat. The Croatian expat poet Boris Maruna hit the nail on the head when he wrote:

Number one, they all know everything.
Number two, they leave garbage behind.
Number three, they won't stop talking about revolution and women...

The above is the opening stanza of his poem about the Croats. It is clear, however, that any assessment of the character of a nation cannot be grounded in poetry, however poignant and witty it may be, or in any given set of stereotypes. Not all Scotsmen are parsimonious, not all Austrians are avid dancers of the Viennese Waltz or prone to yodeling at every opportunity, not all Swiss are punctual or have a sweet tooth... Not all Croats are cultured, politicized and aloof as our neighbors the Serbs insist on perceiving us, or envious, lazy and hospitable as the Slovenes, our neighbors to the northwest, like to characterize us. There is at least some truth in every stereotype but, paradoxically and by the same token, every stereotype, by its very definition, is as far removed from reality as could be. One thing is clear enough, though; the characteristics and traits of the mentality of the Croatian people have been forged by one millennia of living on the Balkan Peninsula and surviving every curve ball the turbulent history of the region threw at them. Many different and opposing influences shaped the Croatian national character. For example, in every Croat there are traces of Mediterranean jauntiness,

Austro-Hungarian penchant for ceremonious and conventional, and brutishness harking back to the time when Croatia was the bulwark of Christendom, which the Ottomans, for centuries, tried to bring down in their bid to impose Islam on Western Europe. It has to be pointed out that the peoples of the Balkans resemble one another more than they do other European peoples, just as the British have more in common, historically, temperamentally and genetically with the Danes more so than they do, say, with the French or Italians.

There are many websites devoted to rehashing national stereotypes. On most of them under the heading *Positive Traits of Croats* or words to that effect one can read adjectives the likes of *hospitable, open, informal, helpful*. On the opposite end of the spectrum there are always adjectives which square neatly into the Croatian expression for what all Croats agree is the incurable malady that afflicts all Croats and is the source of everything negative that has ever befallen the nation – Croatian Envy. I, as a full-blooded Croat often disagree with my fellow countrymen, but in this case, again as a full-blooded Croat, I wholeheartedly agree. Croatian Envy is ever present in our everyday lives. We envy our neighbors, colleagues, even friends. We find enterprising and successful people suspicious and it seems that we cannot come to terms with other people's happiness… There is another Croatian expression that goes well with Croatian Envy. The expression is "A pair of Croats always means three political parties". At this point there are 123 registered political parties in Croatia. The Croats are in love with politics and politicizing is their favorite pastime.

Unity seems to be an alien concept to the Croats. By way of comparison, the Americans are content with only two political parties. Why are the Croats allergic to anything that smacks of unity? Why are the Croats so averse to working for common good? Why are the Croats unable to share a vision?

Before I attempt to answer these questions I have to point out that there are examples of situations when the Croats have been united, worked together for common good and shared a vision. And the results were always impressive. There are two cases in point: sports and war. We will always fanatically support our national teams or individual athletes, regardless of the sport. During the Croatian War of Independence the nation was united behind the desire for independence – history does not record such monolithic unanimity achieved for the purpose of driving an invading army out of the country. Today, there isn't even a trace of that unity left. Croatian society is divided along many fault lines, most of them ideological. Foreigners who visit Croatia cannot help but conclude that our country is a paradise but that we are so ignorant that we don't know what we've got, let alone what to do with it.

The impulse to engage in destructive behavior is not present in the collective psyche of the Croats. It comes from a different source. In this particular case nurture completely trumps nature. The aforementioned examples regarding sports and war irrefutably testify to that. There are other instances where the Croats will always jettison Croatian Envy and unite. The Croats function perfectly whenever they have to organize themselves to help somebody in need. But, unfortunately, when it comes to politics and economy they just don't have it in them to present a united front, express support or understanding for a higher purpose or common goal. The name of the game is always "my way or the highway", translating, in practical terms, into "if I don't get something out of it, then I'll make sure nobody does - I'll rather ruin everything than have somebody else earn more than me from the enterprise". We have a significant number of able and brilliant politicians and economists. But, they just cannot bring themselves to cooperate with one another. Paradoxically, they are all aware how the Finns united to make Nokia one of the most successful brands in the world market and how the Icelanders defied the United Kingdom when they collectively decided not to finance failed banks with the taxpayers' money. It is interesting to note that individual Croats only show their full potential if they relocate abroad. Only there are they able to unfetter their talents and thrive – academics, scientists, businessmen, artists, people from all walks of life. This brain drain has been a feature of Croatian reality for centuries. In Croatia, only those with the ability to repeatedly get up after being viciously knocked down have a chance to succeed in their chosen profession or field of work. Success exacts a heavy toll on mental health.

There is hardly a walk of life in Croatia where people don't partake in a nasty and endless game of backstabbing and blackballing. Are the Croats a nation addicted to conflict? Is the fact that most Croats live by the feud a result of the vagaries of the country's contemporary history where the economic crisis induced by the transition from a dictatorial system of government to a democratic one wreaked havoc with the nation's moral values? The renowned Croatian academic Josip Županov wrote in 1993 that the Croats completely misunderstood the nature of the democratic system that replaced the socialist/communist dictatorship and as a result could not create any dynamic at the centre of which would not be a blind belief in the equality of outcome. It was precisely in this heritage that Josip Županov detected the seeds of the anti-entrepreneurial philosophy that was destined to hold sway over the country. His words have proved prophetic. The state of the Croatian education system that promotes and perpetuates mediocrity as the highest expression of intellectualism confirms Professor Županov's analysis and the veracity of his predictions. It is safe to say that Croatian academia today is a nest of rabid anti-intellectualism. And it is safe to say that the situation stems directly from the inability of Croats to differentiate between the equality of opportunity and the equality of outcome. Given the fact that the nation was under Communist rule for half a century it isn't surprising that most Croats instinctively lean towards the equality of outcome as a desirable concept. That is why the typical Croat is loath to see his or her fellow countrymen succeed and that is why the typical Croat will never be able to come to terms with the fact that there are people out there who are better at any given thing and more knowledgeable than he or she is. That collective state of mind prevents the development of market economy and arrests all attempts at modernization. Županov asserts that the Croats inherited from their recent past a beguiling susceptibility to all the trappings of autocracy, explains that the Croats are always quick to seek refuge in self-censorship, especially in the political arena, and concludes that the social environment thus created is definitely not conducive to the development of a modern democratic system. It is hard to disagree with Professor Županov. What he points to are the obsolete schemes of conduct and it is painfully obvious that we have to discard these behavioral throwbacks to Communist rule because they are destructive and detrimental to any given constructive impulse. The utter failure of the Communist experiment shows how inherently ruinous the system really was. Unfortunately, the identity of many Croats is so indelibly grounded in the Communist mentality that they are terrified of applying anything that smacks of common sense for fear of being branded "rightists" or ostracized on account of their going against the grain of the anti-intellectual dictates of the Croatian education system. A large number of Croats are deluding themselves by believing that they are free of all things Yugoslav simply on the strength of the fact that Croatia was attacked by the Yugoslav People's Army in 1991. Perplexingly enough, those same Croats, when criticizing the government, are prone to pass judgment on those they deem responsible for the country's woes by the words "it was better before, during the era of socialism". They are unfortunately completely oblivious to the fundamental flaw in the logic – Communism collapsed because it was untenable socially, economically and intellectually. But, since there are a fair few Croats who look back on that time of constant austerity, poisonous fruits of ideological terrorism and state sponsored denial of personal freedoms with nostalgia, we have to conclude that despite the demise of Communism Croatia has preserved most of its negative features.

In 1990, many Croatian Communist politicians hectically endeavored to embrace democracy. They did what they could, based on what they knew. Their renunciation of the Communist ideology and embracing of democracy consisted of replacing their old-style Soviet-style suits with those of Western European makers and changing their rhetoric. But the modes of behavior and thinking remained staunchly Bolshevik. And, unfortunately, the new generation of Croatian politicians is created out of the same mold. They are fond of voicing declaratory statements about democracy and European values, but if they forget themselves and start talking too much, it quickly becomes painfully obvious that they don't know anything about democracy or European values. They are not intellectually equipped to learn anything with understanding – they can only learn by rote and hence their inability to move away from meaningless declaratory statements. Franjo Tuđman said in the 1990s that the Croatian nation was in dire need of a spiritual rejuvenation after the collapse of Communism, a rejuvenation that would sweep away the residue of totalitarianism. At the time people laughed at him but today his words are considered, and for good reason, sage. In fairness, the Croats had really no time to nurse the hangover from half a century of Communist rule; they were immediately thrown into the meat grinder of increasingly rapacious capitalism and globalization. People were hard-pressed to make ends meet during those years. The media and education system failed miserably to prepare the nation for the new circumstances and lead it into a better future. As a result, today the vast majority of Croats, including most characters who are in charge of various ministries and resources and who should really know better, have absolutely no idea what it means to live in an independent nation state and how to act in the country's best interest. The nature of the collective psyche of the Croatian people is still determined by the serf mentality and, by the looks of things, it will be decades, generations before the nation is free of the constraining effects of that castrated mentality. Freedom means different things to different people, but in all its forms and idealizations it is always a challenge. The victory in the Croatian War of Independence gave the Croats their confidence and self-esteem back but the nation was simply not allowed to utilize the spirit of victory and erode the shackles of the serf mentality. The acquittal of General Ante Gotovina at the Hague Tribunal was just too long in coming. By the time the judge set the general free, most Croats had started to believe, against their better judgment, that there was something fundamentally wrong with the Croatian War of Independence, that somehow our struggle to chase the invaders out of our country and prevent more massacres on the scale of Srebrenica from happening was somehow wrong, or evil. But, all is not lost. Not yet, anyway. Now that Croatia is in the European Union we'll just have to raise our game and focus on our strengths as opposed to weaknesses and show the world what we can do!

One of the most renowned Croatian theologians Tomislav J. Šagi-Bunić wrote about the Croats back in 1981: "Croatian society is not afflicted only by Croatian Envy. There is another, equally crippling malady that retards the nation and I would call that malady perfectionism and it stems, it would seem, from the inferiority complex. Maybe the defect has roots in our history – we have been overshadowed for too long by, and dependent on, our more powerful neighbors. We demand nothing less than perfection from our people and we are quick to discard truly brilliant people on account of a single flaw, no matter how insignificant or small. This mentality simply precludes any given individual to grow and thrive in his or her chosen profession…" The astute Šagi-Bunić concludes: "Because we are sentenced to live in such environment where people are automatically degraded upon showing a peripheral flaw, many inadequate people have the courage to rear their heads and build careers on defaming those who posses genuine talents and are trying to create something positive. For this reason, our society is unable to spawn true experts and committed professionals…"

Maybe one day, hopefully soon, we will be able to overcome our weaknesses, become tolerant and appreciate other people's successes and ideas. Then, we will stop to instinctively reject different points of view and we will have the power to collectively visualize a better future and duly proceed to make it happen. If history teaches us anything, it teaches us that we are capable of that. It has to be pointed out that Croats exhibit many more positive traits than they do negative ones. These positive traits make the character and identity of the nation unique. Eduard Kale listed five invaluable features that the Croats had managed to retain despite all the hardships they were subjected to during the course of their history: patriotism (solely thanks to this characteristic were the Croats able to survive numerous calamities history imposed on them), willingness to sacrifice themselves for others (the story of Crucifixion and belief in Christ the Savior are the main pillars of Christianity but, no other nation is so piously devoted to the ideal of sacrifice for the benefit of others and for one's country as are the Croats), love for one's mother (due to numerous wars and cataclysms the Croats were exposed to throughout history and the resultant high mortality rates, especially among men, the desire for survival focused on woman the mother and consequently the love for one's mother was elevated to one of the fundamental values of the nation; at the same time the love for one's mother became tightly intertwined with the Christian cult of the Mother of God), readiness to help a fellow human in need (caring for the old and infirm members of the community is considered essential for the survival and wellbeing of the community), rectitude (righteousness as a moral value is traceable to the early Middle Ages in various codes of law and is present in numerous literary works and in the ideology of the Croatian Party of Rights). Kale points out that many other peoples exhibit the same traits but qualifies the observation by stating that only the Croats have incorporated the traits into their everyday lives and lifestyle and thus shaped their unique national character.

Many authors note that the Croats are freedom-loving, jovial, hardworking and diligent (this last trait is especially present in millions of Croats who have, for one reason or another, left Croatia in search of a better life to all corners of the world). Bravery is another characteristic that is often associated with the Croats. Napoleon recognised it and many NATO member countries uphold the Croatian version of martial valor as the ideal to men and women in their armed forces. Another character trait the Croats exhibit is joviality. To an extent, that readiness to engage in gaiety is offset by their susceptibility to corruption. Small wonder, in light of the fact that the Croats hadn't known independence for centuries. Any manifestation of defiance to foreign rule had been deemed as the highest of virtues and old habits, as we all know, die hard. With all that in mind it could be argued that one adjective that best fits the Croats is incongruous. On the flip side it means that the Croatian nation is an inexhaustible well of creative energy but on the down side incongruity constantly undermines unity and fuels self-destructive inclinations.

If You Don't Behave, a Croat Will Come Get You

European stereotypes about Croats throughout history

"Heaven is where the police are British, the lovers French, the mechanics German, the chefs Italian, and it is all organized by the Swiss. Hell is where the police are German, the lovers Swiss, the mechanics French, the chefs British, and it is all organized by the Italians." That cute absurdity showcases the European penchant for embracing stereotypes. We unthinkingly tend to perceive the garrulous Italians as good cooks, stuck-up Brits as having a sense of humor, disciplined Germans as industrious makers of quality automobiles and hedonistic Frenchmen as athletic lovers. However, we are all aware that not all Scotsmen are penny-pinching misers and that not all Italians are excellent cooks but that awareness is, for whatever reason, not potent enough to preclude us from subscribing to the established national stereotypes to the point where they actually govern our lives in the context of how we interact with people belonging to any given nation. It is safe to say that all Europeans are victims of stereotypes of, ironically, their own making. We even find some stereotypes funny and neat without ever realizing that they are actually detrimental to the image of the nations in question. Again, the paradox is that most of us are actually well aware of how unsubstantiated those stereotypes are. Some stereotypes remain etched in the collective psyche for centuries. Others are of a fleeting nature, especially if they are formed as a result of a conflict or a deliberate smear campaign, like those pertaining to the nations of the former Yugoslavia. The negative impact of said stereotypes has been the less enchanting the further in time we move away from the conflict that tore Yugoslavia asunder. But, most national stereotypes are resilient and assertive. For a time, as the process of creating a village of the once wide world began to gather pace, it seemed that the reign of stereotypes would soon crumble under the sheer weight of available information. However, no such thing came to pass. People have to cope with information overload and they enjoy ever less time to deal with it in any meaningful way. Therefore, most people tend to oversimplify and hastily pigeonhole. It helps them to function in a world they increasingly fail to understand and makes them able to form an identity. In that sense, we have to examine what stereotypes and resultant prejudices the Croats have lived with during the last few centuries.

One of the oldest stereotypes about the Croats dates from the 17th century and depicts the Croats as warlike, brave and cruel. Mothers of the Protestant persuasion, during and in the wake of the Thirty Years' War, used to admonish their children with: "If you don't behave, a Croat will show up and take you away!" For centuries after the internecine religious conflict Protestants implored the Lord in their prayers to keep them safe from the plague, hunger, war and Croats. Words to that effect are still visible on a wall of the Protestant cathedral in Magdeburg[1]. It has to be pointed out that the war was not only a confessional conflict; political considerations more often than not determined its course and the constellation of alliances. The light cavalry contingent of the Catholic side consisted mostly of Croatian units. The Croats distinguished themselves in many pitched battles and skirmishes and were feared by their enemies. As had been the case in many wars before, and would be since, the Croats had no stake in the Thirty Years' War. Essentially, they fought for the interests of their overlord. During the Thirty Years' War the overlord in question was the Habsburg Monarchy. One reason the Croatian light cavalry was so effective and feared was because they had honed their skills in numerous battles with the Ottomans. The Swedish, German and French troops were quite unprepared for the tactics the Croats excelled in: ambushes, rapid advance and retreat and surprise attacks. It could be argued that the Croats were the shock troops of the emperor – they took part in numerous battles all along the Rhine, around Prague, Leipzig and Dresden. Some Croat light cavalry units advanced as far as the outskirts of Paris. There wasn't a ruler or a soldier in the anti-imperial coalition who did not fear the Croats. Most Swedes are convinced that it was the Croats

---

[1] The city was mercilessly sacked during the Thirty Years' War by the Catholic forces.

who killed their beloved king and arguably one of the finest military leaders in history, Gustavus Adolphus, at the Battle of Lützen. Historiography provides no proof one way or the other as regards the veracity of the theory that Gustavus Adolphus was felled by a Croatian musket ball or saber and we have no other recourse but to consider it a myth, maybe incepted by the king himself when he praised the combat effectiveness of the Croats: "Not even the devil himself is safe from them on the field of battle!" Despite the death of Gustavus Adolphus, the Battle of Lützen (1632) was a Protestant victory, but the Croatian contingent in the battle soundly defeated every unit Gustavus Adolphus threw at them on that, for him, fateful day. At that time the Swedish army was considered the best in Europe but no unit of that army could match the Croatian light cavalry. The name "Croat" soon became synonymous with the light cavalry in the Imperial army, even though the army comprised light cavalry units from all Imperial domains: Hungary, Poland, the Ukraine… The impact the bravery and effectiveness of the Croatian light cavalry had, and still has, on the collective consciousness of European peoples is demonstrable in the title of an Austrian elite cavalry unit in the popular computer strategic game Cossacks: European Wars – the name of the unit in question is, not surprisingly, Croat. In the Thirty Years' War the Croat units were known as brave and effective, but also as cruel and merciless. The legend about "rivers red with blood after the depredations visited by marauding Croat horsemen upon the citizens" is still being told in the Belgian city of Liege. Jean Delhotel, the then parish priest of the pilgrimage site in Avioth, in what today is northern France, wrote that "the rampaging crazy and cruel barbarian Croats" torched, in 1636, the village and its church with about 300 civilians in it. The Thirty Years' War was an extremely violent and cruel conflict and barbarities similar to the one Jean Delhotel described were not the sole preserve of the Croats. For example, the single worst atrocity of the Thirty Years' War was the sack of the Protestant city of Magdeburg in which more than 30,000 people were killed. Magdeburg was sacked on the orders of the Belgian Marxshall Jan't Serclaes, Count of Tilly, the commander of the Catholic force that had been besieging the city for two months. The Croats played no part in the sack of Magdeburg. I am not trying to portray the Croatian soldiers who took part in the Thirty Years' War as less bloodthirsty than any other group of soldiers that participated in the war. The Croats were perceived as exotic soldiers, hailing from a faraway land. That perception, coupled with their reputation for bravery and fierceness in battle made the creation of a whole plethora of legends and myths about them inevitable. One such myth circling around Germany during the war insisted that there was no point in trying to shoot at Croats because they were impervious to musket balls. The myth was so potent that another one soon sprouted from it – people started believing that somehow the Croats were protected by the devil himself.

The Croats were not only seen as brutal soldiers, they were also widely renowned for being honorable. The Slovenian educator Primož Trubar wrote, addressing the King of Bohemia and Archduke of Austria Maximilian II, in 1562 in the introduction to the New Testament written in the Glagolitic script that "the Croats, also known as Hussars, are known as honorable, strong and sturdy men. Every Croat, who reaches middle age, regardless of whether he is a noble, a count or a common soldier, is so courageous and spirited that he is more than a match for any Turk, either fighting against him on foot or on horseback. Croats are also very eloquent when in a position to speak in their mother tongue and imbued with a strong sense of justice. They don't seek the company of women when on campaign but they are fond of drinking and toasting to the health of their rulers and friends, wishing them luck, long life and safe passage into the afterlife." The Croatian soldiers at the time were not mercenaries, adventurers, bandits or unwilling conscripts, but men staunchly committed to the profession of arms. They took pride in the immaculate state of their uniforms. It was the Croats, distinguishable by their red capes, who created quite a stir in European fashion circles by adorning their necks with a scarf tied in a knot. In 1635 about 6,000 Croatian soldiers arrived in Paris and visited the court of Louis XIII. The king was impressed by the fashion detail and his enthusiasm for the "necktie" rubbed off on his heir the Sun King – Louis XIV. Soon the fashion detail, known today as the *cravate*[2], was all the rage at the French court and the fad quickly spilled to the streets of Paris and thence all over Europe and the world. And thus today, as the British historian Norman Davies points out, the Croats, in a fashion sense, have the world by the throat.

---

[2] The French word *cravate* derives from the word "Croat". The English speaking peoples call this fashion item "necktie" but in almost every other European language the word for "necktie" corresponds to the French *cravate*: krawatte (German), krawat (Polish), cravata (Romanian) etc.

The Croats did not earn their martial reputation solely through the agency of the Thirty Years' War. They had been known as fierce fighters for centuries before the war and confirmed the reputation in every war they took part in since. Zrinski turned the Ottoman tide and saved Europe in the Battle of Siget in 1566. Napoleon said that he had never seen fighters "more brave and reliable than Croats". "If only I had 100,000 Croatian soldiers, I'd conquer the world!" he used to say. The Croat Svetozar Boroević, one of the greatest strategists and officers of World War I, rose through the ranks and became a field marshal in the Austro –Hungarian Army, despite the fact that he was a Slav and not a German. At that time only officers of German ancestry could hope to attain the rank of Field Marshal in the armed forces of the Dual Monarchy. The greatest achievement of Croatian soldiery is definitely the victory in the Croatian War of Independence (1991 – 1995). The Croatian soldiers who took part in it continued the victorious tradition of Croatian warriors, putting an end to the imperialistic aspirations of Serbia. In a bid to destabilize the new country, the secret services of the aggressor launched a smear campaign against Croatia after the war. The campaign drew heavily on the perpetuation of the "cruel, bloodthirsty Croat" stereotype. The Serb-dominated Communist party of Yugoslavia had been actively reinforcing the stereotype by demonizing out of all proportion the admittedly criminal Independent State of Croatia (1941 – 1945), which fought on the Axis side during WWII. However, the Communist propaganda makers conveniently chose to omit the fact that the Croats had started the anti-fascist movement in Yugoslavia and that far more Croats had fought against the Independent State of

Croatia than for it. The Serb-dominated Communist regime in Yugoslavia needed to create a boogeyman and a whipping boy in order to consolidate its hold on power. The Croats qualified perfectly on both counts. Small wonder then that the Serbian Secret Service endeavored first to justify Serbia's attack on Croatia and later to reverse the verdict of the Croatian War of Independence by relying heavily on the established stereotypes of Croats as essentially evil people. The smear campaigns in both instances were fairly successful. In 1991, when the YPA (Yugoslav People's Army) and hordes of Serb paramilitary formations attacked Croatia, the then President Mitterrand ludicrously justified mass killings of Croatian POWs and civilians by YPA soldiers and Serb paramilitaries, saying that the Croats had been fascists during WWII. The French philosopher Alain Finkelkraut acerbically wrote in an article for *le Monde*: "The Croats were fascists yesterday and they are fascists today; they nominally prosecute extreme right-wing elements in the their midst whilst in Serbia Fascism blooms undeterred, but that only means that the Croats are better at gimmicks; proclivity to commit genocide is in the Croatian DNA, racism is in their blood, it's a national character trait. This racial perspective of racism makes the aggression against Croatia a legitimate act of self-defense; is there any other way to fight those who are culturally and biologically programmed to kill but to strive to wipe them all off the face of the planet?"

The American sociologist Tom Cushman claims that due to the aforementioned stereotypes and prejudices, the West, at the beginning of the 1990s, simply could not perceive Croatia as a victim of aggression as it did, for example,

Bosnia and Herzegovina. When the world finally realized what the actual state of affairs was the creators of the smear campaign changed tack a bit and started propagating the stereotypes according to which the Croats where "an ancient people with rightist and nationalistic leanings, backward and opposed to modernization", as the Croatian sociologist Slaven Letica astutely observed at the time. It is actually mystifying and disconcerting that many people still subscribe to the inherent nonsense of these stereotypes. To be sure, some people in Croatia, by acting precipitously, or deliberately, give credence to the idea that the Croats are somehow programmed to be fascists. The individuals, and some organizations, in question are always ready and willing to vilify Croatian society. They are fond of describing frivolous incidents as the systematic process of creating a Fascist state and frown upon any display of patriotism, branding the sentiment as a manifestation of primitivism. One case in point is the same-sex marriage referendum; in every other country such referendums are treated as an expression of the right to free speech but in Croatia the detractors of everything Croatian called the referendum a "Fascist agenda". Reality, however, paints a completely different picture. Croatia is one of the few countries in the world where the extreme right exists at the margins of the political spectrum. Unfortunately, certain people, for their own venal gain, insist on seeing the Croats as unrehabilitable fascists. Fortunately, European public opinion is ever less susceptible to being duped by nonsense about the Croats. Some tour guides still describe Croats as fervently nationalistic individuals. However, many more accurately state that the patriotic fervor from the 1990s has waned significantly and that public holidays are significant only because people don't have to go to work on those days.

Many Europeans still regard Croatia as a country situated on the backward Balkan Peninsula, a part of Europe which still functions on the principle of tribalism... But, ever since Croatia joined the EU the trend has been to depict Croatia as a Central European or a Mediterranean country, as opposed to a Balkan one. That doesn't mean that the Croats have completely shed their Balkan character, but it does show that many Europeans are becoming aware of the positive sides of the Croatian national character. Unfortunately, Croatian politicians are not knowledgeable or skillful enough to capitalize on the trend; they are only aware of the Communist dynamic of governance. This is not surprising because the education system they came out of didn't prepare them for the task at hand. Political careers in Croatia are still not open to talent. For this reason Croatian politicians commit one blunder after another – they don't honor agreements, they are militantly opposed to common sense, out of sheer incompetence they rather embezzle than create, often they act contrary to democratic standards and everything they do is, ultimately, detrimental to the country's image.

On the other hand, many Europeans perceive the Croats as reliable, diligent and adoptable people devoted to their families. That perception stems from the fact that large numbers of Croats have been immigrating to Western Europe since the 1960s. Croatia's tourism industry also offsets significantly the negative impact the incompetence of

Croatian politicians has on the image of Croatia. Millions of tourists who have visited Croatia have stated that Croats are friendly, hospitable, talkative, somewhat conservative but at times assertive and argumentative... Clearly the best antidote to negative stereotypes is first-hand knowledge. Only when armed with personal experience do we begin to understand that our nation is no better or no worse than any other. In conclusion, regardless of how proud we are of our martial past (oftentimes in the service of our overlords) it is high time we understood that we are no longer in the first line of defense of Christian Europe and started utilizing our vast intellectual potential and in that way give our contribution to modern Europe.

The Destroyers of Yugoslavia

The potency of Yugoslav and Serbian propaganda during the early 1990s

As the YPA and Serb paramilitary formations were ravaging Croatia, besieging the city of Vukovar, pillaging and destroying towns and villages the length and breadth of Croatia and committing numerous mass murders, crimes against humanity and war crimes, the world indifferently observed the agony of the newly formed Republic of Croatia. As the outnumbered and outgunned defenders of Vukovar heroically tried to ward off the Serbian tide from the east in a bid to gain time for the Croatian army to arm and organize itself, the young republic implored the world to come to its aid and make a stand against Serbian imperialism and the concomitant depredations of the YPA and Serb paramilitaries. But, Europe stood silent, dazed and befuddled, pretending not to understand who was attacking whom in the former Yugoslavia... And all the while media outlets all over the world were showing footage of YPA soldiers and Serb paramilitaries shelling cities and cultural monuments to rubble, killing civilians, including children, committing massacres and atrocities not seen on the continent since the end of WWII... Why did Europe consciously opt to ignore reality?

The question is complex and I doubt there is an easy, let alone overarching, answer to it. However, maybe one possible answer is that we were blissfully unaware of the country's image abroad and how potent the negative stereotypes regarding Croats, reinforced for centuries in public imagination, really were. It certainly took countless months of desperate fighting until we realized that in order to pluck the fruits of victory on the battlefield we had to be triumphant in the arena of public opinion. It is a fact that Croatia was not perceived abroad as a victim of aggression (as we in our ignorance staunchly believed). The vast majority of media outlets around the world insisted on depicting, no doubt upon subtle or subtle not at all instructions from the global powers that be, the situation as "a continuation of the centuries old ethnic and religious strife of Balkan tribes", "civil war", "secessionist republic's bid for independence", "an attempt to rescue Yugoslavia", "a war to protect the Serb minority", etc. (one only has to flip through old issues of the world's most influential newspapers from that time to find that almost all articles about what today we rightly call the Croatian War of Independence are replete with similar spins). It is no wonder then that most people around the world perceived the Serbs as the good guys and the Croats as the inveterate villains who had resurrected the Nazi agenda of WWII. Again, it was easy to dupe the world public because the spin masters had been preparing the ground for the disinformation coup ever since the end of WWII. For example, the Croats had been always saddled with the stigma of being allies of Nazi Germany and resultantly portrayed as Jew haters and co-perpetrators of the holocaust – never mind the fact that there was no all-out state-sponsored persecution of the Jews in the Independent State of Croatia (NDH) and the fact that the Nedić regime in Serbia exterminated all the Serbian Jews in record time (it was the first country in Europe, and arguably the only one, that "successfully solved" the Jewish problem). The Chetniks did the bidding of their Nazi masters throughout the war but their role in what was essentially the Yugoslav civil war from 1941 to 1945 was conveniently glossed over in post-war historiography.

It is not surprising then that, when the YPA attacked Slovenia and Croatia, the world saw the beleaguered republics as wanton destroyers of Yugoslavia whilst in reality they were victims of Greater Serbian imperialism. And the ideologues of the idea of Greater Serbia were the actual destroyers of Yugoslavia. They insidiously used the federal institutions of the country to subvert and ultimately destroy Yugoslavia both politically and economically.

Yugoslavia enjoyed a positive image in the world. It is worth stressing that Western politicians regarded the existence of Yugoslavia as absolutely essential for their geopolitical interests. For that reason the totalitarian nature of the Communist regime was overlooked because it ensured the continued existence of Yugoslavia as a non-aligned state. As such Yugoslavia was a useful pawn in that part of Europe to be utilized as needed to ward off Soviet aspirations to control the Mediterranean. For example, between 1990 and 1995 (when the Internet was still in its infancy) more than 180 books were published in the USA about the Balkan conflict. Most authors were enamored with Yugoslavia and they were determined to ram their perspective according to which Slovenia and Croatia were the evil destroyers of the paradise that was Yugoslavia mercilessly down their readers' throats.

"At the start of Croatia's bid for independence, Croatia's friends among the foreign correspondents in Belgrade and those shaping public opinion in America were few and far between," Berry Brkich wrote in 1994, analyzing the American perception of Croatia. Neven Štimac, in the same year, stated that public opinion in France was shaped, in large measure, by a combination of the negative stereotypes about Croats, disseminated widely by the Serbian propaganda machine, and sheer French ignorance regarding the history of Croatia and Serbia. The French public, including even those who really should have known better, like the vast majority of French journalists, for example, swallowed all the stereotypes and falsified history served by Belgrade, lock, stock and barrel. The proselytizers of Serbian propaganda did a very successful job. Stjepan Malović commented in the 1990s: "Official propaganda was in the habit of omitting and/or ridiculing the national values of all the constituent nations of the SFRY, except those of the Serbian nation, of course. Furthermore, they systematically spread lies about Croats, describing them as prone to hate crimes and genocide. In the West, under the umbrella of Yugoslav diplomacy, the Greater Serbian lobby endeavored to prepare the ground politically for a future Serbian military aggression against Croatia."

The results of the propaganda campaign were painfully obvious. We only need to call to memory the shameful interview the then President of France Francois Mitterrand gave to the German *Allgemeine Zeitung* in December 1991, shortly after the fall and sack of Vukovar: "As far as I am aware, the history of Serbia and Croatia is replete with such dramas, especially in the context of WWII when many Serbs were killed in Croatian concentration camps. As you know, Croatia was allied to Hitler, whereas Serbia was not. After Tito died, the animosity between the Serbs and Croats that had been simmering in Yugoslavia came to the surface. I don't believe that Serbia intends to conquer Croatia. Serbia just wants to redress the issue of the internal boundaries of the former Yugoslavia and have a say in the affairs of the Serbian minority in Croatia."

Philip Cohen's book *Serbia's Secret War* was published during the Croatian War of Independence and created quite a stir in many diplomatic and academic circles in the West. The author mercilessly debunks all the major tenets of Serbian propaganda and provides irrevocable evidence that the Serbian regime enthusiastically served Nazi Germany and exterminated the Jewish population of Serbia in record time. Cohen also reveals that Serbian propaganda heavily relied on manipulation and forgeries to promote lies geared towards duping the international Jewry, and after 1949 the

Israeli public, into believing that it was the Croats, and not the Serbs, who were rabidly anti-Semitic during the war. We know that many Serb media outlets deliberately mistranslated into English and other languages passages from Franjo Tuđman's books in order to portray him as an anti-Semite. The KOS (the Counterintelligence Service, under direct command of the leadership of the Yugoslav People's Army and later Slobodan Milošević), from its inception, was actively engaged in anti-Croatian activities, including political assassinations. Worth mentioning, in the context of the goals of Serb propaganda, is the KOS's attempt to blow up the building of the Jewish Community in Zagreb and put the blame on "Fascist Croats". However, the attempt failed and the main perpetrators fled to Belgrade. Unsurprisingly, the Republic of Croatia, for years, faced the uphill struggle of trying to prove to the world that it wasn't a Fascist-sponsored entity like the NDH had been, and that the kuna (marten) was not a Fascist currency, but that the animal's pelt was used as a means of payment in the olden days, and that the Croatian coat of arms originated centuries before 1941. (In the Benedictine monastery Saint Paul's Abbey in the Austrian state of Carinthia there is a fresco from 1493 which shows the Croatian coat of arms in its present form. The coat of arms was first officially used on the seal on the Croatian-Austrian Settlement of 1526). From today's perspective we can say that for all the successes of the KOS and Serb propaganda, their efforts have ultimately failed. These days almost nobody in the world believes the nonsense still promulgated by the Serbian state sponsored media and its politicians who continue to be hooked on the idea of Greater Serbia.

Serbia has been increasing its propaganda efforts against Croatia proportionately to the pace of losing its hold on the international media. The latest attempt focused on convincing the world that Croatia and Serbia were equally guilty for Serbia's aggression against Croatia! The Serbs engaged the services of a number of leading PR agencies for the purpose. Jerry Blaskovich, in his book *Anatomy of Deceit*, proves that Serbia hired the Saatchi & Sachi PR company and that SerbNet, the official Serbian lobbying group in the USA, hired Manatos & Manatos for its operations in Washington. McDermot/O'Neill & Associates, an influential American public affairs and strategic communications firm, has worked with the David A. Keene company on improving Serbia's image in the USA. There are indications that many American officials have been on the Serb lobbyists' payroll. There is no doubt that the results of Serbia's investment in the services of lobbying agencies included the large chunk of territory the Serbian side gained by the signing of the Dayton Accords 25 years ago. We still live in the shadow of that nefarious outcome of the war in Bosnia and Herzegovina.

On the other hand, the men in the Croatian government were blissfully oblivious to the fact that there existed such things as lobbying companies. The Croatian diaspora made the first steps to improve the country's image and launched various initiatives and campaigns to promote the truth of what was happening in the former Yugoslavia. Croatian emigrants, unlike Croatian politicians, were acutely aware of the importance of how the country was perceived in the West. A number of former Croatian expats opened the

Foreign Press Bureau in Zagreb. Slowly but surely, these efforts started to erode the effects of Serb propaganda. But, trying to reverse the results of decades of systematic state-sponsored vilification supported by acts of political terror at home and abroad was a gargantuan task, as Vladimir Peter Goss indicates in his book *Washingtonska fronta (Washington Front)*. Luckily for Croatia, the conscience of a number of foreign intellectuals compelled them to help the country in its hour of need. It is safe to say that Croatia owes a debt of gratitude to Philip Cohen, who I have mentioned in a preceding paragraph, to the American professor Michael McAdams, whose book dispelled Serbian myths about Croatia and Croats, and especially to the renowned French philosopher Alain Finkielkraut who, during the first two years of the Croatian War of Independence, when the outcome of the conflict hung in the balance with the odds stacked against Croatia, wrote numerous articles for a whole plethora of French papers and magazines in which he defended Croatia's right to independence, freedom, self-determination and self-defense and ridiculed the ignorance and incompetence of many world leaders, including the French president. In one of his essays, triggered by the tragedy of Vukovar, he ironically points out: "In post-communist Europe there are two types of peoples: legitimate nations who write history and enjoy the right to freedom and countless useless nations. The latter do not have a place in histories written by the former; they are not even allowed to make an appearance in the literary tragedy genre, not even when they are slaughtered mercilessly for their belief in freedom! For a long time Europe was locked in various systems of alliances and for that reason any regional conflict carried the seeds of a world war. Now that we have a united Europe, that danger is no more: mass murders are done behind closed doors and civil disobedience is expressed at football games. We cannot and will not allow a mere ethnocide to burst our precious European bubble! Drop dead, Croats! Europe salutes you!"

It has taken Croatia years to mount a viable defense against Serb propaganda and all the concomitant negative stereotypes. And, it is going to take many more years to repair the damage done by decades-long systematic vilification of everything Croatian. The potency of Serb propaganda is visible in the case of the Archbishop of Zagreb, cardinal and martyr, Blessed Alojzije Stepinac. The Communists, after the end of WWII, arrested Stepinac on trumped-up charges and tried him in a kangaroo court. Ever after Serb propaganda has portrayed Stepinac as a mass murderer of Jews and Serbs. In fact, Stepinac was vocal in his opposition to the Italian-sponsored Fascist regime in Croatia. The Croatian War of Independence ended in our victory and the world now knows the truth of what really happened during those years. On the other hand, it seems that we still haven't learned how potent a tool propaganda is and how important it is to have competent and skillful public relations people working for Croatia's diplomatic service. Twenty five years have passed since Croatia became independent and we still do not have a state-run agency whose brief would be to promote a positive image of the country and public diplomacy is still an unknown concept for the people in charge of the country. We still don't create nearly enough content in the media and new media in foreign languages about Croatia and the Croats, mistakenly believing that everyone in the world knows, or should know, by default, everything there is to know about us, even those things we ourselves don't know. At the same time our eastern neighbors, who are better versed than we are at self-promotion and more savvy when it comes to utilizing both state-run media and new media for propaganda purposes, are very fond of defaming us in the eyes of European audiences. It is high time we started learning from our evidently costly mistakes.

Builders of Europe – Captives of the Past

Committees for confronting the past and committees for confronting the future

"The Croat nation has monuments in its language older than any of its brother Slavic nations: hundreds of writers cloaked the Croatian language in eminence during the time when the enlightened leviathan nations of today were but an illiterate mob," wrote Ante Starčević, the father of the homeland. And his claim was right on the money! When many European nations that are powerful today were irrelevant backwaters the Croats had their own language and a rich literary tradition – at that time Croatia was a powerhouse in relation to art, culture, science, politics... Croatian lawmakers passed enlightened laws, Croatian architects and builders designed and erected monuments that are today protected by UNESCO, Croatian philosophers predicted, accurately, the future of Europe, gave birth to Pan-Slavism and etched the concept of freedom into the hearts of Croats. Humanism as a philosophical concept would not have taken hold in Europe had it not been for the efforts of Croatian scholars of the Latin language and literature!

Throughout history Croats played a pivotal role in the development of Europe. Arguably, Croats were instrumental in the development of Humanism in Europe. The Croatian philosopher Herman Dalmatin introduced, in the 12th century, the Arabic concepts of geometry, mathematics, astronomy and other new and re-discovered ideas to Europe. Ivan Stojković, an eminent Dominican priest born at the beginning of the 15th century, was among the first learned men to advocate European unity, unity of Christian denominations and reform of the Papal States. The theologian Juraj Dragišić was another notable reformer. At the beginning of the 16th century he proposed a calendar reform (Pope Gregory XIII later accepted Dragišić's idea and the result was the Gregorian calendar). Benedikt Kotruljević invented double-entry bookkeeping and thus significantly improved European mercantile practices. Ivan Vitez of Sredna as Archbishop of Esztergom and High Chancelor to King Matthias Corvinus was the founder of the Budim Academy and the University in Bratislava. One of the most influential Croats in European politics was Antun Vrančić. Born in Šibenik in the 16th century he was, for 20 years, the key figure in the court of the King of Hungary John Zapolya and after that advisor to the Holy Roman Emperor Ferdinand I. Antun Vrančić's writings, which were extremely influential, were published by the Hungarian Academy in 12 volumes. Juraj II Drašković, an important reformer of the Diocese of Zagreb and later bishop, king's chancellor and a favorite of the Holy See, also made a huge mark on Hungary. The most renowned poet of Humanism outside Italy in the 15ᵗʰ century was Ivan Česnički, better known as Janus Pannonius. The works of this Slavonian ban, Hungarian diplomat and Bishop of Pécs were widely read by European elites. It is not widely known that the writings of the father of Croatian literature Marko Marulić were amongst the most popular literary works in Europe in the 15ᵗʰ and 16ᵗʰ centuries. 19 editions of his *De institutione bene vivendi per exempla sanctorum* (Instruction on the life of purity modeled on the lives of saints) were printed in the 16ᵗʰ and 17ᵗʰ centuries. Marulić was the favorite author of the future saints Francis Xavier, Francis de Sales and Ignatius of Loyola, of Pope Adrian VI, the English King Henry VIII, the French Queen Margaret of Navarre, Thomas More and many other notable figures. Croatian scholars of the Latin language and literature translated the works of Homer into Latin. Filip Ivan Vezdin was a pioneer of European Indology. The most influential Croat in the Vatican in the 17ᵗʰ century was Stjepan Gradić, who was in charge of the Vatican library.

Many Italian cities are favorite destinations to millions of tourists every year. Many of the architectural attractions these cities have to offer were designed and built by Croatian architects and artists. For example, Lucijan Vranjanin built the Pesaro fortress and the palace of Duke Federico III da Montefeltro in Urbino. The palace is considered a masterpiece of Renaissance architecture and it is a UNESCO world heritage site. The brother of Lucijan Vranjanin was an artist. He specialized in making beautiful busts of 15ᵗʰ century European princesses. Julije Klović was one of the most renowned Renaissance painters. Andrija Medulić was the founder of Italian Mannerism and precursor to Baroque. It is indisputable that the achievements of numerous Croatian nobles, archbishops, diplomats, military leaders, poets and educators are etched in the glory and glimmer of Venice and Rome, Austria and Hungary. Most of those prominent Croats were at the forefront of the European Enlightenment, culture and scientific development. Talented, knowledgeable and astute men from Croatia were also active and influential in the European political arena. Croats played important, sometimes pivotal and instrumental roles in the shaping of European history. At the end of the day, Croatia, alongside Slovenia, was the most developed republic of the former Yugoslavia. For years after the break-up of Yugoslavia, Croatia boasted a higher living standard and levels of development than most of the other countries in transition of eastern and central Europe. But, nobody can live off yesterday's glory!

Ivan Franjo Biundović (Giovanni Francesco Biondi), a native of the island of Hvar and a renowned author, historian, diplomat, the founder of the Italian chivalric romance novel and the author of a history of the English civil wars, was, naturally, aware of how important Croats had been and were for Europe. However, he was astute enough to warn us, at the beginning of the 17th century that "we should not be blinded by the cult of our own homeland, we should abstain from despising the achievements of other nations and we should be careful not to boast about the accomplishments of our forefathers." It is as though he is reaching out to us from the past, warning us not to appropriate the glory of long gone Croats and beseeching us to be wise and brave in utilizing our potential, knowledge, energy and imagination to build on the shoulders of the greats and leave another lasting legacy the future generations can build on too.

On closer inspection, however, it becomes clear that Ivan Franjo Biundović's injunction is lost on most Croats simply because they do not bask in the glories of the past – the legacy of the time when Croats shaped the intellectual, philosophical, scientific and artistic face of Europe seems to be long forgotten or, at best, deemed irrelevant. We, unfortunately, find it, for whatever reason, convenient to remain psychologically in WWII and burden our souls with trying desperately to justify the role of somebody in our family who fought for the totalitarian and criminal ideology of Communism by vehemently vilifying those who subscribed to the equally abhorrent and gangsterish ideology of Fascism. As a result, we're in a situation where we argue about which regime killed more people and thus, unwittingly, perpetuate the dehumanizing agenda of both evil ideologies. At one point the situation got completely out of hand and the government had to react – in 2017 it established the Committee for Confronting the Past. The irony of the situation is lost on most people in Croatia though. While it is imperative for the nation to be able to rise above petty hatreds and learn from the past, the fact that the government took it upon itself to do accomplish the task and ram whatever truth it finds convenient down people's throats harks directly back to the time of totalitarianism the legacy of which is responsible for the situation in the first place. We cannot change the past, regardless of how much we would like to. For that reason, we need to start studying history and use the knowledge gained to ward off the demons of Communism and Fascism that still, it is painfully obvious, lurk in the souls of many Croats.

Maybe we can learn a thing or two from Spain. The Spanish Civil War, which lasted from 1936 to 1939, was arguably one the bloodiest civil wars in the history of Europe. It completely tore the fabric of Spanish society asunder. The war started when the nationalists and conservatives, led by General Franco, rebelled against the leftist republican government. Soon after the start of the conflict Fascist Italy and Nazi Germany sent military help to General Franco and the Soviets did the same for the Republicans. The NKVD soon infiltrated the governing structures of the republican forces and ran the war effort along Stalinist lines. Franco won the war and established a Fascist dictatorship that lasted until his death in 1975. During the last ten years various Spanish governments established a number of commissions, removed monuments and attempted to fabricate history in a bid to smooth over the ideological fault lines dating back to the Civil War. But the attempt ignominiously failed – there are still two distinct versions of history and two different collective memories in Spain. In that sense, the situation in Spain is similar to that in Croatia. There is one crucial difference, however. The Spaniards have developed immunity to the ghosts of the past and go to great lengths to avoid being perceived by others in the context of the Civil War. That is why most people associate

Spain with things such as flamenco, bull fighting, siesta, sangria and Almovadar. We should take a leaf out of the Spanish book and start looking toward the future as opposed to the past.

The Croats are one of the few European nations that are loath to make any plans for the future. Some countries, incredibly as it may sound, have already established ministries of the future. For example, South Korea has a ministry called the Ministry of Science, Information and Communication Technologies and Future Planning. The ministry is tasked not only with monitoring successful scientific and technological trends, but also with predicting the future and defining the role South Korea and its citizens will play in that future. Sweden, up until recently, had the Ministry for Strategic Development and Nordic Cooperation, popularly known as the Ministry of the Future. Kristina Persson headed the ministry and this is how she explained her task: "My job is to create new political ideas and long-term development analyses. We try to understand what will happen before it happens, in order to be able to deal with potential problems before they actually occur." When she left the government Sweden established the Department for Strategic Development with the Prime Minister's Office.

At the World Economic Forum in Davos, Switzerland, in 2016, Marc Benioff, the executive director of Salesforce, a successful American company, said that every country should have a ministry of the future. If not a full-fledged ministry then at least a governmental department responsible for strategic planning. At the moment Canada, India and a whole slew of other successful states are working to establish such ministries or departments. The pace of change in today's world is rapid and is getting progressively quicker and countries that want to remain or become successful have to gear their strategic planning accordingly, hire experts and set up think-tanks.

Thoughtful individuals in Croatia realize that strategic planning for the future on the level of the state is a pipe dream. However, there are dreamers and idealists who are not afraid to visualize a better Croatia and, undaunted by institutionalized mediocrity, are trying to act on the visualizations. Unfortunately, there are precious few of these individuals. It seems that most Croats are oblivious to the fact that the country is going down the tube and that the reason for this deplorable state of affairs is a lack of any viable strategic planning. For example, demographers have been warning us for years that the only logical outcome of the current demographic trends is the extinction of the Croatian nation. The European Union, which most Croats perceived as manna from heaven, is slowly but surely falling apart. In Bosnia and Herzegovina the Croats, one of the three constituent nations, are inexorably being supplanted by Muslims from the Middle East. Bosnia and Herzegovina has for years been an important market for Croatian exports. Now, Bosnia and Herzegovina is turning into a strategic threat because the government of Bosnia and Herzegovina is increasingly susceptible to the ideology of militant Islam. Croatia does not boast strong national brands with which we could make significant inroads into the European market.

We don't know how to attract foreign investors and create jobs, become energy-independent, institute a dynamic of sustainable development so as not to destroy the most precious thing we possess – natural diversity and pristine environment...These are acute problems that have not been seriously addressed by the government. To solve them we need to implement long-term strategies as soon as possible. So far, the successive governments have only been able to form futile committees composed of useless so-called experts and academics whose only concern was to pretend to be doing something in order to justify spending the taxpayers' money. So far, no government agency or committee has come up with a clear set of goals, vision and unambiguously defined strategic steps, with clearly defined tasks, projects, deadlines and contingency plans.

In order to put Croatia on the map we have to decide where we want to see our country in 10 or 20 years. We need a national vision – we need to know where we are going and we need to agree on a common goal and motivate the citizens. Joining NATO and the European Union, in and of itself, doesn't mean that much. We can use the country's membership in the EU and NATO to facilitate the realization of certain goals and aspirations. The problem is, we have no idea what our goals are. The time is ripe for recognizing who the truly creative, knowledgeable and entrepreneurial individuals in the country are and use their potential to find solutions to the country's many problems. Maybe we should take a leaf out of Australia's book – in 2008 Australia organized the Australia 2020 summit for the purpose of clearly defining the country's strategic goals and mapping the way to achieving them.

1002 delegates, renowned Australian experts from all academic and scientific fields, gathered in Canberra in order to "help shape a long term strategy for the nation's future". Many meetings of think tanks and various groups preceded the summit and every Australian citizen was invited to share his or her opinion. Ten key areas were the subject of discussion at the summit ranging from productivity, economy, sustainability and climate change, rural Australia, health and aging, communities and families, indigenous Australia, creative Australia, Australian governments, democracy and citizenship to security and prosperity. Most committees were headed by renowned Australians, mostly from the scientific field. The famous Australia-born Hollywood actress, Oscar winner Cate Blanchett, headed the "Creative Australia stream. It has to be pointed out that there was no preaching to the choir at the summit. The experts present there subscribed to different political options and harbored differing and sometimes opposing opinions about Australia's future. However, the differences of opinion only raised the quality of the discussions and facilitated the creation of a viable strategy. That strategy encompassed a clear vision for the future, precise guidelines and coherent ideas. The successive Australian governments then used the vision, ideas and guidelines to create viable programs for their implementation. Australia managed to bring together many Australians from the country and abroad who had something to say and who could contribute to map out the country's path to a successful future. As I have mentioned above, Croatia should follow in Australia's footsteps. But, I fear that this could prove impossible. There are too many useless people with inflated egos in positions of power and influence in Croatia. Any summit similar to the Australia 2020 in Croatia would immediately deteriorate into a clash of ideologies and an orgy of personal insults. Many capable people would refuse to participate for fear of being branded fascists by self-styled government-appointed *scientists* who have never seen a microscope. Government-supported institutional primitivism has forced a huge number of competent people to emigrate and it is doubtful whether they'd be willing to lay themselves open to being insulted by half-literate, self-styled experts at some hopeless summit. The situation would be hilarious if it wasn't tragic – Croatia is a small country that cannot afford to shun a single competent individual. Unfortunately, Croatia is shunning capable, intelligent and gifted people in droves.

If we compare the situation today to that when Croats were the builders of Europe we can say that now we have the whole world to compete with, as opposed to just Europe. Existing in the village of the once wide world also means that the range of opportunities is wider. In any event, excellence, in whatever constellation of factors, demands commitment, hard work, dedication and dogged determination.

We'd be doing ourselves a favor if we learned the lessons from our history. Our famous forefathers, irrespective of the political entities they lived and worked in and the challenges they faced, were able to make a name for themselves and influence trends, political developments and the fate of Europe. They were agents of Europe's development regardless of the fact that an independent Croatia during those centuries was a distant and unattainable dream. For that reason our politicians have to ask themselves – What will our legacy be in the context of the development of modern Europe and what will the role of Croatia be in that process? Our politicians have to be aware that now, when Croatia is both independent and a member state of the European Union, there is no excuse for failure. The lessons of our own history teach us that we could reverse the current deplorable state of affairs if we found the courage to use the knowledge, talent, imagination and energy present in many Croats who now have to exist under the radar. If we did that then we would be able to show Europe that Croatia has what it takes to be an indispensable factor in creating a better Europe. If only we could throw off the shackles of the past and learn how to fly on the wings of the future. If only...

Do Croatian Politicians Love Their Country?

Patriotism and politics

In the context of Croatia, politics is one of the rare fields of human endeavor for which no special qualifications are needed. To be a politician in Croatia one doesn't have to be college-educated, doesn't have to speak a foreign language, doesn't have to be literate in the sense of being able and willing to read books, doesn't have to know the country's constitution and doesn't have to know a thing about Croatian history... Simply put, anybody in this country can be a politician. Since Croatia won its independence many chancers have tried their hands in politics, often with spectacular results – in the negative sense, of course. All they had to do to get into the political arena was suck up to someone high up in any given political party. This begs the following question: Is it required from those who govern our country, its regions, cities and municipalities to love Croatia and its people and strive to work for their benefit? Or is loving Croatia perceived in the political community as a disqualifying factor?

Pope Francis insists on the importance of patriotism and modesty as key preconditions for being able to work for common good and the benefit of all. Many Catholics, those subscribing to different sets of beliefs and/or religions and atheists, beleaguered by the dog-eat-dog nature of today's world, have found solace and a beacon of hope in Pope Francis' philosophy. "Do I love my fellow countrymen, my fellow humans? How can I help those in need? Am I humble, do I respect and appreciate other people's opinions so that I can modify my own and better myself? If those in power are loath to ask themselves these questions then their rule will have disastrous consequences!" claims the pontiff. Pope Francis was selected as person of the year by a whole plethora or media outlets and organizations throughout the world.

Croatian politicians should take a long look in the mirror, dig deep into their souls and ask themselves these questions: Do I even love Croatia? Am I doing this out of love and respect for my country and my people or to satisfy my own venal desires? Some people may say that the questions are irrelevant in the scheme of things. You get elected and you try to achieve results. If you fail, no bother, someone else will get the gig and do better! Love of one's country has got nothing to do with it. At face value the logic may appear sound. However, experience teaches us that politicians who do not love their country and do not possess a sense of responsibility for future generations never accomplish anything positive. Even, from a purely political standpoint, good moves that create something seemingly constructive and productive in the short term are ultimately detrimental to the country's interests because such moves are more often than not made with some populist agenda behind them and for the purpose of obtaining financial gain by the political party or politician in question. Those politicians who care about their country will do everything necessary to secure the country's future prosperity, even if that means losing the next election. Actions of conscientious politicians, even if initially misunderstood, will always be vindicated by history. And for conscientious politicians that is the only reward that matters...

Patriotism is a sentiment much derided in Croatia. Many people in Croatia, absurdly, equate patriotism with nationalism. Those Croats who do not care too much about their country, its independence, values and interests, tend to perceive patriotism as something unnecessary, backward and abstract. They justify that point of view by saying that patriotism is not compatible with cosmopolitanism, that they love all people as opposed to just their fellow countrymen and they claim that patriotism means uncritical devotion to one's place of birth. It is clear as day that they mistakenly equate patriotism with nationalism. Patriotism means respecting your own language and culture, your country's history and natural beauty without disrespecting the culture, language and values of other peoples. Moreover, true patriots recognize the rights of other nations and respect them as much as those of their own country. Therefore, patriotism means love of one's country without any need to glorify it and perceive it as better than any other country. Patriotism also means recognizing one country's flaws. Love of one's country should never take precedence over the truth about the state of the country and common sense. The more we love our country, the more we strive for the truth and justice the better to improve it.

If we all agree on the above definition of patriotism then we'll make it that much more difficult for venal politicians to do harm to our country. If a politician, for whatever reason, values his or her party or interest group more than his or her country then that politician will inevitably be irresponsible, lackluster and biased and his or her actions will actually be detrimental to the country's interests. If a politician is not imbued with patriotism he or she will, without any qualms and for a hefty kickback, sell off the country's assets to foreign companies, corporations or banks. If patriotism does not form a part of a politician's moral make up then that politician will be bought by the country's enemies and, if so bidden, even give up portions of the country's territory, betraying all those who have toiled, bled and died in the service of the nation. Jason Matthews, a former CIA operative, states in his book *Red Sparrow* that any initiative to stifle patriotism is ultimately devastating for the country and its interests. In the book Matthews reveals compelling details about his career as a spy. Maybe the most poignant part of the book is when he describes the process of finding people, in various countries, capable of serving the interests of the USA by betraying their country and then recruiting them as spies. The author claims that the most important thing in the recruitment process is to kill all patriotic sentiments in prospective moles and informers and adds: "In recruiting an agent or *asset*, we were asking him to ignore the instinct of self-preservation, to break the laws of his own country – to become a traitor. And we were asking him to trust that no leak or mole would ever expose him." After the prospective spy has completely jettisoned his loyalty to his own people and his country's interests, all you have to do is play upon his weakness of choice. There are four motivating factors in this regard and one will always do the trick – money, ideology, conscience and ego (MICE), Matthews concludes.

To be sure, not every individual who is prone to fervent flag-waving is a true patriot at heart. Patriotism is displayed through meaningful actions. Unfortunately, there are too many people in Croatia who think that they are patriots by birth. These people are quick to sing patriotic songs, wave flags and display religious symbols in their cars and around their houses. But, when it comes to actions, their behavior unambiguously shows that they do not care nearly as much for Croatia as they do for their wallets, jobs, popularity... No wonder these people rub many Croats the wrong way. Basically they give patriotism a bad name and bring to mind Samuel Johnson's maxim: "Patriotism is the last refuge of a scoundrel." Many countries abuse, and have abused since the invention of nationalism, patriotic sentiments to start wars of conquest, turning their citizens into cannon fodder. There are those who give zealous lip service to the notion of patriotism while ignoring their poverty-stricken fellow countrymen, as if patriotism has absolutely nothing to do with humanity. But patriotism is all about humanity, as Mahatma Gandhi said.

One thing has to be made clear though; those who truly love Croatia cannot allow abuses of patriotism, no matter how crass and vulgar, to turn them into cynics. If that happens then all hope is gone. The temptation to give up becomes even more potent in the face of the fact that there are a huge number of people in Croatia who do not care about the country and would gladly work against Croatia's interests, especially if there was money in it for them. There are also those who still haven't realized that Croatia is an independent country and that the grass is not greener on the other side and those who are still haunted by the ghosts of the past, expecting that Tito will rise from the grave and drag them into the deepest pits of hell should they dare to express love for Croatia. Then there are those who claim they are patriots but by their behavior they signal their deep-rooted belief that they were predestined to rule a powerful Western country but that somehow God mixed things up and as a result they were born in Croatia and now they have to endure the company of lesser men, meaning their fellow Croats. One cannot claim to be a patriot and at the same time be ignorant of the country's position in the world. Some nominally have nothing against patriotism but believe that any expression of it is boorish and that respecting national symbols is retarded. There are those who think that globalization and cosmopolitanism have somehow miraculously rendered patriotism obsolete. They are not aware that the most powerful nations in the world, the very agents of globalization, promote and nurture patriotism and consider it one of the most important strategic assets.

It is important to be aware that patriotism, especially during economic crises, is the prime mover in the developed countries, because it inspires the citizens to raise their game, work harder, be more responsible and more cooperative. In that way patriotism protects the country's assets. Simon Anholt, in his bestselling book *Competitive Identity*, ventures further and claims that countries which want to recover from an economic crisis have to stimulate benevolent patriotism in order to motivate their citizens to work more diligently for the national interests and realize that the future of the nation depends on them. For this reason, Germany, a few years ago, launched a campaign to foster national consciousness and patriotism called *Du bist Deustchland! (You are Germany!)*. The goal of the campaign was to provoke a change in the mood of the nation, bolster national pride, motivate the citizens and their representatives in the institutions to stand up and take responsibility for the future of Germany and in that way contribute to the country's development. The campaign culminated during the 2006 World Cup. The results were impressive – the Germans, after decades of bearing the burden of guilt for the two world wars, were finally free of that burden. Every city was draped in German flags. Millions of euros were spent on marketing and public relations, and many celebrities, leading institutions as well as 25 leading media corporations lent a helping hand. There is no doubt that the campaign was an important factor in the process of the country's recovery from the effects of the financial crisis.

The Germans had realized that nothing should be left to chance and that the initiative to foster patriotism had to come from the top. "If the government is not patriotic, then the citizens have no reason to be patriotic either," the German philosopher Immanuel Kant said. The issue of national pride, patriotism and respect for national symbols is crucially important in all viable democratic countries. And all the Western countries have long realized that a strong spirit of patriotism directly translates into the strength of the nation and healthy economic development. Only an informed, content and motivated citizen can contribute to his or her country's development and participate in its promotion in the world. And in that process of taking responsibility and strengthening of patriotism the state run media, education system and state institutions play the crucial role.

Give everything to Croatia, take nothing from Croatia was the motto of Croatia's first president, Franjo Tuđman. *I love my country* was the slogan of the Croatian Peasant Party during the 2003 election campaign. *Croatia above all* was the rallying cry of the players of the Croatian national handball team and their supporters during the European Handball Championship in Denmark in 2014. Lofty words indeed but also an incentive to ask ourselves whether those who are in charge of things in Croatia are acting in the country's best interest or trying to satisfy their own unscrupulous needs. Judging by the actions of most of the individuals in question, the latter holds true. However, they would do themselves a huge favor if they pondered the importance of patriotism, in politics in particular but also in everyday life in general.

Some Croats say that they cannot be patriots on an empty stomach. They may have a point. However, it is not the nation that is responsible for their empty stomachs, but corrupt politicians who are, and have been, in charge of the country. In that sense, we should take Mark Twain's dictum to heart – Loyalty to the country always, loyalty to the government, when it deserves it.

Woes with Statehood Day

What we celebrate when we celebrate

Croats love public holidays because they get paid time off. If a public holiday falls on a Monday or a Friday, prospecting a long weekend, unbridled happiness reigns in Croatia. Most Croats do not have an emotional stake in Statehood Day or Independence Day, unlike the Americans and the French, who cherish deeply their Independence Day and Bastille Day respectively. A majority of Croats have no idea what any given public holidays commemorates and they don't care. That's why there are no Croatian flags in evidence on Independence Day and Statehood Day.

According to the survey I conducted in 2013, only 35 per cent of Croats know that Croatia's Statehood Day is celebrated on July 25. Two thirds of the respondents didn't know why they get paid time off on that day. A staggering 27 per cent of respondents thought that May 30 was still the main public holiday. Only 15 per cent of the respondents knew that October 8 was Croatia's Independence Day. Almost 23% of the respondents actually thought that Independence Day falls on August 5, when the Croatian Army liberated the occupied territories after four years of Serbian occupation. The poll results shouldn't surprise us, though. October 8 was hastily chosen as the new Independence Day in 2001 – from 1991 to 2001 Independence Day had been celebrated on August 30, commemorating the constitutive session of the Croatian Parliament and the birth of Croatian democracy. For years it was considered normal, on August 30, to hoist a Croatian flag from a window, sing patriotic songs, attend celebrations commemorating the constitutive session of the Croatian Parliament, invite friends over for a BBQ or simply take a road trip. To be sure, there were some people who were annoyed by such displays of patriotism, maybe because the whole thing reminded them of Republic Day, a public holiday celebrated in the former Yugoslavia (November 29)... But first Croatian president Franjo Tuđman was acutely aware of the fact that all normal countries put a lot of stake in symbolism and national pride and he therefore insisted on pomp and ceremony during public holidays. Sometimes he even went too far. On two occasions he organized a military parade, he insisted at every opportunity that a guard of honor, wearing historical uniforms, be formed, at his request the new currency, kuna, was introduced on Statehood Day, he presided over the opening of the National and University Library in Zagreb, he dedicated the Altar of the Homeland monument... Tuđman's opponents sneered at him, arguing that he was engaging in unnecessary posturing simply to satisfy his vanity. Be that as it may, there is no doubt that Tuđman's insistence on pomp and ceremony bolstered national pride. And we should never forget that without national pride a young state has no hope of ever establishing itself as a truly sovereign political entity.

In 2000, when Stjepan Mesić was elected President, the symbolic iconography Tuđman had so painstakingly created in order to cement national pride and national self-esteem started to tumble down. Mesić, immediately upon taking power, set out to stifle every trace of patriotism in the country. He forbade forming guards of honor, claiming, ludicrously, that they cost too much money, he proclaimed that celebrating historical events was tantamount to falsifying history, he refused, at his inauguration, to wear the sash (even though he was bound by both protocol and law to wear it), he discontinued the tradition of laying flowers at the Altar of the Homeland monument and deliberately consigned it to neglect and inevitable dilapidation. And then, Ivo Škrabalo, an influential member of the Croatian Social Liberal Party, the ruling party at the time, in a display of almost Byzantine sycophancy, suggested that Statehood Day should be abolished. The bizarre suggestion was quickly accepted by the ruling coalition. The whole thing was really done to publically humiliate the HDZ (Croatian Democratic Union) party. It has to be remembered here that Croatia won the Croatian War of Independence under the leadership of the HDZ party. The ruling coalition justified its decision by claiming that it made more sense to celebrate Statehood Day on June 25 than on May 30 despite the fact that the vast majority of the population actually thought that the latter date actually marked the point at which Croatia broke away from the Communist system and embraced democracy.

The leadership of the SDP (Social Democratic Party) party at that time consisted of former Communist Party members. It shouldn't really surprise us then that the SDP party jumped at the chance presented by Ivo Škrabalo's proposal to reverse the course of history and also, in a sense, the outcome of the Croatian War of Independence. Ironically, the HDZ party had insisted that May 30 also be commemorated as the day of national reconciliation. On May 12, 1990, the leadership of the HDZ party issued a proclamation to the citizens of Croatia, stating that "(May 30) is the day when the Croatian Parliament was convened and when the leadership of the sovereign Republic of Croatia was elected" and adding that "...the day should remain henceforth etched in the tradition of the Croatian people as the day on which Croatian statehood is celebrated. The day should also mark the moment of spiritual reconciliation of all those who have fought for Croatia under different and sometimes opposing banners and ideologies and serve as a pledge to endeavor diligently and selflessly in a spirit of unity to lead the country into a better future". In national memory May 30 remains as the day of the birth of the Republic of Croatia. We remember how, during the celebrations in Ban Jelačić Square, the newly elected President of Croatia Franjo Tuđman, laid a loaf of bread, quill and a golden ducat as symbols of prosperity, knowledge and wealth, into a crib which was then blessed by Cardinal Kuharić and the Grand Mufti of the Islamic community in Croatia, Ševko

Orembašić. Unfortunately, the importance and symbolism of that event has been lost on the prime ministers, ministers and many other Croatian officials ever since Franjo Tuđman died…

Effectively, former Communists "killed" a pivotal public holiday, one that meant a lot to the majority of Croats. It is reasonable to assume that they acted deliberately, but even if we are to give them the benefit of the doubt we have no recourse but to conclude that tinkering with Statehood Day was irresponsible at best. In any event, the former Communists in question acted against the interests of the Croatian nation, all the more so because they did not do anything to promote in any way, shape or form the events the new date for Statehood Day was supposed to commemorate. The Croatian people, as a result, sort of adopted August 5, Victory and Homeland Thanksgiving Day, as the main public holiday. The holiday commemorates the Croatian Army's liberation of the city of Knin in 1995. For that reason August 5 is, to many Croats, the real Statehood Day and Independence Day. In that sense most Croats reject the public holiday imposed by the former, and arguably, current oppressors of the Croatian people.

Different countries have chosen different days for their public holidays and often the dates do not commemorate a pivotal moment in a country's path to sovereignty or independence. Strictly speaking, July 25, from a historical perspective, has nothing to do with Croatia's independence. Granted, Croatia declared independence on that day, but it did not gain statehood. Historically, Croatia's statehood dates back to the 9th century. Also, after the declaration of independence on June 25, Croatia, under pressure from the European Community, introduced a three-month moratorium on independence and because of that October 8 is commemorated as Independence Day. Croatian politicians remain divided over the issue of which date is more important.

The shenanigans surrounding Statehood Day left many Croats confused and in that sense the results of the poll I conducted are not surprising. Adding insult to injury, the neglect and derision the successive Croatian governments have lavished on the national symbols and national pride have reduced the public holidays to nothing more and nothing less than days off work. The events the public holidays are supposed to commemorate have slowly but surely faded from the collective memory of the Croats. That is why we see no celebrations or ceremonies on public holidays and that is why Croatian flags during those days are so conspicuous by their absence. Many Croatian politicians have publically stated over the years that expressions of national pride are a thing of the past and that there is no place for such boorish behavior in the modern world. The ignorance of those politicians is staggering. And insulting. The politicians behave as if most Croats are mentally impaired, as if nobody realizes with how much pride, love and creativity the French, Americans, Canadians, Germans and even temperamentally reserved Scandinavians celebrate their independence days. They pull out all the stops on their independence days – there are festivities, fireworks, pageants, political speeches, concerts and organized picnics. They celebrate, in an unbridled and festive manner, their history, political traditions, victories, and they bask in their patriotism. Common sense tells us that patriotism is essential for creating a self-conscious and successful community in the globalised world of today. A sage and conscientious politician embraces the values, traditions, and symbols of his or her country. No wonder, because the sovereignty of each country is grounded in the country's traditions, values and political and national symbols. Only stupid politicians, suffering from delusions of grandeur, or those on the payroll of a hostile government, dare to compromise the country's sovereignty by deriding the patriotic impulses of its citizens. Unfortunately, Croatian politicians are very fond of pouring scorn on everyone who expresses love for Croatia. The Altar of the Homeland monument is in a sorry state. Why did Mesić forbid the ceremonial laying of flowers and wreaths at the monument? The location of the monument is appropriate, its upkeep is cheap and while it was regularly maintained it was a tourist attraction. So the only logical explanation is the well attested fact that Mesić hated Franjo Tuđman and wanted to undo everything Tuđman had created. That means that Mesić set himself the task of dismantling the legacy of Franjo Tuđman, ranging from the sovereignty of the country to monuments commemorating the country's struggle for independence, out of sheer envy. If it's not that then we must conclude that Mesić was on the payroll of forces hostile to Croatia. Mesić served two terms as President of Croatia. During his incumbency he never visited the Altar of the Homeland and he only once, towards the end of his second term, visited Franjo Tuđman's grave. By way of comparison, Mesić's successor, Josipović, a committed Communist, laid a wreath at the grave of Franjo Tuđman a few months after his inauguration and he even had decency to honor those who fought and died for Croatia's independence by visiting the Altar of the Homeland in 2011. Mesić wasn't particularly concerned with the fact that the monument at Medvedgrad was going to ruin and he couldn't be bothered with finding another location for a similar monument (Mesić justified his ambivalent attitude towards the monument in Medvedgrad by claiming that it was too far away from the city center). Many foreign politicians, when visiting Croatia, have expressed their wish to lay wreaths at the Altar of the Homeland to honor the Croatian soldiers and civilians who lost their lives during the Croatian War of Independence. In such cases, after Mesić took office, Croatian politicians had to find ludicrous excuses because they were too embarrassed by the dilapidated state of the monument in Medvedgrad. Ivo Josipović, during his first official visit to the USA in 2011, was disconcerted by the experience. He wrote about it in his diary, published in the Croatian daily *Večernji list* on May 9, 2011: "Washington impresses with the representative grandiosity of the state institutions, with the somber self-respect of the state expressed through, amongst other things, architecture and the veneration of the history of the USA, especially of those who gave their lives for the country. The formal, utterly dignified and solemn ceremony of laying wreaths at the Arlington National Cemetery eerily accentuates the absence of a similar ceremony in Zagreb. It would be nice if we in Croatia venerated those who fought and died for Croatia with such respect. It is sad, really, and there is no excuse for the fact that in the capital of Croatia, a country that won its independence only 15 years ago in a defensive war, there is no monument for the fallen for our freedom, a monument at which we, and foreign statesmen and diplomats could lay wreaths in honor of our legitimate struggle for survival." Josipović proved that his powers of observation were sharp. However, during his mandate he did nothing to repair the monument at Medvedgrad nor did he take steps to build another one at some other location. At the time of the writing of this essay a monument commemorating Croatia's independence is being built in the city centre of Zagreb. It is incredible that the wreath laying tradition at the monument in Medvedgrad was discontinued before another monument had been built at another location, especially as one of the justifications for abandoning the Medvedgrad monument was that it was too far from the city centre. (It took 13 years until someone finally decided to rectify the situation – a paradoxical state of affairs because nothing was wrong with the monument in Medvedgrad in the first place!)

The leadership of the HDZ party has announced that they will move Statehood day back to May 30. A noble initiative. However, the damage has been done. We have embarrassed ourselves in front of the world and compromised our sovereignty by tinkering with things that in normal countries are sacrosanct. Changing the date of Statehood Day means another round of fighting among ourselves and another instance of demeaning our sovereignty. Unfortunately, we do not have much choice – the citizens should decide on what date they want to celebrate Statehood Day. One other option is to imbue the current date for

Statehood Day with the symbolism and solemnity it deserves. Having said that, it is hard to believe that most Croats would agree on one date. Maybe all the controversy that has been plaguing Statehood Day for years could have been avoided had Franjo Tuđman convened the constitutive session of the Croatian Parliament one week later than he did – on July 7, 1990. On that day, 1,111 years before, Croatia was internationally recognised for the first time – in 879 Pope John VIII recognised and blessed Duke Branimir. Also, exactly 888 years before 1990 Croatia had lost its independence – in 1102 it entered into a personal union with Hungary. July 7 would have been the date with dual symbolism and nobody could have ignored it. Unfortunately, the date today marks Croatian Diplomacy Day.

In any event, Croatia's new President Kolinda Grabar Kitarović rescued Statehood Day from the doldrums of irrelevancy. However, the controversy behind Statehood Day and Independence Day continues to persist. It is high time we gave the dates and the events the dates commemorate the meaning, purpose, symbolism and pageantry they deserve. The Republic of Croatia and its citizens deserve that, as do all those who gave their lives for our freedom.

How Does One Become a Croat?

Croats by nature or Croats by nurture

I've known my friend Joe, an American, for years. Some twenty years ago he moved, on account of work and family, from New York to Croatia. He says he's reinvented himself in Croatia – the slow pace of life in Croatia agrees with him, he has learned a lot about the history of Croatia, he has mastered the Croatian language, he is an ardent supporter of the Croatian national football team, he adores Croatian beer and traditional Dalmatian music. He raises his kids in Croatia and says that now he can evaluate his homeland from a Croatian perspective. But, the most interesting thing about Joe is that he considers himself a Croat. He introduces himself as a Croat to everyone, including his American friends who have known him for decades. It is important to note that Joe, for all intents and purposes, has become a Croat without losing his American identity – something he cherishes and will never jettison. For him the whole thing is simple and straightforward – he has decided that his future lies in Croatia and, as he is fond of saying, home is where the heart is! I am genuinely delighted by his attitude. It has also given me some food for thought. Regardless of how he feels, do the Croats around him perceive him as a full-fledged Croat or as an American with an eccentric streak? How does one become a Croat anyway? Simply by being born in Croatia? That criterion is too exclusive for my taste. Maybe all those who respect and cherish Croatia should have the right to call themselves Croats. To be sure, Americans view these matters more liberally than Croats. For them, all those who live, work, respect American laws and values, consider the USA their home and pay taxes are Americans, regardless of where they originally hail from. By the same token, those Americans who relocate to another country always remain proud to be American but also acquire respect for their adoptive homelands and take pride in being citizens of the countries in question. Who can say that Julienne Eden Bušić, an American and renowned Croatian author and wife to the late Zvonko Bušić (who spent almost 40 years in American prisons for Croatia's freedom) who has selflessly devoted her life to the struggle for the freedom and independence of Croatia and suffered terrible hardships in the process, is not a full-fledged Croat?

Croatia is not, by its Constitution, defined as a political nation. In that sense, it could be argued that one can be a Croat only by ethnicity and not by any political criteria. That logic inevitably forces us to make a distinction between Croats and Croatian citizens. In the Historical Foundations of our Constitution it says that "the Republic of Croatia is constituted as a nation state of the Croatian people and a state of members of national minorities". Therefore, in Croatia we have ethnic Croats and members of a number of minorities who are, more often than not and due to ludicrous political initiatives, perceived as citizens of their mother states rather than as Croats, even if they have been living in Croatia for generations. To make matters worse, the concept of nation is not clearly defined in Croatia and there is no clear distinction between national and ethnic minorities. Members of minorities are ethnically connected to other peoples, but not necessarily with the political nations in question because they have never lived in the mother countries and are in no way, shape or form affected by the political processes in the mother countries. The idea that nation states are in fact political constructs which give precedence to loyalty to the state and political identity, meaning citizenship, over cultural, ethnical and/or some other identity, has taken hold throughout the world. Besides, the Larousse Encyclopedia says: "A nation is a legal person encompassing the totality of individuals who abide to one constitution and which is different from a single individual because it is the carrier of sovereignty. A people is the totality of all human beings living in one territory and sharing a common origin, history, mentality and language." For example, in France, which is a modern political nation state, everyone holding French citizenship and living in France is perceived as a Frenchman or a Frenchwoman, regardless of his or her place of origin, ethnicity, religion or affiliation with any given group of people. The situation is similar in Italy and Spain, regardless of the fact that the countries are federal political entities. In many European countries issues such as defining national community, assimilation, multiculturalism, immigration and identity are analyzed and debated. In Croatia, unfortunately, these matters are ignored. To be fair, we have started amending the Constitution. Maybe Croatian politicians are afraid that dealing with the above mentioned issues would open a can of worms in the form of the issue of political identity and force them to define what we really want as a country and society. And we are all acutely aware that there is no consensus in the country regarding these crucial questions. The late academic Županov, a renowned commentator on Croatian current affairs, in an interview he gave to *Večernji list* in 2000, stated that "Croatian political elites have not yet tackled the issue of national identity". The situation has still not improved.

Since there are no Croats in Croatia in the context of political nation, what shall we do with all those members of various minorities and immigrants who declare themselves political Croats but at the same time are conscious and protective of their ethnical identity? Most members of minorities see no contradiction in perceiving themselves as political Croats and ethnic members of whatever minority they belong to. And they have every right to consider themselves Croatian – they are part of the Croatian culture and way of life, they are integrated into Croatian society and they respect Croatia... There are also people who have never lived in Croatia but should by rights be considered Croats; like the young Frenchman Jean-Michel Nicolier, who volunteered to serve in the Croatian army when Croatia was attacked by Serbia. The young Frenchman had had no connection to Croatia prior to traveling to the war-torn country to defend it against

Serb aggression. He was captured by the YPA and bestially killed as a POW at Ovčara in Vukovar. Many Croatian Serbs fought for Croatia during the Croatian War of Independence. Can we, in all honesty, say that they are not political Croats, especially if that is how they, rightly, perceive themselves? How else can we perceive ethnical non-Croats who live in Croatia and respect the country and form part of our culture, like my American friend Joe, than as political Croats? To say that someone who has chosen Croatia as his or her new home and enriched the country with his or her expertise or cultural heritage is not a Croat because he or she was not born within the country's borders is to discriminate against them in the name of the dubious ethnic purity. Today, Croatia would be a lot worse off without the contribution of members of other peoples who considered themselves Croats or who have retained their citizenship but lived, and died, unreservedly for Croatia. Insisting exclusively on ethnic background or religious affiliation would be sanctimonious in the extreme. By the same token, insisting on belonging exclusively to a minority would be equally sanctimonious, as the former President Josipović cautioned, in a debate with the President of the Serbian National Council Milorad Pupovac, saying that putting undue emphasis on someone's ethnicity was reducing members of ethnic minorities to pawns in the ethno business. At the end of the day, can anyone, in the right mind and with a moral compass, who was born in Croatia and enjoys the rights and freedoms guaranteed by the Croatian Constitution, decide to act against the interest of Croatia for the benefit of his or her mother country? The equation is, of course, not as clear-cut as it may appear –

members of minorities may feel, to a lesser of higher extent, ostracized or, due to changing geopolitical circumstances, may decide to hedge their bets and have a foot in both camps. Inevitably, everything boils down to good will. Without good will on the part of everyone concerned, Croatia will continue to carry the burden of civil strife and pointless and ultimately purposeless referendums.

Today, the greats of the Croatian National Revival are synonymous with honest Croatianness and complete devotion to the idea of national unity. Ironically enough, a number of those great individuals were not ethnic Croats. Some were not even born in Croatia. But, that did not prevent them from loving Croatia and did not diminish their patriotism and sense of belonging to the Croatian nation. For example, the great Croatian leader of the National Revival Dimitrije Demeter was an ethnic Greek and Ferdo Livadić was born in Celje (Slovenia) as Ferdinand Wiesner. The first Croatian professional writer and one of the leaders of the Illyrian Movement was a Slovene. His real name was Jakob Frass, but, enchanted with the ideals of the Illyrian Movement he renounced his mother tongue and his Slovene ethnicity. It is interesting to note that France Prešeren[3] resented Frass' infatuation with the Illyrian Movement. Vatroslav Lisinski, a great Croatian composer and the author of the first Croatian opera *Love and Malice* was born in Zagreb into a Slovenian-Jewish family as Ignac Fuchs. Like Frass he was also enraptured by the intellectual and, it is safe to say, spiritual weight of the Illyrian Movement to the point of changing his name. Thanks to Vatroslav Lisinski the

[3] France Prešeren (1800 – 1849) was a famous Slovenian poet.

Croats became the third nation in Europe, after the Germans and the Russians, to have a national opera. The Croatian beatus Ivan Merz was a Sudeten German on his father's side and his mother was a Jew. The great Croatian composer Boris Papandopulo was the son of a Russian-Greek noble named Constantine and Maja Strozzi-Pečić, a successful Croatian opera singer who was Italian on her father's side and Czech on her mother's side. If we followed the argument by which one has to be of pure Croatian blood to be called a Croat to its logical conclusion then we would have to dig up all the mentioned Croatian greats from their graves and perform a DNA analysis on their bones to see if we can call them Croatian. Let us take a closer look at the Strozzi family. The Strozzis were originally Italian nobles who fled from Florence to Zagreb. Their descendants have an honored place in Croatian culture: stage actress Marija Ružička-Strozzi, her son, actor, director and writer Tito Strozzi, her daughter, opera singer Maja Strozzi-Pečić and her son, actor and conductor Boris Papandopulo. One would be hard-pressed to find in the history of European culture, a family that made such an indelible mark on art in one country over the course of several generations. When Tito Strozzi, before the outbreak of World War I, wanted to leave Zagreb and continue his career in Vienna his mother Marija, flabbergasted by her son's intentions, wrote him a sharp letter, in German: "Tito, how can you, as a Croat, even think of leaving your homeland?" Can anybody in their right mind claim that Marija and her son were not Croats?

Many people in Croatia are not aware of the fact that the composer of the Croatian national anthem, Josip Runjanin, by profession an officer in the Austro-Hungarian army, was an Orthodox Christian who spent his retirement years in Novi Sad, where he died and was buried. His faith did not prevent him from loving Croatia and did not, in any way, shape or form weaken or curtail his loyalty to Croatia. His example clearly shows us that we cannot equate Catholicism with Croatian national identity. The Austro-Hungarian Field Marshal Svetozar Boroević was also an Orthodox Christian but he unequivocally declared himself a Croat. The great poet, author of *Kameni spavač* (Stone Sleeper) and *Modra Rijeka* (Blue River), Mehmedalija Mak Dizdar was a Muslim from Herzegovina. By nationality he was a Croat. There are also cases of Croats, Catholics by birth, who converted to other religions and considered themselves belonging to different ethnicities. Josip Pančić, a renowned botanist, known to every schoolboy and schoolgirl by his Serbian spruce (Picea omorika), was born in Bribir as a Catholic and Croat, but later in life he converted to Orthodox Christianity and became a naturalized Serb, changing his name to Josif. Religion and ethnicity should not be agents of exclusion, or disqualifying factors. Many Croatian greats were not born in Croatia and were not ethnically Croatian. The German Hermann Bollé, born in Cologne, spent most of his working years in Croatia, building some of the most imposing pieces of architecture in Croatia; the Mirogoj Cemetary arcades, the Museum of Arts and Crafts, the Basilica of the Mother of God in Marija Bistrica and the Đakovo Cathedral, to name just a few. Slavoljub Eduard Penkala is another case in point. He was born in what is today Slovakia. He and his wife decided to move to Croatia, where he was offered a job in the state administration. Soon he was so taken by Croatia and its people that he added the name Slavoljub to his legal name and became a naturalized Croat. Another example is Gustav Janeček. He was born in what is today the Czech Republic and is considered the father of the chemical sciences in Croatia. In 1879 he was appointed Associate Professor. He prompted the building of two chemical institutes and he established the precursor of what is today the Faculty of Pharmacy and Biochemistry. In 1918 he founded the Isis pharmaceutical wholesaler– the precursor of what is today the *Medika* factory, and in 1921 he founded the *Kaštel* factory, today's *Pliva*. In 1998, commemorating the 150th anniversary of Janeček's birth, a memorial plaque was put up on his house in Zagreb. It reads: "By birth he was a Czech, by life and deed he was a Croat." The same could be said about many great Croats.

On the other hand, can anyone prevent the Slovaks from considering Penkala their own, the Czechs from celebrating the greatness of Janeček, the Hungarians from hailing Zrinski as their hero? Of course not, because what we rightly consider our own, other people can rightly consider their own as well. One thing by no means excludes the other. The greatness of the individuals mentioned above, and many others, their creativity, their ability to tolerate, appreciate and celebrate differences among peoples can build new bridges of friendship and cooperation among nations. Can we afford to call those great people who gave their utmost for the benefit of Croatia and who embraced Croatia as their homeland something else than Croats? There are thousands of people like them living in Croatia right now. Giving them the status of political Croats would change nothing at all in their professional lives and in and of itself would not enhance their love of Croatia. But, they would not feel, in their dark hours, like second-class citizens. For that reason, the legislators and those responsible for amending the Constitution should do what they are paid for and redefine the Preamble to the Croatian Constitution.

The Sellers and Buyers of Freedom

*14 object lessons from the Republic of Ragusa Croatia
cannot afford to ignore*

Researching the history of the Republic of Ragusa (present-day Dubrovnik), I found myself thinking that most countries in the world would gladly give their national gold reserves to have something like the Republic of Ragusa in their history. I think it is fair to say that the national gold reserve of any country does not match the tourist, financial and political potential inherent in the story of the Republic of Ragusa. That tiny state managed to retain its freedom and independence for centuries in the face of acquisitive aspirations of great powers in the region that many consider to be the crucible of history, irrespective of any particular time-period. As many political entities and peoples, big and small, disappeared from the map of Europe, the Republic of Ragusa prospered, developing its economy and agriculture, culture and science. Its education system spawned many great historical figures. The Republic's diplomacy was audacious and highly effective. It created an efficient spy network. The abilities of any intelligence agency today fall way short of the feats the Republic of Ragusa's spies achieved. The Republic of Ragusa had the smallest war fleet and largest merchant fleet in the Mediterranean. Its merchant fleet was the third largest in the world and the Republic was one of the rare states that traded both with the East and the West. Based on successful trade and mediation the Republic got rich. The wealth of the Republic was considerable but the Ragusans were not in the habit of flouting it, especially not in front of uninvited guests. The Republic of Ragusa had a unique system of governance. The Republic issued its Statute, grounded in the traditions of the Republic and the ideal of sovereignty, as the basis of the legal order in 1272. It managed to stamp out corruption and nepotism and create a political system that guaranteed equal protection of the law to all citizens (the Ragusans were fond of saying that justice creates unity and fosters peace and that their city was protected both by its laws and its walls). The Ragusans built imposing city walls (for a time anyone entering the city was required to bring a stone of a certain size for the city walls). Today the city walls are one of the most famous tourist attractions in the world. The city had a sewage system in the Middle Ages (1296). In 1377 the Republic started to quarantine travelers, in 1416 it abolished slave trade – 400 years before Britain. The Republic of Ragusa was among the first to recognize the independence of the United States of America (1783). It published the first European treatise on trade and accounting (Benedikt Kotruljević, 1458). The Ragusan Maritime Insurance Law (1568) is the oldest such law in Europe. The first orphanage in Europe was opened in Ragusa (1432). The *Mala braća* pharmacy is the third oldest in Europe. It was opened in 1317 and has been continuously in business to this day. The granary of Ragusa, built in 1590, is a unique architectural structure – an underground silo three levels deep, where 1,500 tons of grain could be stored, enough to feed the entire population of Ragusa for over a year. For centuries the Ragusans enjoyed a significantly higher standard of living than any other community in Europe. For example, in 1438 they built a complex aqueduct system, over 12 kilometers long, which ended in a fountain in the city centre. The fountain is called Onforio's fountain. It was named after its builder, Onforio of Naples. Architects today are astonished by the fact that the drop from the source to the fountain is only 20 meters. In many ways the Ragusans were well ahead of their time... They did not try to emulate other European peoples and communities; they invented their own solutions and thus were at the forefront of scientific, social and economic development in Europe.

In 2016, Croatian Television (HRT) produced a documentary series about Dubrovnik called *Republika*. The director, Domagoj Burić, used re-enactment to great effect and the show became very popular in Croatia. The show also runs on a number of foreign TV networks. The episodes were met by positive reception from critics and viewers. The show actually brought Dubrovnik, a jewel of world and European history, out of obscurity and introduced it to millions of people around the world. The educational aspect of the show gelled well with its high entertainment value, and Croatian tourism and, at least to an extent, diplomacy, will reap the benefits of the show's international popularity for years to come. The producers of *Game of Thrones* recognised the visual value of the city walls and used the city as the setting for King's Landing. Needless to say, the exposure Dubrovnik got from the *Game of Thrones* show is incomparably higher than that provided by the documentary series, but for me personally, it was much better to see Dubrovnik play itself in the documentary than King's Landing in the TV rendition of George R.R. Martin's books. Despite the success of the documentary and the popularity garnered from appearing on the Game of Thrones show and despite the fact that Dubrovnik is the most famous Croatian city and, hands down, the most favorite tourist destination in this part of Europe, we have to be honest and acknowledge that we, and the world, know far too little about the history of the Republic of Ragusa. That state of affairs is rather sad because those well-versed in the subject of Dubrovnik's history will tell you that many legislators, diplomats, merchants, artists, seamen, and intelligence officers around the world could draw inspiration from Dubrovnik's example. Dubrovnik is not only the city walls that millions of tourists visit every year. The city's story, if told the right way, has the potential to become the best and most viable Croatian export and serve as a remainder to everyone that Croats were ahead of the rest of Europe for centuries in many different fields of human endeavor. "The internal system of the Republic of Ragusa was a fascinating and enduring combination of governing rationality, pragmatism and staunch patriotism. The words of the maxim written on a wall in the Rector's Palace: *Obliti privatorum, publica curate* (Forget private, take care of public interests) were, forgive the pun, cast in stone. Every citizen was prepared to give his or her all for the benefit of the Republic," said the director of the *Republika* documentary series in an interview for *Slobodna Dalmacija*.

Dubrovnik was, from the middle of the 11th century, closely connected to the Croatian kingdom and its successor polities and the sources from that period unequivocally tell us that the citizens of the republic considered themselves Croats. Today's independent and sovereign Croatia should really act as the defender of the political, economic, scientific, cultural and social practices of the Republic of Ragusa. Unfortunately, the leaders of modern Croatia seem to be completely unaware of the history of the Republic of Ragusa. If they are then the lessons that history teaches are lost on them. I have taken the liberty of picking 14 lessons the history of the Republic of Ragusa gives us that the Croatian politicians should take to heart: Liberty and independence are sacrosanct – liberty and independence should not be compromised, no matter what; The country cannot prosper if its citizens and leaders are not imbued with a sense of patriotism; Diplomacy is one of the most potent weapons a country could utilize, and every move in that arena has to be carefully thought through and nothing should be left to chance; Information, if used correctly, translates into power; Small countries are not necessarily at a disadvantage on the world stage; It is important what others think about you – image is all-important and it is of paramount importance to invest money and effort into presenting the country in the best light possible; The geopolitical position between great powers can be a significant source of income; Alliances in politics shift according to current interests and global developments; Everyone should respect the law and laws should not be frequently changed; Power corrupts and there should be checks and balances; Public interests take precedence over private interests and the community is more important than the individual; Personality cults should be opposed tooth and nail, but, at the same time it is necessary to give credit where credit is due; Culture and science, as assets of the state, are not absolute values; constant improvement and development are necessary and stagnation leads to disaster.

Ivan Gundulić, the most prominent Ragusan poet and playwright, wrote in the 1620s:

Oh beautiful, dear, sweet Freedom,
The gift in which the God above hath given us all blessings,
Oh true cause of all our glory,
Only adornment of this Grove,
All silver, all gold, all men's lives
Could not purchase thy pure beauty!

Many people in Croatia consider the poem as the most alluring and elegant work of poetry ever written. Be that as it may, the real strength of the poem, in my opinion, lies in the fact that the lines testify to how much the citizens of the Republic of Ragusa cherished their liberty and independence. The word *libertas* (liberty) takes the pride of place on the flag of the Republic of Ragusa. This is not a coincidence because the belief in liberty was the driving force on which the existence of the Republic of Ragusa was predicated. Many citizens gladly sacrificed their lives for the freedom and independence of the Republic. Many others worked tirelessly to preserve it – by hook or by crook... On numerous occasions the Republic paid tribute to other rulers. At times the Republic even recognised the authority of this or that potentate. However, it never bent its knee under duress; it was always a calculated decision to gain some political or economic advantage and the leaders of the Republic always made sure that the subordinate status was not binding in the long run. The French consul to the Republic of Ragusa André Alexandre le Maire wrote in 1764: "The Republic of Ragusa is the only polity that has discovered the secret of how to subordinate itself to many rulers but still retain its freedom. The Republic recognizes many masters at the same time, without actually serving any." The Republic was threatened by the Byzantine Empire, the Ottoman Empire, various Christian kingdoms of Western Europe but it was never formally a part of any empire, kingdom or larger state... The Republic of Ragusa recognised the suzerainty of the Republic of Venice from 1205. In 1358, unhappy with the Venetians, the Ragusans pledged allegiance to the Croatian-Hungarian king. Formally that meant recognizing the king's authority but in practice it marked the birth of the independent Republic of Ragusa. The Republic signed a number of treaties with the Ottomans before they invaded Europe. The treaties proved extremely advantageous to the Republic when the Ottomans conquered large portions of the Balkan Peninsula. The Ragusans knew that alliances were fragile agreements and were good at predicting changes in the geopolitical situation of the region. Croatia should really follow the Republic of

Ragusa's example. Since Croatia's independence was internationally recognized, successive Croatian governments have been making wrong diplomatic moves with, to put it mildly, regrettable results. We did show that we appreciate our freedom and independence during the Croatian War of Independence. The sacrifices the Croatian nation had to make during the war were great. Unfortunately, since emerging victorious from the war Croatia has lost its economic freedom and independence and entered into a relationship with foreign banks and international institutions that can best be described as indentured servitude. The Republic of Ragusa was very careful to avoid such traps. Modern Croatia, for whatever inexplicable reason, is not.

The leaders of the Republic of Ragusa were consummate professional statesmen and patriotic to a fault. Many of them risked life and limb in the interests of the community – like ambassadors Nikolica Bunić and Jaketa Palmotić, who willingly submitted themselves to torture and humiliation by the Turkish vizier Kara Mustafa while trying to negotiate a deal favorable to the Republic of Ragusa. The question we need to ask ourselves is whether any of the Croatian politicians would be prepared to risk their lives for Croatia. I don't think they would. They have proven time and again that they value their tenures and salaries above the Croatian nation. It is actually ironic that the salaries the Croatian politicians enjoy come from the very tax payers whose interests these nefarious characters are supposed, and are actually obligated, by the Constitution of the Republic of Croatia, to fight for. Yet the results of everything they do are demonstratively detrimental to the interests of the Croatian tax payers.

"Whereas almost all other peoples strive to increase their power by force, sword, weapons and treachery, this Dubrovnik community has increased its sphere of influence solely through friendliness and the means of peace. (...) They harbor the attitude that it is better to keep the existing peace by any means necessary than to seek redress through more injustice and injury. The attitude is laudable," wrote Philip de Diversis in 1440 in his treatise *Description of the Famous City of Ragusa*. He did not hide his astonishment at how the Republic of Ragusa was spreading its influence and bending other communities and empires to its will solely by means of diplomacy.

The diplomacy of the Republic of Ragusa was widely considered one of the finest and most efficient in Europe. Those who were deemed fit to enter the diplomatic service were carefully picked and painstakingly trained. When, after years of preparation, they were finally ready to serve as diplomats, they were given precise and clear instructions. The Ragusan diplomats were extremely knowledgeable individuals and exceptionally skilled negotiators. The other qualities a diplomat in the service of the Republic of Ragusa had to possess were cunning and the ability to act and perform. Whenever it was needed the Ragusan diplomats would burst into tears in front of European rulers to provoke sympathy for the Republic. When dealing with Ottoman sultans and administrators the diplomats used all their powers of eloquence to lavish endless streams of compliments on the Turks. Whenever the Republic was threatened by a kingdom or an empire, its diplomats offset the danger by finding a sympathetic ruler and then playing both sides against the middle. The goal of the Republic's diplomacy was to keep the Republic neutral in order to ensure safe passage for the ships of its merchant navy everywhere and thus protect its trading interests. In the 12th and 13th centuries they signed trading agreements with a number of Dalmatian, Italian and Balkan cities, solidifying their trade monopolies in practically the whole of Southeast Europe. In the 13th century the Republic of Ragusa traded with Egypt, Tunisia and other communities in North Africa. It is safe to say that Ragusan diplomats were the architects of the Republic's golden age in the 16th century. They adroitly took advantage of the geopolitical position of the Republic at the time, nestled right between the respective spheres of interests of the great powers of the age. The pivotal diplomatic coup was a treaty with the Ottoman Empire according to which the Republic of Ragusa was to pay tribute to the sultan and nominally accept his suzerainty. In reality, the Republic retained its independence and freedom and, more importantly, received the right to trade in all the territories of the Ottoman Empire, thus retaining all its key bases and trading outposts on the Balkan Peninsula – essential as sources of raw materials needed for the Republic's international trade. The Republic of Ragusa at that time enjoyed a privileged status in the Ottoman Empire. An example of the influence of the Republic of Ragusa on the Ottoman Empire is St. Mary's Church in the Bulgarian capital Sofia, also known as the Ragusan church. For a long time this was the only church in the East where Catholics were allowed to go to Mass. Important trading partners of the Republic of Ragusa were communities of Italy and Spain. The latter was a true friend and protector of the Republic of Ragusa.

Croatian diplomacy, it is painfully obvious, is still in its infancy. The example of the Republic of Ragusa means nothing to the leaders of the modern state of Croatia. The Ragusans knew that a large diplomatic corps was not a drain on the treasury, if the diplomats were talented and adequately trained. Even though the territory of the Republic was very small, with a total area just over 1,000 square kilometers, in the 18th century it had more than 85 consulates all over the globe, twice as many as some of the significantly larger countries. It is hard to resist jibing at the Republic of Croatia's diplomats here; the diplomatic corps of the Republic of Ragusa did not consist of half-literate people, yes-men completely oblivious of even the dictionary definition of diplomacy, bureaucrats at heart who are only interested in covering their backside, and similar weirdoes. The jibe may seem unwarranted, but given that the Republic of Ragusa's diplomats achieved impressive results time and again, that they were constantly under scrutiny from their peers and superiors and that mistakes were not tolerated, the stark difference between the diplomatic corps of the Republic of Ragusa and modern Croatia is simply too imposing to ignore. The diplomats of the Republic of Ragusa were well ahead of their time. Only about 15 years ago did modern European countries start insisting that a modern diplomat had to also act as a PR agent of his or her country.

The diplomats of the Republic of Ragusa knew that 500 years ago.

Ragusa, in the Middle Ages, was the spy capital of Europe because the Ragusans were well aware that information translates easily to power and influence. Ragusa was positioned right between the Ottoman Empire and Christian Europe and many spies from both sides traveled to Ragusa to glean as much information about the other side as possible, and maybe gain an insight into the other side's intentions. The Ragusans were shrewd intermediaries. They sold, dearly, information about the situation in the West to the Ottoman Empire and equally dearly information about what the sultan plans were to the West. Of course, they were careful to use whatever piece of information to their utmost advantage. Both Christian Europe and the Ottoman Empire perceived the Republic of Ragusa as an indispensable ally. Little did they know that the Ragusans were duping them both. That game of hide and seek with the great powers was deadly, dangerous and did not suffer fools. A single mistake could prove fatal to the Republic. The Republic of Ragusa had to, in order to ensure its survival, hone its intelligence system to perfection. And that was exactly what it did. It is safe to say that Ragusa's spies invented industrial espionage. The Republic of Ragusa's spy networks utilized everything and everybody, even the monks (Benedictine monasteries were built on top of cliffs and other vantage points for the purpose of monitoring shipping in the Adriatic). No expense was spared to acquire useful information that could be in turn peddled for profit or other tangible political gain. Traitors were punished severely. The intelligence services of the Republic of Croatia have a lot to learn from the Republic of Ragusa; instead of wasting time, money and effort on wiretapping the phones of political analysts they should use their infinite resources to finally start pulling their weight and gain political advantage for Croatia. Even the tiniest of successes in that regard would be a huge improvement.

The Ragusans had a reputation as trustworthy dealers of reliable information in espionage circles. They also took great care to present themselves to others in the most favorable light – they were aware of the importance of image. The Ragusans were careful not to flaunt their wealth because they wanted to be perceived as modest. It was important for them to come across as honest, principled and friendly. The charm and charisma thus established was then turned into what Joseph Nye would term "soft power" five centuries later. According to Nye, "a country may obtain the outcomes it wants in world politics because other countries – admiring its values, emulating its example, aspiring to its level of prosperity and openness – want to follow it. In this sense, it is also important to set the agenda and attract others in world politics, and not only to force them to change by threatening military force or economic sanctions. This soft power – getting others to want the outcomes that you want – co-opts people rather than coerces them". It is as though Nye had the Republic of Ragusa in mind when he came up with the definition. The Ragusans spent a great deal of money on culture and science, far more, relatively speaking, than most developed countries do today. The notion that culture and science should be used as leverage to establish the Republic as a major player in the geopolitical landscape of the age was a generally accepted article of faith in Ragusa. That dogged determination to be a successful political player spawned many European leviathans of science and culture – Sorkočević, Božidarević, Nalješković, Bunić, Vučić, Držić, Bošković, Gradić, Getaldić, Gundulić, Palmotić and many others. The accomplishments of these natives of Ragusa serve as a more potent tool of country branding than anything our government has been able to come up with. Does our current government, then, need any more incentive to make alterations to the system of budged distribution?

The Ragusans realized early on in their history that the small size of their polity was not necessarily a disadvantage and that their position between the East and West was not a curse but a blessing – and one that could be very lucrative. The Republic of Ragusa's insistence on neutrality, favorable geopolitical position and the decline of Venice established Ragusa, in the first half of the 16th century, as the main link between the East and the West. The Ragusans were presented with the opportunity to monopolize trade in the Mediterranean basin and they were hell bent on making it happen. The Republic of Ragusa's merchant navy consisted of about 180 vessels and more than 40,000 seamen. They shipped goods the length and breadth of the Mediterranean, but also to the shores of England in the north, India in the east and the west coast of the North American continent in the west. Croatia, by contrast, does not utilize its geopolitical position to any advantage. Croatia is a maritime country but for all practical purposes it may as well not be. The port facilities in the ports of Ploče and Rijeka lie for the most part idle and are slowly but surely turning to ruin.

The laws of the Republic of Ragusa were followed to the letter. Criminals were punished severely and no mercy was given. The Ragusans knew that the key to the Republic's survival as an independent polity lay in their putting the interests of the community before their aspirations as individuals. That attitude was clearly regulated and enforced by law. The citizens of the Republic of Ragusa were aware that political legitimacy rested, among other things, on legal tradition – laws were seldom changed or significantly amended. The Ragusans were not concerned with minute and irrelevant inconsistencies in their laws and in that regard subscribed to the principle "if it ain't broke, don't fix it". And the history of the Republic teaches us that they were absolutely right. Another comparison with modern Croatia is warranted here: one Croatian government, in its four-year term of office, made changes to the tax law several times. Furthermore, in the Republic of Ragusa perjurers were forced into permanent exile whereas the legal system of the Republic of Croatia introduced the category of state witness with the inevitable result that criminals belonging to that category lie through their teeth to save their skin, more often than not under instruction from corrupt judges.

Who can call to memory the name of a duke (or "rector") of the Republic of Ragusa? The mandate of a rector lasted only one month. For that one month rectors were required to live in the palace without any contact with their families and friends (the Ragusans were aware of the fact that power corrupts and the idea was to shield rectors from being unduly influenced in their decision-making by their family and friends). There was absolutely no chance a cult of personality would develop around any given rector, regardless of his achievements. The citizens of the Republic of Ragusa were extremely careful not to elevate, and thus really degrade, their deserving citizens to the status of celebrities. It is interesting to note here that Croatia's politicians desire to achieve celebrity status without being aware of how the attainment of that goal degrades them both as human beings and professionals. The Ragusans gave credit where credit was due without any undue pomp and circumstance (there was, however, an official period of mourning in the city when Ruđer Bošković died). Only God and saints were publicly celebrated in Ragusa. The first statue of a citizen of Ragusa was erected in 1633, 450 years into the existence of the Republic of Ragusa. The man in question was Miho Pracat, a wealthy banker and merchant who bequeathed his enormous wealth to charity. Here is some food for thought for our well-off entrepreneurs and an incentive for the Croatian public to start differentiating truly great individuals from buffoons in suits sitting in the Croatian Parliament.

And lastly, the example of the Republic of Ragusa confirms Percy Bysshe Shelley's musings about change; naught may endure but mutability. If you want to stay relevant, you have to continuously be able to adapt to new circumstances. Otherwise, you'll become antiquated. And that is exactly what happened to the Republic of Ragusa – it aged out of relevance. That circumstance, coupled with a number of unfavorable changes in the geopolitical landscape of the world, spelled the Republic's demise. By the same token, Dubrovnik will not be able to live off the touristic value of its walls and legacy forever. The time has come for new visions and new trends to emanate from Dubrovnik. And the time is also ripe for Croatia to finally become a viable country on the map of Europe, a markedly better, wiser country than it is at this point in time. A country that is both assertive and more pragmatic in its relationship with others, a country that is actively engaged in creating a brighter future for its citizens. It is not as though we have no one to learn from!

Unknown Croatian Greats

History lost

Every people, every nation on the face of our planet has its
heroes and great men, individuals to whom generations owe
a huge debt of gratitude. The memory of these worthy
individuals is safeguarded and their lives and achievements
are celebrated; some even became legends in their lifetime.
Some, on the other hand, died in obscurity and poverty,
their deeds recognised only centuries after their demise from
the mortal realm... Some of them did not hail from the
country to which they bequeathed the substantial benefits of
their achievements or improved the country's standing by
achieving extraordinary feats of arms, succeeding in politics,
leaving their mark as successful artists, becoming
outstandingly prosperous businessmen or excelling in any
other field. Some great men left their mark not in their
homeland but all over the world and are remembered and
revered by their countrymen as national heroes nevertheless,
simply on account of spreading the good name of the

country wherever they went. Many countries celebrate the achievements of those wandering great men and covet the glory of their names. All these great individuals we simply call *greats*. In their honor we name squares and streets, create works of art, build institutions and compose operas. They are our role models and objects of aspiration. The names of some greats are instantly recognizable all over the world, thanks, to a lesser extent, to the magnitude of their achievements and, to a larger extent, to the competence of their countries' propagandists. On the other hand, some truly great individuals and their marvelous accomplishments get lost in the shuffle of history. Their destinies and their lives are shrouded in mystery and available historical facts about them are few and far between.

Croatia, considering its size, has given the world a disproportionate number of scientists, writers, educators, inventors, warriors, saints, successful sportsmen and talented individuals in many other walks of life, whose contribution to the development of Europe, establishment of Western civilization and affirmation of Croatia is substantial and extensive. Unfortunately, many of these worthy individuals have slipped our collective memory and we know not nearly enough about many others. It could be argued that we tend to show far too little respect for many of our greats. Maybe that state of affairs originates in the fact that we cannot agree on who exactly is the greatest Croat of them all and the question *To which individual does the nation owe the greatest debt of gratitude?* is a point of constant contention and source of many recurring controversies. The

Croatian media outlets have been fuelling a number of controversies regarding the issue by conducting a number of dubious polls and surveys. The results were not surprising in the sense that they reflected the points of view of those who commissioned the polls and surveys in the first place. The four names in contention for the top spot appeared more often than others: Nikola Tesla, Ruđer Bošković, Franjo Tuđman and Josip Broz Tito. Franjo Tuđman and Josip Broz Tito occupy the opposite sides of the political spectrum so it is small wonder that the Croats cannot agree on which individual should serve as Croatia's calling card in the world. The issue is simply too politicized and, for want of a better phrase, apolitical figures from the country's history get glossed over in the political mess. Croatia has many greats comparable to Goethe, Cervantes or Dante. Unfortunately, these Croatian greats are virtually unknown outside the county's borders.

It is painfully obvious that we are useless when it comes to using our greats to promote our country. In a broader sense, each and every of Croatia's greats is a potential cash-cow, so, from that perspective, we are losing a lot of money in the situation. For example, Nikola Tesla is very popular in the world today, but almost nobody knows that he was a Croat. His legacy is discussed in many scientific articles and books, he is the subject of many documentaries and, as a supporting character, he appeared in a number of Hollywood films. To our chagrin, his name is more often than not connected to the USA than Croatia. So, that's one of our cash cows another country is milking. Another great we can cash in on is Ruđer Bošković. A native of Dubrovnik,

Ruđer Bošković is said to be the most versatile Croat to have ever lived and it is safe to say that his achievements turned Europe into the scientific powerhouse of the world. Yet, we are not doing nearly enough to promote Croatia through his legacy. Nikola Šubić, a Croatian war hero without whose exploits during the wars against the Ottomans the official language in Vienna would today be Turkish has been actually abducted, as a national hero, by the Hungarians. And fair play to them because we haven't done anything to let the world know about his heroic deeds. Only recently did we erect a statue of him in Zagreb – a classic case of too little, too late. If any military leader from history deserves a film, that leader is Nikola Zrinski. Unfortunately, it is obvious that his life will never be reenacted on the big screen. So, there goes his legacy out of the window. Inexplicably, we have no problem with accepting the myth that Marco Polo was an Italian. The Croatian politicians who received the Vice-Premier of the State Council of the People's Republic of China Liu Yandong during her official visit to Croatia in 2014 were pointedly embarrassed when she visited Marco Polo's birthplace on the island of Korčula and announced China's intention to open a consulate there. Antun Lučić (Anthony Francis Lucas), from Split, was the first to discover oil in Texas and start the mass exploitation of the resource. He is on the list of 200 greatest Americans. In Croatia, practically nobody has ever heard of him. Vinko Paletin was a translator, historian, Dominican, theologian, naval theoretician, mathematician, travel writer, jurist, diplomat and conquistador. He participated in the Spanish conquest of the Yukatan, translated from Spanish into Italian the work about navigation written by the Spanish cosmographer

Pedro Medina (L'arte del naviger, Venice, 1554), wrote *De jura et justitia belli contra Indias*, preserved as manuscript in Latin, and created, based on his own measurements, the first map of Spain, to name just a few of his achievements. He is a celebrated historical figure in Spain but in Croatia only a few intellectuals are aware of him and his accomplishments. Filip Vezdin (Paulinus of St. Bartholomew) was one of the first people who studied the relationship between Indian and European languages, but in Croatia there are some trusted and respected – say their diplomas on the wall – professors of literature who have never heard of the man. Sad but true. We all learned about the father of Croatian literature Marko Marulić at school but only a few people in Croatia are actually aware that his literary works were translated into many languages. He was the favorite author of many rulers and kings in Europe in the second half of the 16th century. The English King Henry VIII found solace, inspiration and solution to his problems in Marulić's literary works. Croatian Latin literature, especially during the Renaissance, was very influential in Europe at that time. The tourist attractions in many Italian cities that draw millions of tourist every year were actually built or created by Croatian artists, builders and craftsmen. The splendor of old Austria would have been significantly less grand without the contribution of many Croatian nobles, bishops, diplomats, military leaders, poets and educators. The Croatian National Revival, and the years leading up to it, spawned many gifted and great Croats in all fields of human endeavor and motivated many equally gifted and brilliant people from other countries to declare themselves Croatian and give their contribution to their adoptive homeland. In the 20th century

Croatian writers, artists and scientists were at the forefront of global trends. The lives and achievements of most of those talented and influential individuals seem like tailor-made narratives for novels and films. But, in order for that to happen we need to make ourselves learn more about the lives of those Croatian greats and then find people creative enough who can actually make them live again on pages of books and on the big screen.

The importance of many Croatian greats and the treatment they have received over the ages can be gleaned from many architectural designs, works or art, books, honors given at various events and similar. We just have to analyze everything with due diligence. I deal with the subject extensively in my book *Hrvatski velikani* (Croatian Greats). For example, the names of streets and squares in Croatian cities are a good gauge. In order to ascertain which Croatian greats have received the most acclaim we listed the names of the main squares, main streets or promenades (in coastal cities without squares) in all 127 cities in Croatia. The most represented names are: King Tomislav, Franjo Tuđman, Ban Josip Jelačić and Ante Starčević. King Tomislav has 17 main squares and one main street, Franjo Tuđman – six main squares and one promenade, Ban Josip Jelačić – six main squares, Ante Starčević – six main squares, Stjepan Radić – four main squares, Zrinski, four main squares, Josip Broz Tito – four prominent locations in four different cities; three in Istria and one in Opatija, Josip Juraj Strossmayer – two main squares and King Zvonimir – one main square and one main street. Also, many military and civil decorations, manifestations and awards, postage stamps, coins and banknotes, monuments and many other things bear the names of Croatian greats. We can also track the rankings, as it were, of the Croatian greats through numerous editions of various publications – from the first publication written by Ivan Kukuljević Sakcinski to the present. We made a multi-varied analysis based on the instance of representation of names regarding everything mentioned above. The idea was to establish who the most popular Croatian greats are. It was easy to figure out which names are most represented in the various lists. If squares, streets and institutions are named after this or that historical figure, if every generation erects monuments in honor of the same people, if books are written and songs sung about them, if their names crop up in various top ten or top whatever lists in the media, it is logical to assume that the individuals in question are rightly called *greats*. Their achievements cast long shadows and in that sense they are important in the scheme of things and still relevant today. Their names are instantly recognizable because most people have learned about them at school and are indelibly ingrained in the collective psyche of the Croatian nation. On a purely emotional level, these greats serve as beacons of aspiration, we consider them ours and they are objects of our admiration... I divided the results of my survey into three categories: consensus, popularity and respect. The following names are positioned prominently high in all three categories: King Tomislav, Nikola Šubić Zrinski, Ban Josip Jelačić, Ante Starčević, Stjepan Radić, Nikola Tesla, Ruđer Bošković, Marko Marulić, Josip Juraj Strossmayer, Cardinal Alojzije Stepinac and Ivan Meštrović. We can consider the aforementioned individuals as being in the top tier of Croatian greats. The second tier comprises those with somewhat lower values in the consensus category but equally high values as regards the other two categories: Marco Polo, Ivan Gundulić, Marin Držić, Ivan Mažuranić, Miroslav Krleža, Ivo Andrić, Julije Klović, Juraj Dalmatinac, Slavoljub Eduard Penkala and Faust Vrančić. In the third tier are those who scored high in the popularity and respect categories but poorly in the consensus category: Franjo Tuđman and Josip Broz Tito. In relation to the consensus category, Tuđman and Tito are mutually exclusive. Having said that, the popularity of Tuđman, as the first Croatian president and the founder of modern Croatia is on the rise whereas that of Josip Broz Tito is on the wane, due undoubtedly to his dictatorial rule and the fact that, during the course of the past few years, it has been proven beyond any doubt that he was responsible for the deaths of hundreds of thousands of innocent people.

Many of the mentioned names appear often in popular culture and in various TV programs and documentaries and in that way they have achieved a sort of immortality in today's world of instant gratification, 15 minutes of fame and information saturation. And therein lurks the key methodological flaw when it comes to ascertaining who the most deserving greats, in any given European country, really are. TV producers and editors of print media outlets know that some names can generate more interest, and therefore increase viewer rating and sales, more than others. That puts the greats in question at a distinct advantage in terms of their popularity and it also means that the magnitude of one's achievements represents just a minor, not to say insignificant variable in the equation. The real value of one's achievements inevitably gives way to what appears good on screen and what may be turned into controversy in the newspapers and many great men and their deeds are slowly but surely being reduced to obscurity and irrelevance. Unfortunately, in today's world knowledge derives ever less from books and ever more from the mass media – and the qualitative difference between the two is clear for all thinking individuals to see. Many Croatian greats, because we're too lazy, sloppy or incompetent to honor them, are celebrated in other countries as national heroes, and their names are tweaked in accordance with the language of the country in question and their ethnicity is never mentioned. There are too many of our greats who have been unjustly consigned to obscurity. Therefore, it is our duty and moral obligation to do something about it and allow ourselves to become wiser and better men and women in the process.

PART II

Croatia and Europe

The Battle of Siget and the *Cravate*

Not only did the Croats defend Europe, they also educated Europe

We like to perceive our homeland as inconsequential in the context of the wider world due to Croatia's small size. But, if we examine the history of Europe more closely we will see that many Croats played instrumental roles in events that both shaped and determined the course of European history. Two anniversaries, marked in Croatia in 2016, testify to that. One was the 450th anniversary of the famous Battle of Siget. In that battle Nikola IV Zrinski, commanding a force vastly inferior to the Ottoman host both in numbers and materiel, repulsed the Ottoman offensive aimed at the heart of Europe – Vienna. Siget was right in the path of the Ottoman's advance and Suleiman the Magnificent decided to lay siege to the town. He expected to overrun the defenders in a matter of days and duly proceed to the capital of the Austrian Empire. Suleiman had every reason to be confident: his army numbered around 90,000 soldiers and the garrison of Siget, commanded by Nikola IV Zrinski, consisted of some 2,500 soldiers, for the most part Croats. But, Suleiman miscalculated. The defenders resisted fiercely for over a month. On September 7, 1566, when the Ottomans breached the outer wall, Zrinski led a suicidal charge against the invaders. He died preserving European values and freedoms. Before the Battle of Siget Zrinski had gotten the better of Ottoman forces in a number of skirmishes and inflicted two signal strategic defeats on Suleiman's armies; defending Vienna in 1529 and Pest in 1542. Suleiman considered these defeats as a slight on his martial honor and his decision not to bypass Siget and continue on to Vienna was informed, to a significant degree, by his hatred of Zrinski IV. The decision to lay siege to Siget would unravel the plans to attack Vienna and prove fatal; Suleiman did not live to bask in the glory of finally defeating his archenemy Zrinski IV; he died three days before the fall of Siget. The grand vizier kept Suleiman's death secret from the troops – he was afraid the news would completely demoralize them. He need not have bothered – the casualties inflicted on the Ottoman army by the defenders of Siget and time spent besieging the town put Vienna, the main objective of the offensive, out of the Ottomans' reach. The Ottoman army retreated eastwards and Zrinski IV's name entered into legend.

The story of Zrinski's bravery, of a man who had refused the position of Croatian Ban so that he could defend Europe from the Ottoman scourge, soon spread all over the continent. Every European ruler and politically prominent person publicly declared his admiration for the Croatian hero (the Hungarians consider him their national hero too under the name Zrinyi Miklos). The French Cardinal Richelieu wrote: "A miracle was needed for the Habsburg Empire to survive. And a miracle did happen. At Siget!" It has to be remembered that Zrinski counted on help from the new Habsburg Emperor Maximilian (1564 – 1576), but the venal potentate never issued an order for a relief force to march towards Siget (ironically, Zrinski's descendants, Nikola VII and Peter, were executed on the orders of the emperor in Wiener Neustadt in 1671 – their crime was agitating for greater Croatian autonomy within the Habsburg Empire). Generations of Croats and Hungarians have been celebrating Zrinski IV as one of the most important European military leaders. And rightly so. The defenders of Siget, with their heroic defense of the town, bought much needed time for Hungary and Vienna. Had Siget fallen within days as Suleiman the Magnificent originally planned, Central Europe would have been at the mercy of the Ottoman army. Siget fell late in the campaigning season and the Ottoman army had no choice but to return to Istanbul. Nikola Zrinski, by holding out for over a month, saved Vienna.

Many works of art have been created in Nikola Zrinski's honor. A monument to Nikola Zrinski decorates the central square in Budapest and one of the main streets in the Hungarian capital bears his name. In his honor the city fathers of Zagreb named one of the main squares, and arguably the most beautiful square in Zagreb today, after him – Zrinjevac. The square was opened at the celebrations of the 300th anniversary of the Battle of Siget. One hundred and fifty years later Zrinski IV received his monument there in the alley of the greats.

The 450th anniversary of the Battle of Siget presented an exceptional opportunity to rekindle our knowledge of and admiration for this great historical figure and also to remind the rest of Europe of the fact that Zrinski IV, a Croat, had saved Europe from the Ottomans. As a side note it is worth mentioning that Croats have always been ready and willing to die for European freedoms and "ideals"! Some people perceived this important anniversary as conducive to a "war of all against all" situation between the Croats, Magyars and Turks. There is no doubt that Zrinski IV is a controversial figure because for the Hungarians he is a Hungarian while the Croats consider him a Croat. For the Turks he is that nefarious character that caused the death of their celebrated sultan, Suleiman the Magnificent, made even more magnificent in the eyes of many soap opera devotees around the world, including Croatia, by the Turkish TV series *Muhteşem Yüzyıl* (The Magnificent Century). The Hungarians stake their claim on the fact that Zrinski IV was born in Croatia, at that time part of their lands. The Croats' case is grounded in the fact that Zrinski IV was a nobleman from the Croatian Šubić family. The Hungarians counter that it was their state that gave Zrinski IV military commission and authority. Both the Croats and Hungarians agree, unsurprisingly, that Suleiman the Magnificent is the bad guy in the story of Zrinski IV. The Turks, in a bid to change that perception, reconciled, at least to an extent, the mutually exclusive positions of the Croats and Hungarians as regards the ownership of Zrinski IV. The Turks initiated the erection of a monument honoring both Zrinski and Suleiman in the Park of Turkish - Hungarian Friendship in Siget. Many Hungarian and Croatian committees helped organize the event and the Croatian and Hungarian presidents participated in it. From this example it is clear that Zrinski IV can be, with no undue contention, both a Croatian and Hungarian national hero. The Turks obviously respect him as a worthy adversary of their hero Suleiman. It is also obvious that the manifestation did not, in any way, shape or form, glorify the European struggle against the Ottomans and therefore Islam or vilify the Turkish territorial aspirations from the same period. The manifestation celebrated a story of chivalry, a story of a few against many, a story of the heroism of an able military leader, a story of one small nation defending Europe.

Seemingly unconnected to Zrinski IV, another anniversary was celebrated in 2016 – the 360th anniversary of the first "official" use of the *cravate*[4]. According to Britannica and other relevant encyclopedias, 1656 is the year when the *cravate* made its first appearance as a fashion item, even though it is known that the *cravate* had been worn in Croatia for quite some time before. Most relevant sources tell us that the *cravate*, as a fashion item, originated in Croatia – the word *cravate*, in many languages, is derived from the word Croat. The Croats made a name for themselves in the Thirty Years' War (1618-1648) as fierce warriors. The reputation

---

[4] See footnote 2. For the purpose of clarity, I use the French word *cravate* instead of the English word *necktie* whenever the fashion item is mentioned in a historical or linguistic context (the latter in relation to both the Croatian and French languages).

was well deserved because the Croatian contingents of the Imperial forces, especially light cavalry units, had honed their lethal skills in merciless engagements with the Ottomans. The French King Louis XIV noted the unusual red scarves worn by the Croatian mercenaries in his service. Fascinated by that Croatian clothing item, he introduced the fashion to his court. Shortly afterwards he created a special regiment composed mostly of Croats and named it Royal Cravates. The rest is history. But, that history would be lost to us today had it not been for the Croatian entrepreneur Marijan Bušić. Early in the 1990s he created the brand *Croata* in Zagreb and decided to remove the cobwebs from the history of the *cravate* and make it shine in its full glory and splendor. Some time later *Akademija Cravatica* started successfully promoting the *cravate* as a Croatian invention. As a result, CNN and Japanese television ran shows on the history of the *cravate*. Undoubtedly the *cravate* is one of the most beautiful European symbols because many nations participated in the establishment of the *cravate* as the ubiquitous fashion item that it is today. "After the Croats had given the world the product, the French took care of the marketing and promotion side of things and commissioned the Spanish and the Dutch to do a lot of legwork and heavy lifting in that regard. The English gave the *cravate* a cult reputation. The Americans improved on the original design and the Italians enriched it artistically... At the end of the 20th century even Germany gave its contribution to the *cravate* culture: in the city centre of Frankfurt, the financial heart of Europe, they erected a bronze monument a few meters high in honor of the *cravate*..." writes Stefan Bencak in his fantastic book *Illustrated History of the Tie and Its*

Antecedents published in Austria. There is no doubt that the Croats, unwittingly to be sure, in the 17th century gave the world a fashion item that is worn by more than 700 million people every day as a mark of elegance, professionalism and civility. The *cravate* has become much more than a mere symbol of civilization. The elevation of the fashion item to that status started and it still continues, as a joint venture of all the nations that comprise the civilized world, to this day. The whole world bows to the *cravate*. It is no wonder that the father of the modern Turkish state Ataturk made it a point to always wear a tie and instructed all the civil servants to do the same in an effort to show the world that Turkey belonged to the civilized world. The example of the former Greek prime minister, Alexis Cipras is even more striking. The energetic politician, at the beginning of his term of office, jettisoned the tie to show that it was time to break a serious sweat with the promise that he would put it back on when the country is safely out of the financial crisis. Unfortunately, he never had the occasion to put the tie back on. The promise was, however, deftly exploited by the Italian Prime Minister Matteo Renzi who, during his first official visit to Greece, gave a blue tie, the color symbolizing the Italian tenure of the presidency of the EU Council, to his Greek counterpart, stating: "When the occasion arises, I would like the Greek prime minister to put this particular tie on!" Renzi displayed excellent statesmanship and showmanship and thus promoted his country and its tie making industry. Italy is the largest manufacturer of cravats in the world. In a way, the tie has become a symbol of the European Union. During the handover ceremony, the officials of the country taking up the presidency give cravats adorned with their country's symbols to the visitors. Some of those cravats are made by the Croatian fashion brand Croata.

The Croats have not taken full advantage of the fact that the *cravate* originated in Croatia. The 360th anniversary of the first "official" use of the *cravate* was a good opportunity to remind Europe that Croats did not underline European values and freedoms just as cannon fodder but also in the context of culture, science and, in the case of the cravat, fashion and civilized values. At first glance there is no correlation between Zrinski and the *cravate* but on closer inspection it becomes clear that both have become symbols of Croatian contribution to all the facets that make Europe what it is today. We have many such symbols. Many Europeans are blissfully unaware of at least some of those symbols, due, first and foremost, to our complacency. However, the history of Croatia is eternally intertwined with that of Europe and in that sense both Europeans and Croats can learn a lot about themselves from the example of the other.

Part of Western Europe or a Post-Communist Neighbor

How Croatia presents itself to the European Union and how the member states perceive Croatia

Croatia joined the European Union on July 1, 2013. Many people in Croatia were surprised and offended by the lukewarm welcome Western Europe extended to their country. Contrary to popular expectations in Croatia, Europe did not perceive the new member as a country belonging to Western civilization. The European public, for the most part, saw Croatia as a poor neighbor haunted by the ghosts of Communism and plagued by woes inherent in trying to abandon central planning and embrace market capitalism. Some member countries even clearly expressed their opposition to accepting Croatia into the fold. Some European politicians and media outlets poured scorn on Croatia…

We all know that making a first impression only happens once. And Croatia did not take the task of adequately presenting itself to its new European neighbors seriously. In light of that fact we shouldn't really be surprised that Old Europe tends to look down on us. By the same token, the process of enlargement of the EU that started in 2004 has produced some nasty surprises for the old member states and, realistically speaking, the accession of Croatia as the 28th member of the European Union was bound to be met with a healthy dose of skepticism. For example, Romania and Bulgaria joined the EU in 2007, but the countries are still perceived by many in older member states as unfit to be part of the EU – the popular perception is that they were admitted out of political pragmatism or pity. For once, the popular perception just might be completely accurate.

Is it any wonder then that most people in the EU perceive Croatia as part of that slew of poor and insufficiently Europeanized newcomers rather than as a regional leader and historically integral part of Old Europe which has met all the criteria and successfully carried out all the requisite reforms and brought a nice chunk of underpopulated territory – lands of outstanding natural beauty and rich in cultural heritage – back to Europe? It is hard to give a simple answer to the question but it is perfectly clear that Croatia has a long way to go to be perceived as a country that is deservedly part of the EU and one that has made the Union better by joining it. In comparison with Romania and Bulgaria, Croatia enjoys four distinct advantages – it is a small country with, in a wider European context, small population, it is a popular tourist destination with the cleanest and warmest sea in Europe, it is a relatively stable democracy situated on the historically politically unstable Balkan Peninsula and it is a country whose cultural and historical heritage was part of the Western European cultural circle for centuries. Despite all the derision lavished on Croatia as a new member, the European Union is well aware of all the advantages Croatia possesses. On the other hand, Croatia, so far, has not offered a single argument that could charm EU citizens sufficiently to turn them into willing advocates of Croatia, buyers of Croatian products or lobbyists for this or that Croatian cause. There are isolated and individual attempts in that regard, like the promotion of Croatian culture in Paris, the festival of Croatian music in Vienna, the odd exhibition or tourist fair in London. But there is no concerted effort to bring Croatia closer to millions of EU citizens who know nothing or, at best, very little about Croatia.

What could Croatia offer to the general public? Croatia, unfortunately, has not yet made a film good enough to do well at the box office in Europe. We don't have a band, or singer, or music producer, good enough to make it big outside Croatia. Croatian academics, for the most part, are deemed substandard and consequently they are not invited to give lectures at prestigious European universities. The covers of European magazines never feature Croatian intellectuals. Croatian writers and politicians cannot even hope to be considered candidates for a Nobel Prize. Modern Croatia has not produced a single individual Europe could be proud of – someone Europe would embrace with enthusiasm and make films and write books about, organize symposiums in his or her honor, celebrate his or her achievements...There are a few exceptions, but in Croatia they are considered mavericks because they have achieved their successes outside a strictly Croatian context. We have done close to nothing to promote the achievements of great Croatian historical figures like Ruđer Bošković, Marko Marulić, Miroslav Krleža, Nikola Tesla, Ivana-Brlić Mažuranić, Ivan Meštrović, Julije Klović... Slowly but surely, all of them are fading from the collective consciousness of the Croatian people. By contrast, almost every other European nation would have used such greats, long ago, to establish itself as the leading cultural and scientific force both in the context of Europe and the wider world. We do not have many globally known manifestations that are prestigious enough to attract heads of state or celebrities. Apart from a relatively good tourist promotion, the odd cultural event and fitful promotional activities by the Croatian Chamber of Commerce, we have no strategy to promote Croatian products in Europe. Other countries in transition, like Poland and the Czech Republic, had such strategies in place well before they were admitted to the European Union in 2004. We have to give a good reason to the world to focus its attention on us. Otherwise, we'll sink into the morass of mediocrity which we won't that easily get out of.

What are the results of such poor performance? Relatively undeveloped identity, not entirely positive image, and fear that Europe will regard us as lesser. It could be argued that Croatia's image is much better than its inadequate promotional activities warrant. Croatia is lucky in the sense that its natural beauty is arguably unsurpassed by any other European country. On the strength of that, and that alone, Croatia has managed to develop a fairly successful tourism industry and offset the negative consequences of the war. This is best reflected in the results of the public opinion survey that the Institute for Tourism in Zagreb conducted, before Croatia joined the EU, in a number of European countries among people who had never visited Croatia. The respondents were from the rich Scandinavian countries, countries in transition or from the Mediterranean countries and they all perceived Croatia as a tourist country with a beautiful coastline and clean sea. On the other hand, many people in Denmark and Britain still associate Croatia primarily with war. Luckily for us, war is not the only thing Britons associate with Croatia: high on the list are beautiful coastline, pristine nature and sport. The perception of the Danish respondents is similar to that of their British counterparts: war and all the concomitant imagery contend for the top spot in the association game with sunshine, summer, tourism and picturesque vistas. We can feel pretty smug when it comes to the perceptions of the German respondents – the first things that came to mind at the mention of Croatia were beautiful coastline, tourism, beaches and summer. However, there is a fly in the ointment there; the positive imagery comes in tandem with some negative associations, namely Yugoslavia and its destructive legacy. Most Poles who participated in the survey had nothing negative to say about Croatia – they pointed out that Croatia has a beautiful coastline and that it is a popular tourist destination. The perceptions of the Spanish respondents surprised us because we didn't expect them to know much about our country. They proved us wrong. Unlike the respondents from the other countries, they cited culture and history as our main advantages. On the other hand, they also associate Croatia negatively with war and positively with nice beaches. Had this survey been conducted five or six years before we would have been extremely proud of the results. However, we have to be aware of the fact that the world media started peddling Croatia as a country of outstanding natural beauty and desirable tourist destination more than ten years ago. We still remember that Croatia was, back in 2003 and 2004, among the top unexplored tourist destinations in the world. It is striking, and somewhat worrying, that we haven't been able to show the world that there is a lot more to Croatia than a beautiful coastline and nice beaches. Virtually nobody associates Croatia with a product, innovation, culture, a successful individual, manifestation or spectacular architectural symbol. By the same token, nobody even considers the possibility that a Croatian value could be perceived as a valuable gift to Western civilization. We often feel proud when other people praise the natural beauty of Croatia but we really shouldn't because we didn't create the cleanest sea in Europe and the thousands of islands off our coast and pristine environment – nature did. We should feel gratitude to our ancestors from the 7th century for having recognised the potential of the lands they decided to settle – thus providing us with the most beautiful part of Europe. It is a sad fact that, thirteen centuries later, we build our image on something God has given us and not on something we have achieved. Europe respects and appreciates Croatia's natural beauty and cultural and scientific achievements of our ancestors and scoffs at how inadequate modern Croatian academics and artists are. Small wonder then that on many threads about Croatia on foreign Internet forums many people say that Croatia is the most beautiful country in the world but that Croats are extremely annoying people. These opinions of common people who have visited our country speak volumes about our image in the world.

On the other hand, we shouldn't read too much into any one single indicator. In comparison to many of our neighbors, our image is relatively good. Even in the global context we should be satisfied with how our country is perceived. However, our image is not nearly as good as the potential of the country warrants. It should be obvious to all Croats that we cannot rely solely on the natural beauty of Croatia to improve our standing among nations. We have to put a lot of effort into becoming a politically, economically and culturally relevant country in Central and Southeast Europe. Without succeeding in that endeavor, being a member of the EU means nothing. We ourselves travel as tourists to exotic countries and enjoy their natural beauty and ignore their political failures and disastrous economic policies. We are aware that many beautiful countries have been bought lock, stock and barrel by foreign corporations. The coastline of any given such country is dotted with impressive luxurious hotels natives may enter only if they're employed there as housekeeping staff. In today's world, this is the price small and beautiful countries inevitably pay for their lack of unity, vision, courage and wisdom. Croatia should consider itself duly warned.

CEFTA (Central European Free Trade Agreement) and the region are things of the past and we have to become important players in the competitive European market. We all agree that we do not have enough mass-produced goods to sell to Europe. Maybe we should stop thinking about what mass-produced items we could manufacture and start thinking about offering Europe intellectual property. Culture is an industry worth billions of euros. Developed European countries have realized that long ago. If we have nothing to compete with in that industry, then we should at least define the steps we have to take to avoid being perceived by Europe as nothing more than a pool of cheap labor, threatening to overspill once the work restrictions are lifted. "There's only a few Croats," stated one British MP during a discussion about the ratification of Croatia's EU Accession Treaty. So, luckily for us, the British don't have to worry about hordes of our poor and destitute invading their shores – the whole population of Croatia could easily be lost in the throngs of people in one of their major cities.

We shouldn't really underestimate the fear citizens of Europe have of new member states. *Eurobarometer*, which regularly conducts public opinion surveys in the member states of the European Union, clearly shows that citizens of the member states are afraid of an influx of cheap labor from the new member states, losing their jobs to the newcomers who are prepared to work a lot more for a lot less, increases in crime rates, illegal immigration and political instability that may result from accepting huge numbers of people who hail from societies in which democracy is an alien and unwanted concept. I can fully understand and sympathize with a clerk from England, a shop assistant from Belgium or, say, banker from Sweden when they fear for the future of their countries in the extended EU. For them, we are people from behind the Iron Curtain, their former enemies from the era of the Cold War. Apart from a number of negative stereotypes they know nothing about us. It is, therefore, up to us to break those stereotypes and prejudices. The only way we can do that is to provide those who are afraid of us with enough information about ourselves and then prove to them that culturally we belong to the same society. Dry information alone will not do the trick. Most people have no time to read things they are not entertained by. So, we have to present ourselves to the citizens of the old member states on their own terms. If we can do that, then we will have proven to them, and ourselves, that we indeed belong in the European Union.

It is important to be aware that we have to shed some of the stereotypes and prejudices we harbor about Europe. I remember one survey from 2006 conducted among Croats. The survey was very simple – the respondents were asked who, in their opinion, Croatia's friends in Europe were. Germany and Austria topped the list while Britain and the countries in transition, including Slovenia, brought up the rear. At the same time *Eurobarometer* published the position of citizens of every member state regarding whether Croatia should join the EU or not. The Finns, French, Luxembourgers and Germans were against Croatia joining the EU. We received largest support in countries that went through similar experiences in recent history – Slovakia, the Czech Republic, Hungary and very surprisingly, Slovenia.

Regarding the old member states, Croatia received most support from Sweden and Greece. It is obvious that there are no permanent friends or enemies in the political arena. Everything revolves around national interests and emotions are not a factor in the equation. We have to be aware of the fact that the official positions of political elites do not always correspond to public opinion. In that sense we should have worked simultaneously in the parliaments of EU member states on the ratification of the treaties of accession. We should have launched promotional campaigns to present ourselves to the citizens of the old member states. Simply put, we should have fully exploited the occasion of being admitted to the EU to our advantage. It was a historic opportunity. In the summer of 2013 we, as a newly admitted member of the EU, came under the scrutiny of 500 million people. We had the center stage. And Europe eagerly awaited us to give them answers to the following questions: *Who are these Croats? What values do they have? What is Croatia bringing to the EU? What are the country's riches? What are these Croats we are bringing into the fold like?* And Croatia, to paraphrase the renowned British theorist of identity and country image Simon Anholt, who has written about the accession of Slovenia to the EU in 2007, continued to murmur the corny and dull phrases about pristine beaches, foreign investment, historic cities and competent workforce instead of sending a clear and inspired message about itself and thus making a statement of intent – the intent being to truly become part of Europe, to be a trusted, valued and respected partner in any given European endeavor.

There's no second chance to make a first impression. However, the gods of second chance seem to have a particular fondness for Croatia, against, it may be argued, their better judgment; in 2020 Croatia will take the helm of the EU presidency and we can only hope that our politicians by that time will have learned something from their mistakes.

What Are the Real Capabilities of Croatian Diplomacy?

Subject or object of international relations

According to the results of a survey conducted by the portal *Politico* in the spring of 2016, Croatia is the least influential country of the European Union. Some people in Croatia were incensed by the results of the survey, lavishing numerous insults on the portal and decrying the methodology as faulty. The objections were completely misplaced simply because the survey never claimed to be grounded in the scientific method and the intention was simply to show how people in other EU member states perceived Croatia. The results obviously destroyed some long cherished beliefs of many Croats about themselves, and hence the outcry.

There is no point in being offended by reality. One does not have to be well versed in the game of politics to see to what extent we are the masters of our own destiny in terms of calibrating our foreign and domestic policies according to national interests and to what extent we dance to somebody else's tune – the scale is tipped overwhelmingly in favor of the latter dynamic. Our leaders, in the global game of politics, are nonentities. Croatia has never launched an international initiative accepted and carried out by other member states of the EU (one exception is the Three Seas Initiative launched by the Croatian and Polish presidents). Croatia has never managed to block an initiative, arrest an unfavorable development or incite its friends to support a cause important to Croatia. Croatian politicians have never expressed their own opinions about any given internationally important issue, like the Israeli-Palestinian conflict or the refugee crisis; they always repeated, in a blatant show of sycophancy and incompetence, someone else's rhetoric. Croatia has never managed to install its own man at the top of an important international organization (some Croats have achieved that level of success but thanks solely to their own individual efforts and outside of any official Croatian context). How can anybody in Croatia believe that our vote at the European table has equal worth to that of, say, Denmark, Belgium, Netherlands or even tiny Luxembourg, which gave to Europe the leading man of the European Commission? The above facts clearly testify to the sheer ineptitude of Croatian diplomacy. Croatia has been independent for 25 years; it has been a member of the European Union since 2013; and yet, we have remained on the periphery of European and global politics. The survey mentioned in the introductory paragraph also tells us that some of our neighbors who are not member states of the EU, and will not become member states for a long time to come if ever, have more influence in the corridors of power of that mightiest conglomeration of states on the planet than Croatia. The situation is worrying, to say the least.

The Croatian President Kolinda Grabar Kitarović, at about the same time as the results of the *Politico* survey were published, berated the then Minister of Foreign affairs Miro Kovač, asking him: Are some of our diplomats working for the interests of Croatia or those of the countries to which they are posted? It has been sad, over the course of the last few years, to witness Croatia's debasement at the hands of politicians from unfriendly countries – Croatia has been snubbed, degraded, insulted, used as a sacrificial lamb and the reactions of those paid for preventing such things from happening have been either belated or counterproductive. Sometimes nonexistent... In fairness to the Chief of Diplomacy Kovač, a very able and experienced politician, he could not have, just in a few months, repaired the damage that had been accumulating for decades. However, if there is no marked improvement in the performance of our diplomats in the foreseeable future, the consequences could be dire.

The global geopolitical realities have been significantly altered in the past few years; politicians and diplomats no longer operate behind closed doors but under the limelight. The work of any given diplomat nowadays is a measurable factor. Furthermore, it is required of the diplomats of today to toil hard and achieve results – gone are the days of ceremonious posturing for the sake of ceremonious posturing. Most Croatian diplomats are blissfully oblivious of these new realities; they are 19th century relics, imbued, ironically, with the Communist mentality, lost in the 21st century. They spend their mandates in foreign posts essentially waiting for the plane home, killing time by writing official notes and organizing the protocol for Statehood Day celebrations... Some even do great harm to Croatia by their behavior and almost every time they open their mouths. To be fair, there are also those who doggedly work tooth and nail, utilizing their experience, creativity and expertise, for Croatia's interests, promote the country's tourism, culture and economy and serve as bridges between cultures. Unfortunately, these able diplomats are not adequately rewarded for their efforts and results. It is as though the leadership of Croatia is hell bent on not motivating those who are willing and able to work for the country's benefit. Maybe the leaders of Croatia figured that by joining the EU there would be no need for diplomacy because the institutions of the European Union would do all the work anyway (but the taxpayers still pay an arm and a leg for the salaries of the diplomats and their entourages). The leadership of Croatia simply does not understand that despite the fact that Croatia is a member of the EU, diplomacy is still the pivotal tool in the conduct of foreign policy. And a viable foreign policy is essential for strengthening the country's economy and its image in the world. Our politicians should be aware of that, but, unfortunately, they are not.

Radovan Vukadinović, one of the leading Croatian experts on international relations, wrote in 1998, that diplomacy has been transformed from ceremonial activity into a serious job and that modern diplomacy has shed the romantic nature of its previous incarnations and become a "business of communicating between governments", which requires more experts in various fields and fewer general practitioners of diplomacy. The leaders of most countries in transition realized this on time and started giving precise and clear instructions to their diplomats and, equally importantly, measuring their performance and results – using indexes ranging from increases in exports and numbers of bilateral problems solved to media coverage. The primary function of a diplomat is to build economic relations with, and improve the image of the country in, the foreign host country. Viable political relations between two countries are not possible if diplomats are not successful regarding the above mentioned function. In 2000, the former German Chancellor Schröder called on his ambassadors to consider themselves advocates of German interests abroad because the key to German economic success is a healthy social development. The German Ministry of Foreign Affairs, under the leadership of Joschka Fisher, urged their diplomats to put more effort into swaying public opinion in partner countries in Germany's favor. In September, 2000, about two hundred chiefs of German diplomatic missions met in Berlin. At the gathering the State Secretary Wolfgang Ischinger stated for the *Berliner Zeitung*: "Given the new set of challenges in the ever changing world, the diplomats should be less engaged in compiling economic statistics and more in offensive communication strategies as regards public relations. It is no longer sufficient for embassies to serve as information gathering institutions, they have to be agents of modeling public opinion in host countries (...) A diplomat can no longer expect to conduct his duties in secret, away from the prying eyes of the world media, therefore he has to actively promote the interests of his country in the host country. The ambassadors of tomorrow have to be public relations experts and as such reap the benefits for Germany."

It has to be pointed out that what the Germans started doing at the beginning of this century the Americans have been doing since the 1960s – creating and conducting public diplomacy. The Americans were among the first to realize that it wasn't enough to be on the good side of the politicians of host countries (both ruling and those in the opposition) but that it was equally, or even more crucially important, to be on the good side of the citizens of host countries. Guided by that principle, they began to utilize not just official channels but started relying on music, films, literature, the appeal of the American way of life, tourism and university exchange to influence public opinion all over the world to America's advantage. The Americans essentially create and cultivate buyers of their products, supporters of their way of life, lobbyists for their causes, friends... Small wonder then, as the renowned British theorist of nation branding Simon Anholt writes, that kids from Hong Kong to Paraguay drink Coca Cola, force their parents to take them to McDonalds, play at cowboys wearing Stetsons and sporting toy revolvers (boys) or play with Barbie dolls (girls). Hollywood and *The Voice of America* have done wonders in the context of promoting the American values and way of life. It is interesting to point out that Hollywood, in the best-selling computer game

Civilization IV, features as a world wonder. The Americans consider public diplomacy as a strategic tool of the first order – in 1999, at President Clinton's initiative, the USIA (the United States Information Agency) became part of the US Department of State in order to make the agency more important and increase its budget. Leading marketing and public relations experts were put in charge of the restructured service – politicians were not even considered for the positions in question. The Americans are aware of the fact that the game of politics is played in the virtual world too and that images and words are equally important, if not more important, than facts. In 1999 Evelyn Liebermann was appointed as the first Under Secretary for Public Diplomacy and Public Affairs. This (she sadly passed away in 2015) veteran of public relations and close associate of the Clintons, stated, on the occasion of her appointment, in the Senate that diplomacy, in the modern era of information technology and satellite TV, could not be conducted behind closed doors and that diplomats should be well-versed in communicating with the public and mass media.

It should not surprise us then that public diplomacy is being ever more associated with public relations on the level of the state. Evelyn Liebermann, after the attack on the Twin Towers of September 11, was succeeded as Under Secretary for Public Diplomacy and Public Affairs by Charlotte Beer. Charlotte Beer had honed her skills as the CEO of the famous marketing agencies Ogilvy & Mather and JWT. She spent $15,000,000, an incredible sum, in an effort to improve the slighted image of the USA in the Muslim world. The concept of mediatized foreign policy can no longer be, by any stretch of the imagination, considered as a novelty. By the same token, those countries that do not utilize the full potential of communications technology in their diplomatic endeavors are hopelessly lost in the past. Croatia is one such country. We do not have to aspire to achieve the greatness and success of Germany and the USA in the context of conducting diplomacy in the virtual world. These two countries are true economic leviathans and the USA is still, arguably, the only super power on planet Earth. However, the leaders of Croatia would do themselves a huge favor if they studied how smaller countries had been successfully utilizing communications technology to promote their values across the globe. For example, when cartoons of Muhammad appeared in a Danish newspaper in 2005, 11 Muslim countries blacklisted Denmark. But, Danish diplomacy, using images and words as well as dry facts, managed to regain its positive standing in the Muslim world in no time at all. The Danish exports of seed potatoes to the Islamic world were not disrupted even for an hour.

We would be amiss if we didn't mention the fact that Croatia has had some good ideas and intentions to strengthen its diplomacy along the lines of modern trends. For example, in 2001, when the Račan-Budiša coalition came to power, a strategy termed "Croatia in the 21st Century" was developed. It called for a reform of Croatian diplomacy as the main precondition for the realization of the previously set foreign policy objectives. The architects of the strategy accurately predicted that international relations would swiftly, if gradually, move away from a strictly political context and into any given framework regarding the economy, culture, sports, education, information technology, environment, immigration and emigration. Back in 2001 the world seemed preserved in the moment of the "global victory of democratic principles of liberal internationalism" but the creators of the Croatia in the 21st Century strategy clearly stated that there would be ever less covert types of diplomacy and ever more transparent ones, grounded in economics, culture and other things, ever fewer professional diplomats and ever more experts in various fields fulfilling the role, ever fewer yes-men and ever more creative individuals and ever wider acceptance of the concept of lifelong learning within the structure of diplomacy… Diplomats and creators of foreign policy, the experts at the Institute for Development and International Relations suggested at the time, should give presentations regarding their plans of action, to committees of the Croatian Parliament and submit regular progress reports. The experts further suggested that progress reports should comprise objective and relevant information regarding the international standing of Croatia and not "irrelevant nonsense pleasing to the ear of the political leadership". The Ministry of Foreign Affairs, according to the experts' suggestions, should provide all the necessary analytical and logistical support. The experts also recommended that a special advisory body be set up within the Ministry of Foreign Affairs – a council for international relations, which should consist of experts in all the pertinent fields – and tasked with finding new and creative foreign policy solutions and outcomes and also with establishing a dynamic necessary for a successful reform of Croatian diplomacy. However, almost none of the experts' suggestions have been implemented, with the result that Croatia has been represented by self-styled diplomats who excel at currying favor with those in power and lack in creativity and professionalism.

The former Croatian Prime Minister Ivo Sanader, throughout his political career, was aware that the promotion of Croatia is the main goal of every diplomatic service. Any increase in the international activity in the economic arena, he writes in his scholarly paper published in 2000, puts economic relations into the foreground, thus initiating new foreign policy agendas. Croatia started to put its economic diplomacy on a more serious footing in the summer of 2003, when a special department of economic diplomacy was set up and staffed with experts whose task was to promote the Croatian economy. The new approach did not reap any significant results. However, some diplomats have managed to establish closer trade relations with a number of other countries but their successes are the result of their own individual initiatives and affluence and not any viable effort by the state of Croatia. During the tenure of Vesna Pusić we even had, in the Zrinjevac park, an office of public diplomacy headed by a man perfectly suited for the job. Unfortunately, apart from managing to set up a website, every idea and initiative the office came up with was thwarted by the "expert committee" of the then Prime Minister Zoran Milanović. Yet another case of "back to the drawing board".

What do Croatian diplomacy, Croatian Tourist Board, the Ministry of Culture and the Croatian Chamber of Commerce have in common? The main task of all these collectives is to promote Croatia in the world. Regrettably, there is no cooperation between the mentioned institutions and the government seems unable to come up with a concerted and viable strategy for creating a positive image for the country abroad. Whenever a foreign media outlet airs a segment or publishes an article about Croatia based on disinformation and/or inspired by malice towards Croatia, the governmental agencies whose brief is to react to such misrepresentations and debunk them remain silent. Only individuals and organizations from the Croatian diaspora go to the trouble of seeking redress, but, since they receive no official backing from the Croatian government, their efforts are seldom successful. Unlike all developed countries, Croatia does not have a central state institution tasked with strategically managing the reputation of Croatia and communicating with the world. During the course of the last two decades, Croatia's foreign policy has been completely rudderless. Our diplomats are at a loss when it comes to presenting the country's identity because they themselves are not sure what that identity exactly is (they are reduced to parroting whatever meaningless rhetoric comes from the top). Making the bad situation terrible is the fact that many of our diplomats are incompetent (some of them know close to nothing about their host countries) and owe their jobs to their political pedigree. To be sure, political appointments are a fact of life. For example, even in the USA the former President Obama, and the current President Trump gave a number of ambassadorial posts to their friends and those who had contributed to their presidential campaigns. However, Obama and Trump, by appointing their friends and patrons as ambassadors, did not, in any way, shape or form, jeopardize the national interests of the USA, because the ambassadors in question are competent politicians. Therefore, experts will always be experts and brown-nosers will always be brown-nosers – no amount of reforms or restructuring can change that fact.

I've heard it said that a diplomat is a person who spends half his working life entertaining other diplomats and the other half being entertained by them. Maybe once upon a time – but today such laissez-faire approach to diplomacy is something countries can ill afford. If a country wants to conduct successful diplomacy then its diplomats have to be highly educated, intelligent, imaginative and well-read individuals. Furthermore, they have to possess excellent communication skills, be well informed regarding current social and political developments and extremely knowledgeable about the host country's history and culture. The above requirements are necessary in light of the fact that a diplomat, if he or she aspires to be successful, has to be able to gauge correctly public opinion in the host country in order to influence it to the home country's advantage (for this reason American diplomats prepare for their missions up to one year in advance). Negotiating skills and ability to listen, be emphatic and at the same time aggressively persuasive are also extremely important. Therefore, the personality of a diplomat plays a huge role in the scheme of things. More often than not a diplomat's personality is more important than the official stance of his or her home country. At first glance it seems that in this day and age information is a free commodity. That may be so, but it takes a highly skilled individual to sift through the wealth of information that is out there, recognize what is pertinent and what is not and then turn the relevant intelligence into a viable diplomatic tool – writes the seasoned Croatian diplomat Ivan Šimek in the *Diplomatic Academy Proceedings*, published in 1999. The Croatian government is not in the habit of employing as diplomats graduates from the academy, despite the fact that the Diplomatic Academy is one of the best such institutions in Europe. But, at the end of the day, charisma and ability mean nothing if a diplomat is not fiercely loyal to his, or her, country. A diplomat has to be a staunch patriot, ready and willing to risk life and limb while promoting his or her country's interests, as the experience of the Republic of Ragusa teaches us. The actions, or inertia, of a diplomat have a direct knock on effect on the fate and future of the home country. For that reason, diplomatic posts should not be given to people who put their own interests before of those of their country. We know, from a myriad of books and treatises and thousands of examples stretching back to the invention of writing, that people who are not imbued with loyalty to their country could be easily turned into traitors.

Diplomacy is a business. However, in the diplomatic game it is not advisable to switch allegiance and loyalty as it is in the corporate world – to be given an opportunity to represent and promote the interests of one's country abroad is a great honor and the rules are therefore different. We are not happy with the state of our nation and how our diplomats represent and defend us. The only remedy to this state of affairs is to be highly critical of everything that is wrong at home and focus on everything that is right when presenting our country to foreigners. If we do not talk positively of our country, nobody else will have an inclination to do so either.

Croatian Variety of Cultural Cringe

What is the realistic position of Croatia within the EU?

"Croatia is just a small country and therefore inconsequential in the scheme of things." That assertion has become universally accepted as gospel in Croatia, and Croats apply it to everything – relations with the International Criminal Tribunal for the Former Yugoslavia, limiting overfishing in the Adriatic or limiting imports of the same foodstuffs Croatian farmers produce. The logic according to which we have to know our place because we are too small a country to lock horns with the big players has become a ready-made excuse for all our failures – running the gamut from slaps in the face received by credit agencies to doing badly in the Eurosong contest. We entered the EU suffering from a heavy inferiority complex. Ironically, our belief in our inability to fight for our interests defeats the purpose of joining the EU in the first place. No wonder pessimism holds such a pervasive sway in Croatia. Croatian successes in various sports are a source of some optimism –

in that arena we are universally respected and, in a sporting sense, feared.

Contrary to what most Croats believe, Croatia is not a small country. Nine members of the European Union are actually smaller in area than Croatia – Belgium, Cyprus, Malta, Denmark, Estonia, Luxembourg, the Netherlands, Slovakia and Slovenia. In terms of population two more countries can be added to the list – Latvia and Lithuania. These facts are remorseless and blow the myth that Croatia is too small a country to matter in any given European context right out of the water. No full-blooded Dane or Irishman would ever say that his country is too small to be important for the functioning of the European Union.

Even if we accept, for the sake of this argument, that Croatia is a small country and ignore the fact that theorists are in acute disagreement about what makes a country big or small within the framework of international relations, we cannot use it as an excuse for our lack of vision and creativity, laziness, disastrous economic policies and inept foreign policy. We live in a world in which size doesn't matter – ability is all. Some of the richest countries in the world, in addition to some EU countries already mentioned, serve as testimony to the fact that ability counts much more than size; Israel, Switzerland, Singapore, Kuwait, Qatar, Bahrain… Some of those are wealthy and influential because they are rich in natural resources like gas and oil, some, like Singapore, have deftly taken advantage of their geographical position and some owe their success to their ability to create competitive economies and position themselves as global centers of trade, capital exchange, services and information. These countries have never lamented their small size and have never used it as an excuse to do nothing; they have shown the world, with pluck, skill and determination, who and what they are. There is no doubt that some of those highly successful countries envy the inexhaustible potential Croatia has in its geographical position, the cleanest sea in Europe, arguably in the world, and hundreds of thousands of acres of prime agricultural land in Slavonia. Devastatingly for our self-esteem, in return we envy their able, successful and brave leaders.

We can take Finland as a case in point. Similar in population to Croatia, Finland was, at the beginning of the 1990s, in a situation resembling that Croatia finds itself in today. Throughout the 1980s Finland had been experiencing a steady economic growth. Then, at the turn of the decade, it all came crushing down. Companies and citizens found themselves in crippling debt. When the Soviet Union collapsed so did Finland's main export market. The country sank into a deep economic slump. Unemployment rose from 3.5 per cent to 19 per cent practically overnight. Finland's credit rating dramatically plummeted. Hundreds of Finish companies declared bankruptcy. The Finish Prime Minister at the time, Esko Aho, had enough courage to act decisively. He introduced austerity measures in the public sector and tax reform and at the same time bolstered consumption and the development of the private sector, increasing the country's exports and insisting that Finnish companies have to be competitive and innovative. That meant additional investments into education, incentivizing excellence and protecting the environment. These measures resulted in the global success of Nokia and many other Finnish corporations. Can Croatia learn something from the Finnish, and similar examples? Of course it can, if it drops the "too cool for school" attitude. The former Croatian President Josipović was fond of saying that Croatia, in the context of the European Union, had to shed the small country mentality and replace it with the small power mentality. Josipović's advisor at the time, Professor Dejan Jović, in one of his scholarly papers defined the term *small power* as "a country that has far greater potential to be influential internationally than the size of its territory and other characteristics may at face value warrant". Many small countries are permanently caught in what could best be described as a vassal relationship towards larger, more influential countries. Small powers, on the other hand, wield a lot of influence regarding economic or political issues of global importance. However, the status of small power has to be earned by hard work. Many possibilities, hitherto unavailable, lie open for Croatia simply on account of the country's membership in the EU. To be sure, certain restrictions apply and the EU demands of each individual member state to make concessions but, on the other hand, each individual country is free, and encouraged, to use the EU as a platform to promote its interests. And there is the EU's collective security clause, making each member state that much stronger politically. It is always useful to negotiate from a position of strength, and being a member of the EU definitely secures that position. The act of joining the EU is analogous to a bride from a poor, peasant family being married to a lord – all of a sudden the peasant girl commands respect of everyone who has previously afforded her none. And if she is capable and smart enough, she can influence her husband into doing her bidding, effectively she can be the real ruler of her husband's domains. By joining the EU Croatia gained respect in the global arena. Unfortunately, it hasn't been able to use that respect to its advantage. The official wisdom teaches us that Croatia cannot become an economic force to be reckoned with overnight. On the other hand, Croatia's potential is unlimited and the moment the Croatian national psyche wakes up from its collective slumber the ugly duckling will spread its beautiful wings and fly proudly with its flock. Everyone knows that the global economy is being propelled, with growing momentum, by intellectual services, intellectual property and virtual products. The most important factor in the development of any given country are its human resources. In that sense the lack of traditional investments is not the crippling impediment to economic progress that it once was. For that reason the so-called soft power plays an ever more important role in international relations. It can even be stated that human resources count for more in the scheme of things than the traditional coercive factors, such as economic power, political clout or military might. The term *soft power* is the brain child of the American theorist Joseph Nye. In his book *Bound to Lead: The Changing Nature of American Power* he stated that "when one country gets other countries to want what it wants – might be called co-optive or soft power in contrast with the hard or command power of ordering others to do what it wants". Nye claims that a country could achieve desired results in the global political arena simply by inducing other countries to follow its lead, admire its values, mimic its way of life, aspire to reach its level of technological progress and shape their societies in its society image. Soft power is the ability to attract and draw other societies into your society's orbit. As a result, other societies imitate your own. Soft power, therefore, derives from culture, political acumen and successful representation in the international arena. There are only a few countries in the world that can contend for global supremacy on the basis of hard power. On the other hand, one would be hard-pressed to find a country poor in non-material assets. If viewed from that perspective, the fact that there are many underdeveloped and impoverished countries in the world suggests that dumb luck plays an equally important part as ability when it comes to translating the elements of soft power into economic prosperity.

Where is Croatia then, in all of this? Does Croatia possess enough soft power to conquer the European Union? The answer is undeniably yes. However, it is also true that many Croats, including those who are paid to know better, are not aware of the country's potential. It is a fact that Croatia's natural beauty has been seducing tourists from all over the world for decades. It is a fact that Croatia has passed all the EU's democracy tests. It is also a fact that Croatia's neighbors have no chance in hell of passing these tests for decades, if ever. Foreign media outlets are awash with programs, articles, stories and reports glorifying our culture, gastronomy, historical figures... Our innovators and entrepreneurs, permanent underdogs on a global stage, repeatedly leave their competitors in the dust. Our athletes and sports teams are so successful that even the mighty BBC had no choice but to conclude that the wealth of talent in Croatia is completely disproportionate to the country's size. The masses in the region are mesmerized by Croatian music... If only we had likeable, congenial, wise and honest politicians, efficient and affable administration, enforceable laws, if only there was more tolerance, and respect, if only we were accustomed to working in the spirit of cooperation, if only there were less envy and backstabbing – the Croatian star in the EU flag would burn bright as a thousand suns and conquer the world with its charisma. And no one would care whether we were a big or small country. Besides, it has long been proven that without a healthy dose of self-esteem not much is possible. If we consider ourselves weak and small, others will inevitably treat us as such.

Why the Danes Are Happy and the Croats Are Not

Recipe for happiness and branding a way of life

During the days following the advent of the 2018th year of our Lord, the homes, streets and squares in Croatia resonated with voices wishing a happy New Year, many happy returns and similar greetings and responses. It is notable that all the well-wishing phrases include the word *happy*. Happiness is something we all wish for ourselves and our loved ones. Interestingly enough, there are as many definitions of happiness as there are people. Many a social scientist nowadays subscribes to the view that happiness, whatever it may mean for different people, is something that has to be "produced" or provoked and that attaining happiness means preparing for grasping it when the opportunity presents itself. The Croats are more in need of happiness now than they have ever been. If the United Nations is to be believed, we are amongst the unhappiest countries in the European Union. In the spring of 2017 the

United Nations published the results of its survey in its World Happiness Report. The report was based on the survey conducted in 155 countries within the framework of the Sustainable Development Solutions Network initiative, Croatia was ranked 77th, three places lower than in 2016 and 15 places lower than in 2015. The average value the Croatian respondents put on their level of happiness, on a scale of 1 to 10, was 5.29. Only the Greeks and Portuguese, according to the survey, are less happy than the Croats. According to the same survey, the Norwegians and the Danes are the happiest nations in the world. To be sure, the research was based on the subjective views of the respondents and their individual assessment of the quality of their lives. However, Jeffrey Sachs, director of the Center for Sustainable Development, points out certain tendencies and correlations. He claims that those nations that enjoy a healthy balance between progress, interpersonal relationships and trust in society, efficiency of the state and confidence in the government and equality between the classes are happier than those where there is no balance between the aforementioned factors.

One might be tempted to trivialize the subject by concluding that rich countries top the UN happiness list; countries where people are not encumbered by existential worries, insecurities regarding finding a job or trying to make ends meet from paycheck to paycheck, or from pension payment to pension payment and collective psychosis stemming from bad governance or political divisions. On closer inspection, however, it turns out that such a simplistic explanation is wrong. Other research about the happiness of nations, conducted independently of the United Nations, shows that many nations that cannot be, by any stretch of the imagination, considered rich, are actually happy. For example, impoverished Bhutan often pops up as a decidedly happy nation. The citizens of Bhutan are not fazed by what they don't have – they are content because they don't need much. Their unimpaired state of mind is far more important to them than the state of the economic health of the country. *Gallup World Poll* positions Costa Rica, alongside Denmark and Singapore, as the happiest country in the world. The aim of the survey conducted by *Gallup World Poll* was to reveal three indicators by posing a whole string of questions. The three indicators are: how each respondent perceives the quality of his or her life in its entirety, how content every respondent is with his or her daily routine (for example, are there moments of happiness, how many times a day they laugh and similar things) and how good the health of each respondent is. The survey confirmed that different cultures perceive success in different terms but that the feeling of being happy is universal – it means being happy in one's own skin and unwilling to change anything regarding one's life. Good health, having family members around and faith in God is what makes people in Costa Rica happy. The Costa Ricans are content with the simple things in life; they want to enjoy a stress-free existence, it is important to them to be surrounded by friends and to know that they can always count on their help, to be able to rely on God's providence and the universal and free healthcare system. The price – gladly paid, so to speak – of their happiness is a life without money in bank accounts, expensive electronic gadgets and cars. On the other hand, the source of happiness for the

Singaporeans lies in their willingness to work hard and make sacrifices, giving their lives purpose measured in long working hours and high salaries. Unity of purpose is the name of the game in Singapore and it provides each and every Singaporean with security and assurance that hard work will always be rewarded. The National Geographic magazine wrote extensively about these countries' reasons for happiness. However, the best selling book on the subject is Dan Buettner's *The Blue Zones of Happiness: Lessons from the World's Happiest People* in which the author finds out what makes people around the world happy and healthy. Ever more people are becoming obsessed with finding happiness.

The Danes' has become a global phenomenon. No matter how a given poll or survey is structured the Danes come out as one of the happiest nations in the world. Many books have been written on the subject and the Happiness Research Institute has been established, an independent forum of experts analyzing all aspects of prosperity, quality of life and happiness in Denmark. One of the leading members of the institute, Meik Wiking wrote a book titled *The Little Book of Hygge: The Danish Way to Live Well*. The book is somewhat of a bestseller and explains the Danish hygge lifestyle. Academics, scholars, journalists and politicians from all over the world are frequent visitors to the Institute, trying to figure out how to apply the Danish recipe for happiness to their own countries. Another book about the phenomenon of Danish happiness is Louisa Thomsen Brits' *The Book of Hygge: The Danish Art of Living Well*. The author gives us an engaging analysis of the Danish way of life. Quite a few documentaries have been filmed about the Danish way of life and how conducive that way of life is to a happy existence. One reputable British university even offers courses devoted to the phenomenon. It is clear that the Danes have successfully branded their way of life and their happiness and have turned it into a lucrative export product.

Everyone engaged in analyzing the Danish way of life agrees that the Danes are not only the happiest, but also the most composed, placid and serene of Europeans. The Danes spend most of their time with their families and friends but they also know how to enjoy solitude. The analysts also agree that that the Danes have developed an extremely efficient welfare system, one where state institutions give the citizens a sense of security and foster prosperity. Of course, these state institutions are not a source of happiness for the Danes but provide a solid framework within which the citizens can successfully pursue happiness. And as far as pursuing happiness goes, the Danes have their way of life, their hygge lifestyle that makes them happy and content. This begs the question: What exactly do the Danes have that the Croats do not? Nothing springs to mind. So, the inevitable conclusion is that the Croats have everything they need to be happy but they are not aware of it – or even if they are aware of all the good things they possess they are clueless as to how to translate their good fortune into happiness and all the bliss that goes along with it.

For example, Croatia is blessed with exceptionally favorable climate, seasonal in the north and Mediterranean in the south, along the Croatian coast. It is tempting, in the context of this particular comparison, to embrace the idea Norman Davies proposes in his book *Europe, a History*, in the chapter about ancient Greece, that 'high intensity sunlight may well have been one of the many ingredients which produced such spectacular results – in which case Homer, Plato and Archimedes may be seen as the product of native genius plus photochemistry'. As we have already seen, native genius is plentiful in Croatia and the appropriate climate is there too. The Danes, on the other hand, have to contend with 179 days of precipitation a year and cold, dark, foreboding and depressing long winters. They need to rely on artificial heat and artificial light to ward off the various ill effects of seasonal affective disorder. That quest to defeat nature makes Denmark the largest consumer of candles in Europe. Most Danes spend every second of sunshine outdoors, taking full advantage of every single sunray. The Croats, by contrast, are oblivious to their God-given four beautiful seasons. The Danes are enchanted by light and that fascination with illumination is reflected in the interior design of their houses – everything is subordinate to lighting and the assorted sources of different layers of gleaming glow...One thing the Danes and Croats have in common is sociability. However, the Danes are wary of foreigners and people they don't know in general. An immigrant living in Denmark has to be prepared to wait a long time for the experience of being invited for dinner by a Dane into his or her home. And when that ritual of acceptance is over, the immigrant should expect to be asked to pay for half the cost of the food. The typical Croat is fond of doing exactly the opposite – invite a complete stranger to lunch in a fancy restaurant and pick up the tab. The Danes spend more time

150

in their "humble abodes" than any other Europeans. They prefer relaxing over a cup of tea and coffee, or with a bowl of sweets, by their fireplaces to spending time in pubs and cafés – in Denmark, cafes and pubs, unlike those in Croatia, close pretty early. On average the Danes drink more coffee than the Croats, but they are not in the habit of sitting for prolonged periods of time in cafés – they drink their coffee at home or quickly on the go. The Croats could not imagine a life without spending copious amounts of time drinking coffee in cafes, watching the world go by and shooting the breeze with friends or strangers. Strangely enough, the Croatian obsession with idling away in cafes has become one of the most attractive traits of Croatian life to foreigners. In that sense the trait begs to be turned into a brand or at least a potent marketing tool. The Croats see nothing remarkable in their addiction to that peculiar ritual of idleness. If anything, for most Croats sipping coffee on the terrace of a restaurant or café is almost a religious duty, or something very akin to that.

When analyzing the Danish way of life, especially from the Croatian perspective, it is easy to conclude that the Croatian way of life offers more substance, more flavor, more color... And yet the Danes are happy and we are not. We always find time for other people, we are emphatic, we know how to enjoy the moment and have plenty of joie de vivre. We are open, hospitable, always ready to lend a helping hand...We don't work too hard, we have a universal healthcare and free education system. We eat healthy food. Our gastronomy is rich, a mixture of various cuisines. We have a healthy respect for our national customs to the point that tradition permeates all aspects of life in Croatia. Therefore, no traveler to Croatia can ever get bored. But our way of life, so contagious for most of the visitors to Croatia, we haven't yet been able to brand. What's more, we are completely unaware how rich in quality our way of life is. It is actually pathetic that foreigners have to point out to us how good we actually have it. Most Croats think that the grass is always greener on the other side. Those who have seen the grass on the other side know better but their voices are lost in the din of complaints about all things Croatian and praise for all things foreign. It is no wonder then that the Croats are not a happy nation. The Danes are smart enough to see for themselves what's good and what's not, and they are grateful for every little good thing that comes their way. They are aware, therefore they can be happy and therefore they are happy. The Croats keep waiting for the powers that be to give them something, always frantically searching for something to be discontented about, despite the fact that every Croat knows that being grateful for the good things in life is a sure recipe for happiness. The Croats are never satisfied with anything. The Danes, unlike the Croats, are not fond of displaying wealth because they are aware that the best things in life come without a price tag. The Danes have no need to compare themselves to anyone and are realistic enough to know that great achievements are reached by small steps, by setting the bar low enough at each stage of the journey. The Croats yearn for great results overnight and success is therefore always elusive. And the Croats are consequently always frustrated.

All happy nations have in common the ability to be grateful for the good things in life (regardless of how rich or impoverished a given nation is). Social scientists agree that a healthy balance between private and professional life is an important factor in the happiness equation (the factor actually favors the Croats because they do not work hard by any stretch of the imagination and the number of free days a year is substantial). The concept of overtime is unknown in Denmark and the Danes appreciate their free time. All happy nations on the face of the planet value highly their social life; time spent with their families and friends. Poor people, if they enjoy support from their families and friends, are happy people. As the adage goes – money can't buy happiness. The Croats are very similar to the Danes in that particular regard. Both the Danes and the Croats are creatures of habit. Both nations love rituals. The sense of belonging is strong both in Croatia and Denmark. Knud Jespersen wrote that "the Danes are not a nation, they are a tribe; tribalism unites them and imbues them with unflinching trust in their fellow countrymen". Most Croats are tribal in the context of family. As a society, on the other hand, we are divided. The most striking difference between the Danes and the Croats lies in the fact that the Danes trust each other whereas in Croatia the belief in the good nature of human kind has plummeted significantly in the last 15 years. The same period has seen an ever growing lack of confidence in the state institutions. Maybe there is a correlation between the two trends. Rarely can one see a bicycle locked to the railings in front of a café or a restaurant in Denmark. Prams too are regularly left untended in front of cafés and restaurants while the parents jauntily eat or drink with the toddlers. No one is afraid that someone might steal their bicycle or pram. The Danes have a trust in the state and its institutions and the state gives them freedom and confidence. Denmark's state institutions do not burden the populace with tons of illogical laws and regulations and the state bureaucracy is not geared towards terrorizing the citizens. The state of Denmark lets its subjects exercise total control over their own lives. The politicians in Croatia, by contrast, behave as though their power derived from God himself and perceive the ordinary Croatian citizens as serfs, non-entities fit only to be taxed and terrorized by the bureaucratic apparatus.

Louisa Thomsen Brit in her book states the obvious – the Danes believe that life is beautiful. They can hardly believe anything else because their needs are modest and they do not have to dread privation of any kind. Denmark, from a historical perspective, is a homogenous country and the Danes possess a sense of belonging to their country and one another. They live contentedly in a safe environment. There are no external pressures and only a modicum of state-applied authority is needed to keep the odd deviant in line. The Danes exhibit a great degree of social consciousness and in that regard Danish society is able to transcend the social and economic differences between various groups of citizens. The resultant social equilibrium is conducive to an almost universal feeling of equality in every day life. It should not surprise us, therefore, that the Danes are great patriots. The most common expression of patriotism in Denmark is caring about the community. No wonder, because the Danish hygge state of mind is predicated on casualness, comfort, informality, living in the moment, absence of great expectations…We can learn a lot from the Danish example even though most Croats would not trade their way of life for that of the Danes, regardless of how cool the hygge concept may appear to be. In any event, learning from the Danes can only make us realize how good we have it and teach us how to be happy.

What Did Croatia Bring to the European Union as a Dowry?

Untapped potential

In the few years leading to the accession of Croatia to the European Union, the media space in Croatia was inundated with analyses about the benefits the country would enjoy when it joined the Union; EU funds were often mentioned, the Europeanization of our public institutions knowingly emphasized, the importance of attracting foreign investors was rammed down our throats and the marvel of the Common Market was condescendingly explained by many a renowned academic and economist. But not many talking heads deigned to speak about what the European Union would get from Croatia. And why would they? Most people think that Croatia is a small country and completely inconsequential in the scheme of things. According to that line of thinking, the countries on the continent of Europe didn't even notice that a new country had joined the European Union on July 1, 2013. One British MP, just before

Croatia joined the EU, said to his colleagues who expressed apprehension about the new wave of immigrants, that they needn't fear because there were so few Croats that they could easily be lost in the throngs of people in one of their major cities.

The uninitiated may be forgiven for perceiving Croatia solely on the basis of its, relatively speaking, miniscule territory and small population size, and concluding, based on that perception, that the horse-shoe shaped country perching on the northern end of the Balkan Peninsula is completely irrelevant. However, it is a fact that many Europeans think that Croatia has a lot to offer to the European Union. Recently I came across a serious study about Croatia commissioned by the European decision makers. The authors of the study are of the opinion that Croatia has a lot of potential and advantages and that, despite its problems with bureaucracy, economy and corruption, will prove to be an asset to the European Union.

Reading the study I realized that the authors are far more knowledgeable about Croatia's potential and advantages than many high ranking Croatian officials. I wasn't too surprised though. Croatia still does not have a public database of its national treasures and if you want to know, for example, how much arable land there is in the country you'd get different answers from different institutions. The only relevant overview of the natural and cultural treasures, that is to say, the artefacts, buildings and places of national interest, was published by the Croatian Academy of Sciences and Arts in 2016.

The entry of new countries into the European Union is not unlike the process of acquisition in the business sector, when large corporations are deciding whether to acquire this or that small company. The key issue in the process is whether the targeted small company would prove more of an asset or liability to the big corporation. In terms of the European Union, the question is whether the entry of a new country will enrich or burden the Union. Bluntly put – will the existing members profit more by accepting the prospective entrant or will the prospective entrant profit more by joining? We should not fool ourselves by thinking that the European decision makers decided to accept Croatia into the European Union because they were guided by some altruistic impulse to help a small country in transition. The decision to accept Croatia into the European Union was based on self-interest, nothing less and nothing more. There is nothing wrong in acting out of self-interest in business and politics. For our own peace of mind we have to assume that our political elites were aware of that when they negotiated the terms of Croatia's entry into the European Union. We have to hope that our negotiators protected the national interests and did not obligingly sign on the dotted line proffered by the other side. At the end of the day, in business, as well as in politics, it is essential that both sides are happy with any given deal or agreement. The Croats expressed their wish to join the European Union in a referendum. However, to this day we haven't seen any viable strategy implemented by the state to take advantage of the membership in the European Union. It is actually funny, but at this stage it seems that joining the EU was an end in itself, and not, as it should have been, a means to improving the quality of life in Croatia. On the other hand, it is perfectly clear that the EU analyzed carefully all the aspects of admitting Croatia. And the final tally surely was that Croatia would not prove to be a liability and that European Union would be able to take advantage of Croatia's potential. Again, it is obvious that those in charge of the European Union know exactly what Croatia has and they know exactly how to get their hands on it.

The political reasons behind the EU's decision to accept Croatia into the fold are clear. The EU desperately needed a positive development after a string of setbacks and admitting a new member sent a message that the future of the Union was bright, despite all the recent hiccups. And Croatia behaved like the perfect teacher's pet – it completed with flying colors all the allocated tasks and set an example to its neighbors, showing them that it pays to work on democratization and reforms. Also, Croatia has been a real stabilizing factor in Southeast Europe, because Serbia has become dangerously radicalized and Bosnia and Herzegovina is completely bogged down in the quagmire of futile experiments of the international community and ill effects of the cumbersome system of governance (add to this Islamic radicalism that recently started to boldly rear its ugly head). The favorable geopolitical position of Croatia is also an important factor. Europe cannot, in geopolitical terms, function properly without access to the Adriatic from the east. Croatia is an important member of NATO and that fact, coupled with the already mentioned geopolitical factors, tipped the scales heavily in favor of the accession of Croatia to the EU. However, it is hard to believe that the EU's decision makers decided to invite Croatia to join based solely on political considerations, regardless of how pivotal they may be.

Immediately prior to the accession of Croatia to the European Union the international hacktivist group Anonymous sent a video message to the citizens of Croatia. The message, for the most part, went unnoticed in Croatia. The Anonymous people called on Croats to rebel against the depredations of the Croatian politicians and bankers and warned that membership in the European Union was a dangerous and dubious honor. The message included the following grim prediction: "Your children will be a cheap labor force in the European Union". Another interesting part of the message was a sentence about the EU's agenda regarding Croatia: "Your country is particularly interesting because it contains a range of resources such as water, forests, pristine nature, sea and islands so they are trying to impoverish you and take everything you have..." I'm not big on conspiracy theories and it is my firm conviction and belief that Croatia, based on its history, culture, human and other resources and potential, belongs in the European Union. And it has to be noted that the Anonymous people in their message to the Croatian nation merely rehashed what many European experts had been saying about Croatia's advantages for years. Those European experts list five distinct advantages Croatia possesses: arable land, reserves of fresh water, clean and warm sea with a well-intended coastline, forests and geopolitical position. An impressive list indeed, but not by any means exhaustive. The same experts also regularly mention Croatia's natural beauty, pristine nature and rich cultural heritage. So, the cyber activists did not tell us anything new. However, I simply cannot shake the feeling that Croatian politicians are completely oblivious of Croatia's potential. In that sense, maybe the message was sent as a wake-up call to the political leadership of Croatia. If so, there is no indication that those running the country have any inkling to heed the warning, assuming they are even aware of the message and its content. No wonder the Croatian masses have absolutely no confidence in the country's leadership. What's worse, this lack of confidence, absolutely justified to be sure, produces feelings of despair and impotent anger in the populace. But there is hope. As we have seen, foreign experts are aware of Croatia's potential. Ordinary people in Croatia are aware of how successful and rich the country can become. Therefore, it boils down to replacing the incompetents in power and setting up a system of governance based on merit. The sooner that's done, the better for all concerned, including the incompetents in question.

Croatia boasts huge areas of arable land. That fact, coupled with the favorable climate, creates perfect conditions for producing enormous quantities of healthy food. In exact numbers the phrase *huge areas of arable land* means 1,850,000 hectares of prime arable land – 500,000 hectares of which lie unused and uncultivated. If we include in the equation the land that, for various reasons, is not arable at the moment but can be turned into agricultural land, then the area of more or less readily available arable land is, according to some experts, as high as 2,500,000 hectares. The state owns about one third of all arable land in the country.

Large swaths of arable land in Croatia, due to the war and impoverished state of Croatian farmers, have remained free of artificial fertilizers and pesticides. That means that the cropland is unpolluted – the main precondition for producing healthy food. In this particular regard Croatia enjoys one huge advantage over other, more developed, food producing nations because the organic produce market in Europe, and in the whole world for that matter, is growing at exponential rates due to the fact that demand outstrips supply by a large margin. By way of comparison, Israel has managed to reclaim 1.1 million hectares of arable land from the desert and an incredible 500,000 hectares of land (despite acute water shortages) is under irrigation. As a result, Israel produces most of its food and exports flowers, fruit and vegetables all over the world. During the winter months Israel serves as a veritable greenhouse of Europe, exporting watermelons, tomatoes, cucumbers, peppers, strawberries, many kinds of citrus fruits, roses and carnations to the continent. And Croatia is located in the very heart of that continent and, ironically, has at least twice as much arable land, under which and through which rivers flow, than Israel.

Irrigation should not really pose a problem for Croatia, not with 32,818 cubic meters of renewable supplies of water per capita, which places the country among the 30 most water-rich countries in the world and among the top five in Europe. Croatia, with its vast supplies of clean and drinkable water (in terms of volume we are third in Europe, behind Norway and Iceland), can become one of the main exporters of water in the ever thirstier world and thus secure

162

its financial future. Some people in Croatia have proposed that we should enter into trade agreements with the Arab world on the principle of "water for oil". Regardless of transportation costs it is obvious that Croatia, with its supplies of water, has what it takes to become a major economic player on the world stage in the 21st century.

Not often do we hear in our media that Croatia is rich in forests. Forest area in Croatia measures at 2,690,000 hectares or 47 per cent of total land area. 95% of forest area is covered by natural forests, representing an important part of Europe's natural wealth. Most forests in Croatia are owned by the state (about 2,100,000 hectares) which makes it that much easier to manage them. *Hrvatske Šume* (Croatian Forests), a public company, is responsible for forest management of state owned forests. The company's records are transparent and in the public domain and therefore the numbers cited above are as accurate as they can be. Croatia has the wherewithal, both in terms of raw materials and know-how, to start producing high quality wooden furniture. There's a lot more money in that than in just exporting logs...

Croatia is blessed with one of the cleanest seas in the world, beautiful coastline and pleasant climate. The Adriatic region of Croatia is the country's most precious treasure. But, the Croatian tourism industry hasn't yet realized the full potential of the country's coastline. It is, with 1,246 islands and islets, one of the most indented coastlines in the world. And under the surface of the Croatian sea there is an abundance of fish species. Unfortunately, a fair number of the species of fish that grace our sea are endangered due to overfishing. About 65,000 tons of fish are caught every year, 85% of which are fish belonging to oily fish species. Croatia exports a lot more fish and other sea foods then it imports – we export about half our fish catch every year. In that regard the fishing industry is almost unique in Croatia. About one half of the exported fish ends up in Japan – mostly the Atlantic bluefin tuna. The fish belonging to white fish species we export, for the most part, to Italy and other countries in the region. Many people are probably unaware of the fact that Croatia is the European record holder in the diversity of freshwater fish species. Croatia is home to 113 freshwater fish species. We hold third place in terms of the number of species of invertebrates, fifth place in terms of the number of reptiles and seventh place in terms of the number of mammals. And we also bring to Europe 29 indigenous species of animals (for example, the Istrian cattle breed boskarin, the Lika cattle breed buša, the Turopolje pig breed, the Lika sheep breed pramenka, the Tornjak, the Carniolan honey bee …).

Croatia is positioned right at the crossroads of the East and West, Central Europe and the Mediterranean. This fortuitous geographical location affords Croatia with countless opportunities. But, to fully take advantage of those opportunities we need to come up with a viable transport strategy. We have already done a great deal as regards road transport but we haven't done practically anything to modernize our inadequate rail network and replace the antiquated locomotives and carriages that are currently in service. Once we have done that, then the ports of Rijeka and

Ploče will become strategically important doorways into Europe from the Mediterranean basin.

These God-given gifts are ready made to be utilized for the development of the Croatian economy and turned into important strategic assets to Europe and European markets. We have to be careful though. Bad management and neglect can very well destroy what God in his infinite wisdom has blessed us with. The high rating of a country rich in preserved areas can plummet dramatically as a result of using outdated industrial methods and facilities, bad waste management, environment pollution and unsustainable commercialization of natural resources. This doesn't mean keeping investors and entrepreneurs at bay. It simply means that Croatia should take great care to protect its assets. Croatia has the cleanest sea in the Mediterranean, 12th cleanest in the whole world. In addition to that, Croatia is one of the most naturally diverse countries with the most preserved areas in Europe. At this point in time about 11 per cent of Croatian territory is under some kind of protection. It is of strategic importance for Croatia to have more of its territory protected so as to safeguard its natural wealth from devastation. Many European experts consider Croatia as a large European national park and we shouldn't ignore that opinion. Quite the contrary.

In that respect we ought to focus our energies on encouraging the growth of clean industry, production of healthy foods, development of innovative leisure programs and improvement of the cultural and health tourism. Europe is well aware of the fact the Croats are capable of manufacturing and producing many commercially viable products and items. For this reason, many analysts in Europe think that Croatian food, chemical, pharmaceutical, construction, military and transport industries are loaded with potential. Ditto the country's advanced technology sector and cultural heritage.

It is difficult to understand why, with all our potential and advantages, we keep running around in circles and why the quality of life in Croatia keeps getting lower. Are Croats aware that other countries have achieved a lot more with a lot less? Do we possess enough knowledge, enthusiasm, will and determination to protect, enrich and develop our potential and values in today's world of globalization and commercialization? Or are we simply going to bow our head to those who are more capable than we are and hand over to them what God has given us?

Croats Teaching Europe about Islam

The pitfalls of Europeanization

In most European countries today the far right is on the ascendant. If we listen carefully to the far right rhetoric, we cannot fail to notice that the right-wing parties owe their popularity to the current trend of intolerance towards the minorities, immigrants, foreigners, the other... Many people are taken aback by how fortified feelings and expressions of xenophobia have become in Europe. Some, like the French philosopher Alain Finkielkraut, justify such trends with the fact that some immigrants are averse to adapting to the Western way of life and that such an attitude nips any initiative towards integration and multiculturalism in the bud and inevitably creates a shadow immigrant society that promotes, propagates and perpetuates values incompatible with those of Western civilization. There is no doubt that the recent recession is responsible, at least to some extent, for this desire to find a scapegoat for Europe's myriad problems, be they real or imagined... There are some who propose that Europe's value of multiculturalism has been a sham all along and that European people have never been able to adopt the American mindset with respect to immigration and integration simply because Europe is lost in the mire of its feudal legacy while the New World is structured on a long history of flight from the Old World and its perpetual hatreds and internecine bouts of intolerance. In simple terms, guest workers in Germany can never be perceived by the Germans as anything else but guest workers, that is to say, second-class citizens. It is a fact that Europe, in a political sense, has been propagating freedom, equality and tolerance for decades. It is also a fact that the treatment of minorities and immigrants leaves a lot to be desired in many European countries. There is a fair share of hypocrisy underlining Europe's lofty stance regarding human rights.

During accession talks a lot of media coverage in Croatia was given to EU officials saying "Croatia needs to be Europeanized", "Croatia needs to embrace European standards", "Croatia must look up to developed Western countries" etc. The issue of minority rights was under special scrutiny; Croatia had been perceived by many Europeans as a country where it wasn't exactly pleasant to be a member of an ethnic minority ever since the war. The whole accession talks business actually proved how sanctimonious, in political terms, the EU really is. EU officials berated Croatia for being chauvinistic and xenophobic. At that same time Gypsies were being expelled from a number of locales in the EU, the prophet Muhammad was being ridiculed in cartoons, the ethnic and linguistic identity of immigrants from the former Yugoslav republics was being in turn ignored and belittled all across the EU, building permits for minarets were being denied, citizens of EU countries were being discriminated against, undesirable elements were being made stateless, and African refugees were being left to die of thirst or drown in the Mediterranean Sea. No one in Croatia then had the temerity to ask: Is there a democratic criterion according to which Croatia is more developed than and superior to most European countries? And do we have a democratic practice that Europe can learn from us? Had the questions been posed it would have, undoubtedly, met with derisive laughter from all those EU officials who were busying themselves with admonishing Croatia. They would have poured scorn on the idea that the mighty and infallible EU could learn something from a small country on the backward Balkan Peninsula. But, the question should have been posed. And answered.

"Croatia treats its Muslim population better than any other country in Europe. The Christian world can learn a lot from Croatia and the Muslim world can also learn a lot from Croatia. The former in relation to its Muslim minority and the latter in relation to its Christian minority," said the Croatian Mufti, Aziz Hasanović, while assuming office, just prior to Croatia's accession to the EU. On the same occasion, his predecessor Ševko Orembašić, who had been openly praising Croatia for years, stated that "Islam in Europe is the subject of ridicule and derision." In Switzerland, that paragon of democracy and civilized way of life, it is not allowed to build minarets. In Croatia it is. At the celebration marking the opening of the mosque in Rijeka, the most beautiful mosque in Europe, the following phrase was on everyone lips: "In Croatia, a multi-cultural, multi-ethnic and multi-faith country, all citizens, without exception, have the right to freedom of religion..." The representatives of the Muslim and Bosniak community in Croatia use every opportunity to emphasize how tolerant and devoted to the concept of multiculturalism Croatia is. Already in 1916 the Croatian Parliament recognised Islam as an official religion in Croatia. In 2002 the government of Croatia and the Islamic Community in Croatia ratified the Contract Regarding Special Relations, giving the Muslims in Croatia various rights including the obligation of the Croatian government to finance 22 Muslim parishes. The contract thoroughly protects the rights of the Muslim community in Croatia – for example, a school with as few as seven Muslim kids has to, if the parents of the kids wish so, secure Muslim religious instruction in the school; every Muslim in the Croatian Armed Forces has the right to leave his or her post between 10 o'clock in the morning and 1 o'clock in the afternoon to pray. As a gesture of gratitude Mufti Hasanović has been teaching Croatian soldiers waiting to be sent on peace missions to Afghanistan about the Muslim culture and customs. Many Croatian soldiers owe their lives to what they have learned from him. Mufti Hasanović also gave his contribution to the success of the Center for Halal Quality Certification – the center helps Croatian companies to export their products to Islamic countries. It is a shame that Croatia is not really adept at taking advantage of the fact that it treats Muslims better than any other country in Europe. The possibilities are endless – from establishing more cordial and closer relations with rich Muslim countries to convincing the pigheaded leaders of the Bosniak community in Bosnia and Herzegovina that Croatia, contrary to anti-Croatian propaganda, is well disposed towards the Bosniaks and that their artificial state cannot hope to survive without Croatian help. The latter point is important in many different regards because the Bosniak leaders, instead of working on unity and equality of all constituent nations in Bosnia and Herzegovina, are determined to marginalize the Bosnian Croats.

Croatia is equally tolerant towards other minorities. However, only the Muslim community is brave enough to stand up and tell the truth. The Croatian Constitution lists 22 ethnic minorities. The state of Croatia supports and co-finances all the projects of those minorities. By way of comparison, Croats are not even recognised as an ethnic minority in Slovenia let alone mentioned in the Slovenian Constitution. The Austrian state institutions, 20 years after the international recognition of Croatian independence, still do not find it appropriate to recognize the Croatian ethnic minority outside the framework of *Yugoslav Immigrant Community*. It is obvious that the rights the ethnic minorities in Croatia enjoy are far greater than those enjoyed by ethnic minorities in most European countries. Moreover, the fact that some ethnic minorities in Croatia insist on being a world apart in relation to Croatian society but still enjoy their dual voting rights and have eight guaranteed seats in the Croatian Parliament baffles many European politicians. It is clear that the privileges Croatia generously handed out to all and sundry after the war are being used today by venal politicians representing particular ethnic groups for the benefit of their mother countries and to the detriment of Croatian society as a whole. Inevitably this puts the ethnic groups in question on the path of self-imposed isolation. Ironically, only the venal politicians stand to benefit from this development. They have shrewdly secured their voter base at the expense of the very constituents whose cause they so vehemently pretend to be fighting for. All in all, it is undeniable that Croatia can be, and really should be, the role model to every European country with respect to minority rights, and especially with respect to how Croatia treats its Muslim minority. Speaking of minority rights it has to be pointed out that gender minorities in Croatia enjoy more freedoms and rights than they do in most other European countries. In light of everything I have mentioned above, it is clear that the process of Europeanization is a two-way street.

PART III

Croatia and Its Balkan Neighbors

Two Truths about the Wars

Who is to blame for the wars on the territory of the former Yugoslavia?

In the fall of 2012, at the International Criminal Tribunal for the Former Yugoslavia in The Hague the Croatian generals Gotovina and Markač were acquitted of all charges against them, including that of taking part in a joint criminal enterprise. The acquittal caused a deep political rift between Serbia and Croatia. The Serbian nationalist politicians, backed by the state-run Serbian media and sympathizers of the Serbian imperialistic agenda all over the world, had been waging an aggressive campaign of disinformation about the Croatian War of Independence since 1995, when the Croatian Army soundly defeated the Serbian forces of occupation and paramilitary Serbian formations on the internationally recognised territory of the Republic of Croatia. The disinformation campaign had been, for a time, fairly successful and reaped many spectacular results, one of which was the arrest of Gotovina and Markač on the charges of crimes against humanity and war crimes. The acquittal of the Croatian generals spelled the defeat of Serbia's disinformation campaign, the main aim of which was to shift the international focus away from the Serbian aggressive war against Croatia and the resultant sack of Vukovar, genocide against Croats and other non-Serbs within the internationally recognised borders of the Republic of Croatia and wanton destruction of whole cities, towns and villages and Croatian cultural and historic heritage. The Serbian Army and Serb paramilitary formations had committed war crimes and crimes against humanity on a scale unseen on the continent since the end of World War II. No wonder then that the Serbian politicians panicked when the news of the generals' acquittal reached their ears. The myth that Croatia shared the blame with Serbia for the war had been broken. The disinformation strategy lay in ruins and for the Serbian politicians it was back to the drawing board.

Mentally sane people tend to perceive certain Serbian politicians as unhinged individuals who live in their own warped reality. These Serbian politicians do not seem to remember whose tanks rolled towards Zagreb, who destroyed the city of Vukovar and who committed countless acts of genocide and ethnic cleansing in the Krajina region of Croatia and all over Bosnia and Herzegovina. Despite Serbian propaganda, the truth was bound to triumph in the end. And so it did. But, the situation is not as clear-cut as it should be. The war ended more than 20 years ago, diplomatic relations between Croatia and Serbia were duly established, both countries started investigating war crimes and crimes against humanity committed during the war and life continued; new generations grew up, born in peace and disconnected experientially from the war...The Croatian War of Independence, in certain circles, became a taboo subject and certain people avoided the subject of the recent past so as not to jeopardize their interests in the present, hoping that the truth would find its way to the surface without their help. As we have seen, the truth did indeed find its way to the surface, but, unfortunately, only a few people realize that now it is out there it has to be used to exorcise the demons of the past. Because the demons, if not expelled from the collective consciousness of the peoples in the region, are bound to haunt the peninsula forever. And, again, only the truth can free all of us from that psychological scourge. In that sense, coming to terms with the truth is the main prerequisite for a lasting peace. There are many people, on both sides, who lost someone or something during the war and they desperately try to hang on to the loss because they've got nothing else to keep them psychologically together. They need to come to terms with historical truth so that they can start looking to the future, as opposed to the past. In that regard, recent history has to be studied by everyone and freely discussed in all public forums by everyone. That's what it means to come to terms with historical truth. It is not the fault of a son, or a daughter, if the father committed a crime. It is high time we stopped burdening the new generations with outdated propaganda and thus forcing them to uphold the crimes of their fathers. It is clear, from a political perspective, who and what caused the war, it is clear from a military perspective who attacked whom, and it is clear from a purely human perspective which individuals committed crimes against humanity and war crimes. And it is also clear who benefitted from the carnage. We just have to be brave enough to study the subject and be brave enough to speak the truth. The information regarding all of the above is out there, readily available for anyone interested in picking it up.

One journalist from Belgrade, a dear friend of mine, warned me a few years ago that coming to terms with historical truth might not be possible in the foreseeable future because generations of kids and young people in Serbia during the 1990s had been exposed to diabolical propaganda that viciously demonized Croatia and everything Croatian. As a result, my friend surmised, people in Serbia would be unable to understand what really happened and why during the war for years, maybe even generations to come. It is a fact that the Serbian academic community, the education system and the media find it easier to fabricate history than to come to terms with it. Small wonder then that according to one survey conducted in Serbia in 2017, 64 per cent of the Serbians are unaware of the horrific crimes the Serbian Army committed in 1991 in Vukovar and 71 per cent of the Serbians do not know that Sarajevo was under siege for almost four years... My journalist friend herself admits that she had only become aware of the scale of the criminality of the Milošević regime in 2003 when she visited, on a journalistic assignment, Vukovar and the Ovčara farm, where hundreds of Croatian POWs and civilians were massacred by local Serb paramilitaries acting on the orders of the Serbian government and leadership of the army. To be fair, the former Serbian President Tadić did tentatively try to initiate a number of processes by which Serbia would eventually accept responsibility for the war and everything that happened during the conflict. Unfortunately, due to Tadić's kowtowing to the radical right for fear of losing popularity, Serbia did not go through a catharsis and the truth about the wars the Milošević regime had started (from Kosovo to Slovenia) remained hidden from the Serbian public. Tadić's successors, radicals Nikolić and Vučić, participated in Serbia's attack on Croatia so it would be foolhardy to expect them to come to terms with historical truth and work towards establishing a lasting and just peace on the Balkan Peninsula. The Serbian leaders (apart from a few notable exceptions) simply did not have enough courage to confront the image in the mirror and admit the truth. They followed the path of least resistance and worked for those international institutions that stand to gain money and influence from relativizing the issue of guilt in relation to the Serbian wars of aggression from 1991 to 1995. In light of the efforts of the Serbian media, education system and government, we should not judge the ordinary Serbs too harshly when they fail to understand that the acquittal of Gotovina and Markač was a just decision and that the Croatian War of Independence was a defensive war against Serbia's military aggression. To be sure, many Serbians are aware of what really went on during the war but they are in a minority and it is obvious that quite some time will pass before their voices are heard through the din of official nonsense in Serbia. In 2008 I conducted a survey in Serbia and other countries created after the break-up of Yugoslavia. The central question was *Who is really to blame?* Some results of this survey I published in the book *Hrvatska i susjedi*

(Croatia and Its Neighbors). In short, there was not much difference in perceptions between 2008 and the 1990s... Each country has its own truth and is fully committed to clinging to it at all costs. That said, there is some consensus regarding our collective recent past. The usual suspects, based on all the responses in total, turned out to be the political leadership of Yugoslavia, Slobodan Milošević, Serbs and international community. However, respondents in different countries liked different suspects better and in that sense a few more names, apart from those given above, are worthy of mention.

Serbia and Montenegro were allies in the wars of aggression against Slovenia, Croatia, Bosnia and Herzegovina and Kosovo. The respondents from these two countries, unsurprisingly, held the same people responsible for the wars. However, more Montenegrin than Serbian respondents thought that Milošević was responsible for the wars (25%) and more Serbian than Montenegrin respondents thought that the international community holds the top spot in that regard (36%). About half the respondents from both countries believed that the political leadership of Yugoslavia should be held responsible. 21% of respondents from both countries opined that Franjo Tuđman was the main culprit. 15% of respondents from Serbia and 16% of respondents from Montenegro gave that honor to the then President of Bosnia and Herzegovina Alija Izetbegović. It is interesting to note that 18% of the Serbian respondents thought that Slobodan Milošević was solely responsible for the wars. When it comes to the question of which nations are responsible for the wars the percentages tell a somewhat different story. 15% Montenegrins said the Croats as opposed to 6% of their countrymen who thought the Bosniaks caused the whole mayhem. Some respondents in both countries said that the wars had been the result of an unfortunate set of circumstances – 14% in Serbia and 11% in Montenegro. It is notable that 9% of the Montenegrin respondents perceived the Serbs as a nation as the main cause of the war and 4% of the Serbian respondents shared that opinion.

Bosnia and Herzegovina is a federation of Bosniaks, Serbs and Croats. The country was devastated by the war and still lives in the shadow of that catastrophe. 37% of the respondents saw the Serbs, as a nation, as the main factor that had led to the war and 34% of the respondents squared the blame on the shoulders of Slobodan Milošević because he had been the leader of the Serbian nation at the time. 28% of the respondents chose to blame the international community and 26% of those asked figured that the politicians who had been in power at the time had led the country into chaos and war. Fifth place belongs to the Croatian President Franjo Tuđman – 23% of the Bosnian-Herzegovinian respondents picked him as the main cause of the war. Interestingly enough, 15% of the respondents saw their own president, Alija Izetbegović, the first president of Bosnia and Herzegovina, as the person who had ushered in the horrors of war. Also, 11% of the Bosnian-Herzegovinian respondents saw the Yugoslav People's Army as the main factor that had made the war inevitable. The percentage as regards the YPA is significantly higher with the respondents from Bosnia and Herzegovina than those from any other country included in the survey. Of course, the percentages regarding the respondents from Bosnia and Herzegovina should not be taken at face value because the opinions of the respondents belonging to different ethnic groups vary widely.

Slovenia fought the Yugoslav People's Army for ten days and the country did not suffer any significant damage during that short, and for the Slovenians, exceptionally successful conflict. The Slovenian respondents, for the most part, agreed on who was responsible for the wars that devastated Bosnia and Herzegovina and Croatia. 31% of the Slovenian respondents thought that the Serbs should be blamed. 28% of the respondents blamed Slobodan Milošević and only 10% were of the opinion that the politicians comprising the leadership of Yugoslavia in the late 80s and early 90s were guilty of starting the wars.

Croatia was attacked by the Yugoslav People's Army and countless units of Serb paramilitary formations in 1991. One third of the country's territory was occupied until 1995 when the Croatian Army defeated the YPA and Serb paramilitaries and liberated the occupied areas. The Croatian respondents shared the opinions of their Slovenian counterparts. 54% of the Croatian respondents thought that the Serbs were directly responsible for the wars and 28% of the respondents believed the wars were Slobodan Milošević's brainchild. The Croatian respondents, just like the Slovenian respondents, did not think that the politicians in charge of the country at the time had had much say as regards the developments that led to the wars. Both the Slovenian and Croatian correspondents did not believe in coincidences.

Interestingly, a significant number of respondents from the other countries, unlike those from Croatian and Slovenia, believed that the wars had been the result of an unfortunate set of circumstances (9 – 14%, depending on the country).

Macedonia escaped the attentions of the YPA and Serb paramilitaries. 38% of the Macedonian respondents saw the Yugoslav leadership as the cause of the wars, 29% awarded that role to Slobodan Milošević and 25% thought that the Serbs, as a nation, were responsible for the wars. Not surprisingly and unlike the respondents from the other countries a fair share of Macedonians (13 %) saw the Albanians as the main cause of the wars.

It is interesting to note that most respondents, all across the board apart from Bosnia and Herzegovina, perceived the YPA and its leadership as soldiers and officers just following orders and as such not responsible for the wars.

So, in Slovenia and Croatia most people agree who is to blame for the wars, but in the other countries created after the break up of Yugoslavia there are virtually as many opinions regarding the issue as there are people. On the other hand, according to the results of the survey, a significant number of people in all the countries included in the survey see Slobodan Milošević as the person who engineered the wars. A high number of respondents, excluding those from Croatia and Slovenia, perceived the political leadership of Yugoslavia and the international community as the main villains in the story of how the wars in the former Yugoslavia were made possible. The Serbs, not surprisingly, did not fare well in the survey. It is hard, for most people, to perceive just one man, regardless of how powerful and charismatic he may be, as capable of producing so much evil, pain, misery and suffering on his own, without the willing support of hordes of his minions, followers and worshippers of his hideous ideology. The wave of hatred on which the YPA and Serb paramilitaries rode and committed numerous heinous crimes against humanity spawned a yearning for revenge in many survivors of their depredations. And a number of those survivors sated that yearning. Blood followed blood, evil followed evil the length and breadth of Croatia, Bosnia and Herzegovina and Kosovo. We should not, however, fall into the trap of confusing cause and effect... By the same token, it would be incongruous, in that sense, to put one whole nation in the dock. Guilt can never be collective. As much as the Hague Tribunal tried to get to the bottom of the causes of the wars in the former Yugoslavia, the results of the court's efforts, due to the indolence of some of the officers of the court and blatant partiality of some of the judges, were mixed. The issues, despite a number of just verdicts, were often left unresolved and even more muddied. We put too much faith in historians, we expect them to tell us what happened and why it happened and we tend to accept their verdict at face value. More often than not, they're prone to tweak their opinions and conclusions according to the current political agendas of their countries' governments. Instead of looking up information for ourselves, we expect historians to give us the ultimate truth. And therein lies the conundrum. The information is out there but most people, often for purely disingenuous reasons, would always rather accept a historian's inflammatory rhetoric than doing some research on their own. A truly incredible situation given the fact that we live in an information age. And thus hatred lives on in the region. The only way out of the clutches of hatred for both nations is to turn to the future, instead of being led into the maze of the past by people who sell fake history simply because the political situation allows them to do so.

Dreading the Prospect of Regional Cooperation

Countries created after the break-up of Yugoslavia 20 years on

Immediately after the end of the celebrations marking the entry of Croatia into the European Union in the summer of 2013, the then president of Croatia, Ivo Josipović, in tandem with his Slovenian counterpart Pahor, organized a meeting, in Zagreb, of the presidents of the countries in the region. As the president of a new EU member he chose Bosnia and Herzegovina as the destination for his first official visit. The media outlets in the region hailed his decision to go to Bosnia and Herzegovina as a sign that Croatia had not turned its back to its neighbors now that it was a member of the European club. But, in Croatia, the reactions to the news were mixed. There were many people in Croatia who balked (and still do) at the mention of regional cooperation and who indignantly asked: "Well, haven't we been fighting tooth and bleeding nail to get out of this Balkan mess – so what's with this nonsense message to the world that we are not weaned off this troublesome region and not quite ready to be part of the developed West?" There are others in Croatia who get off on being part of the Balkan community and want to nurture and strengthen Croatia's ties with the peoples of the former Yugoslavia, regardless of the Schengen Agreement. There are even some people in Croatia who think that it is our moral obligation to be on good terms with our former countrymen at all costs because, they believe, Europe wants us back in some sort of neo-Yugoslav fold again so that we can act as a Europeanizing force there.

The terms *region, West Balkan, Southeast Europe* and *former Yugoslavia* denote pretty much the same thing. However, the terms have been extremely politicized and the Croatian public often reacts negatively to them. No wonder because the physical and mental scars from the war still haven't healed. We remember the initiatives of some EU member states to accept Croatia into the EU only as part of the whole former Yugoslav package. And we also remember how insulted we felt by the initiatives, having worked so hard to be considered a worthy member of the European Union. It is understandable then that many people flinched at the mention of the term *Yugosphere*. On the other hand, Europe did insist that Croatia should foster regional cooperation, signaling that Croatia could not hope to join the EU if it didn't bend over backwards to build strong political ties and trade links with its neighbors. Establishing solid political and trade ties in reality meant forgiving crimes against humanity, backing financially and morally other countries in the region and being open to any form of partnership with any given country in the region. To be sure, that approach benefited Croatia – exports rose significantly, new investment opportunities presented themselves, the Croatian police force started cooperating better with the police forces of the neighboring countries. However, when it came to politics, the issue of regional cooperation became the bane of Croatian politicians' existence. They became averse to calling a spade a spade, let alone raise their voices in protection of Croatian interests, lest this or that European politician should berate them for not toeing the line. That servile attitude of the Croatian politicians led them to abandon the Bosnian Croats to their fate. As a result, the Croats, as the smallest constituent ethnic group in Bosnia and Herzegovina, had no chance in hell of competing with the Bosniaks and the Serbs, especially since the Muslim world looked after the interests of the former and the Serbian government championed all the causes of the latter. The Croatian government even chose to let slide a number of serious transgressions committed by Serbia against Croatia, transgressions that actually reflected the almost medieval and definitely uncivilized nature of the Serbian regime. This passive stance of the Croatian government was a constant source of frustration to the Croatian public. Needless to say, the benevolent attitude of the Croatian government was never reciprocated by the Serbian or Bosnian governments.

Today, Croatia is a member of the European Union. No politician in Croatia need be afraid anymore of being criticized for not being sufficiently enthusiastic for making Serbia, Bosnia or Herzegovina or any other country in the region happy. Finally, our politicians can be free to pursue the country's interests unfettered by the obligation to cooperate with Croatia's neighbors. Nobody can dictate policies regarding the region to our government any more. Now is the time for Croatia to come into its own. Of course, we have to realize that Croatia, as a member of the European Union, has to follow, at least to a significant extent, the Union's policies in relation to Southeast Europe. This in no way prevents Croatia from generating its own constructive policies in that regard. It has to be said that with Croatia the European Union has acquired a valuable factor of stability in Southeast Europe. That factor had been conspicuously absent in this part of the world from well before the break up of Yugoslavia until Croatia joined NATO and the European Union shortly thereafter. However, it is a long way from being a factor in a geopolitical equation to tangible results on the ground. Croatia has to step up to the plate and prove to everyone that it is well capable of meeting the expectations of the EU and becoming the guarantor of stability in this part of Europe. Once that task has been accomplished the other 26 member states of the European Union will appreciate Croatia as an indispensible member of the Union and Croatia's Balkan partners will start bending over backwards to be in Croatia's good graces.

Croatia's interests in the region are compatible with those of the European Union. For example, both Croatia and the European Union would like to see all of Croatia's neighbors in the fold as soon as possible. The rationale behind this desire is simple; the Balkan Peninsula cannot be allowed to continue to be the black hole of Europe, constantly threatening to suck the continent into strife and discord.

Both the European Union and Croatia, for obvious reasons, need Bosnia and Herzegovina to develop into a prosperous federation where all three constituent nations could live in harmony together. One of the main obligations of Croatia, in that particular regard, is to protect the rights and interests of about half a million Bosnian Croats. The Bosnian Croats are only nominally equal to the Bosniaks and Serbs, the other two constitutive peoples of the Bosnian-Herzegovinian federation. In reality, 500,000 Croats in Bosnia are marginalized and in many ways discriminated against. Serbia, such as it exists at this point in time, is an eyesore for both Croatia and the European Union in the political and social landscape of Europe. Croatia and the European Union are in agreement about the need to induce Serbia to modernize its institutions and industry and implement the required reforms. The reforms Croatia implemented in order to be accepted in the European Union changed Croatian society considerably for the better. It is in the interests of many Croatian companies to be able to continue doing business without any undue restrictions in the neighboring markets. Also, it is important for Croatia that companies from the neighboring countries continue investing money in Croatian businesses, that there are no restrictions, or as few as possible, on the movement of goods, services and people between the countries in the region, that there is better cooperation between police forces in combating organized crime and the trafficking of people and goods, that minority rights are respected... At the same time, the leaders of Bosnia and Herzegovina, Serbia, Montenegro and Macedonia should really do themselves a favor and accept every offer coming from Zagreb, because they need an advocate in Brussels and an adviser on their road to Euro-Atlantic integration. Even those who were initially envious of Croatia's accession to the EU would have by now realized that Croatia deserves to be a member state of the European Union – if for no other reason than to use its influence in the EU institutions to ease their countries' entry into the European Union. Croatia should not be making statements to the effect that everyone in the region will automatically respect Croatia now that the country is in the European Union. Croatia should make it absolutely clear to its eastern neighbors that they cannot get something for nothing, that they have to work hard to implement the required reforms if they want Croatia to help them on their way to the European Union.

And finally, when the word *region* is mentioned, I think it is time we started perceiving Austria, Italy and Hungary as part of the region too. We share many common goals and aspirations with these countries. Besides, Croatia was in a union with Hungary for 800 years, with Austria for 500. By way of comparison, Croatia and Serbia were together in various incarnations of Yugoslavia for a mere 70 years.

Croats Have Too Many Complexes and Serbs Too Few

Differences and similarities between Serbs and Croats

From 2011 to 2016 Croatia was ruled by a democratic, pro-European left-wing party. During the same period Serbia was ruled by nationalist and pro-Russian politicians. Nevertheless, Serbia got out of recession sooner than Croatia did. To be sure, the Croatian institutions had been reformed and Europeanized, but regardless of that, many entrepreneurs claimed that it was easier for them to do business in Serbia. The standard of living is far higher than that in Serbia but it seems that our Serbian neighbors enjoy life a lot more. During the period in question Croatia became a member of the European Union. Serbia only received a date for opening accession talks. Croatia faithfully completed every task the European Union imposed on it and abided by all the conditions of the international community. Serbia, by contrast, managed to force the European Union and international community to compromise on a number of issues and even ignored some pressures without incurring any penalties from either the EU or international community. Croatia cooperated in good faith with the Hague Tribunal as regards processing cases of war crimes and crimes against humanity while Serbia stalled, protected those guilty of war crimes and crimes against humanity and withheld evidence. At that time Croatia was often described as a regional leader, while Serbia and Serbs were depicted as villains in Hollywood films. The Serbs marveled at how clean and modern Croatian cities were and how modern and developed the road network was and the Croats envied the Serbs' ability to attract foreign investment – the Fiat company alone invested almost a million euros in the car factory in Kragujevac and Austrian investors created 20,000 jobs in the period from 2000 to 2013. The Serbs' knack for attracting foreign investment is best reflected in President Putin's plan, presented in 2013 in Sochi to Serbian President Nikolić, to invest an additional 1.5 billion euros to the same amount already invested in the Serbian NIS oil company. Putin also offered 1.7 billion dollars for financing the Serbian stretch of the South Stream pipeline. In light of the above we simply have to ask ourselves: Where is our INA company and what happened with the promises of our Hungarian partners?

Some people may say – Croats are pedantic, principled, they stick to the rules and like to pretend they're smarter than they really are and, as a result, often botch things up, whereas Serbs are often rude, boorish and like to break the rules but nevertheless make things happen. In the late 80s a theatre play called *Šovinistička farsa* (Chauvinistic Farce) was very popular in Belgrade. The play in a way "embodied" all the stereotypes about the Croats and the Serbs. The typical Croat is depicted as a short and lively man in a white suit, always charming, good-mannered and conflict-averse. The typical Serb, on the other hand, is depicted as a spontaneous and boorish man, tall of stature, unpretentious but bursting with self-confidence. There are many jokes about Serbs and Croats in which the Serb is always rough around the edges but manly, while the Croat is slightly effeminate and overly polite. These stereotypes persist to this day and many Croatian girls perceive Serbs as macho guys as opposed to many Serbian girls who expect every Croatian male to be a romantic lover. We encounter stereotypical differences between the Serbs and Croats on many other levels too. For example, the popular perception is that the Serbs, for whatever reason, are better tennis players than the Croats. But, for equally inexplicable reasons, everyone agrees that the Croats are better football players. Croatian film buffs adore Serbian movies; Croats like Serbian humor. The Serbs look up to Croatian culture and are fans of Croatian music. The Serbs are envious of our coast and we are envious of their joie de vivre. The Croats admire the Serbs' defiant nature and sense of unity while the Serbs commend the Croats for their adaptability and diplomatic tact. From time immemorial the Serbs have always been belligerent and resolute, while the Croats have always exhibited a proneness to compromise and eschewed violence. The great Serbian poet Jovan Jovanović addressed the issue of the differences between Serbs and Croats in his poem *Što se čuje... (What Is Going On...)*

The Croat fights not to pillage, nor to plunder nor to steal
Instead the sacred flame in his hearth he protects with zeal
Come hell or high water he will not be made to falter
For God and justice kneel with him at the holy altar
And the Serb – will he forever astray be led
On the evil path of lawlessness and bloodshed?

The Croatian War of Independence started when Serbia attacked Croatia in 1991. The war lasted for four years and ended in a Croatian decisive victory. During the war the YPA and Serb paramilitaries destroyed many Croatian churches, hospitals, homes. It has to be said that the Croatian Army never set foot on Serbian territory. It expelled the Serbian invaders and stopped at the border. Crimes were committed by both sides. However, the crimes committed by the Serbian side were part of a deliberate campaign of terror, genocide and ethnic cleansing whereas the crimes committed by the Croatian side were the results of the immediate exigencies of war. A good analogy, both in terms of scale and nature, would be the Armenian genocide versus, say, the Biscari massacre[5]. The former was a state-sponsored project of genocide, ethnic cleansing and crimes against humanity on a massive scale while the latter was a case of adrenaline pumped victors of a hard fought and brutal engagement showing no mercy to the defeated soldiers. Ever more Serbian citizens, luckily for all concerned, are becoming aware that the acts of genocide and ethnic cleansing committed by their troops on foreign soil

---

[5] The Biscari massacre refers to two incidents during the Allied invasion of Sicily in 1943 in which soldiers belonging to the 180th Infantry Regiment of the US Army killed 71 Italian and 2 German POWs.

cannot fit into the same sentence with individual acts of brutality committed by Croatian soldiers. It is worthy of note that the Serb ethnic minority in Croatia enjoys more rights than any given minority anywhere else in the European Union and that the Croatian minority in Serbia is marginalized with practically no rights at all. The YPA and Serb paramilitary formations ethnically cleansed large areas of Bosnia and Herzegovina and the international community rewarded them for a job wall done by giving them an autonomous republic within the borders of Bosnia and Herzegovina. Ironically, the Bosnian Croats, who defended the country from Serbian aggression, today have no rights in Bosnia and Herzegovina. The Croat defenders of Bosnia and Herzegovina were rewarded by the international community for their efforts with the stigma of being aggressors in the service of Croatia. The Republic of Croatia conscientiously cooperated with the Hague Tribunal to the point of giving state secrets to the prosecutors whereas Serbia withheld evidence. So, in the end, a huge number of mass murderers and war criminals from Serbia have escaped justice while many Croats have been found guilty on the flimsiest of circumstantial evidence. Croatian naivety and Serbian guile, one might be tempted to conclude. The situation is somewhat paradoxical because for centuries Serb intellectuals were fond of calling the Croats "those shrewd Latins".

Anyway, the war is behind us and, like it or not, Serbia is an important trading partner for Croatia. The Croats export many more products to Serbia than vice versa. Many Croatian companies actually depend on their exports to

Serbia. The Serbian market is saturated with Croatian products. Serbia, it is obvious, will not make much headway in their membership negotiations with the European Union without Croatia's backing. And the Croatian government did pledge to provide that help to Serbia.

Croatia wanted to shed its Balkan legacy. Serbia, on the other hand, is comfortable in its Balkan skin because it continues to deftly exploit the great powers' political aspirations on the Balkan Peninsula. Croatia is ashamed of the fact that the country was run by a Fascist regime during WWII. The Serbs have no problem with extolling their war criminals and mass murderers who fought in the service of Fascist Italy and Nazi Germany as national heroes. It is fair to say that Serbia plays the game of diplomacy more adroitly than Croatia. Serbia even managed to place its man, Vuk Jeremić, at the helm of the United Nations General Assembly. The Croats are prone to disowning everything that is not 100 per cent Croatian (Nikola Tesla, Ivo Andrić, Rade Šerbedžija). The Serbs, on the other hand, will always happily appropriate what is clearly not theirs. It seems that Pulitzer prize-winning journalist Chris Hedges was right on the money when he said that Croats have too many complexes and Serbs too few.

It is hard to imagine a reality where Croatia does not have Serbia to compare itself to and where Serbia doesn't have Croatia to blame for its manifold woes. No wonder because the countries were locked in a macabre dance of rivalry, war and, ironically, interdependence for almost a century. The existence of every incarnation of Yugoslavia was fuelled by the energy generated by the friction between the Serbs and the Croats. The international community was, for about 25 years following the end of the Croatian War of Independence, doing everything in its power to escalate the rivalry between Serbia and Croatia. For example, whenever Serbia made a wrong diplomatic move the West would favor Croatia and bring it one step closer to Euro-Atlantic integration. Whenever Serbia seemed to be in a cooperative mood, Western European diplomats were quick to travel to Belgrade with assurances that Croatia would not become a member of the European Union before Serbia because such a development would seriously disrupt the balance of power in the region. The European Union praised Croatia for its eagerness to cooperate fully with the Hague Tribunal and publically criticized Serbia for not following Croatia's lead. The international community, with regard to Serbia and Croatia, mercilessly played both sides against the middle. At times it seemed that any success by one country can only be achieved at the expense of the other. Only when the international community desisted from creating undue friction between Croatia and Serbia did the abominable symbiotic relationship between the two countries end.

The new political relationship between Croatia and Serbia will not be marred by constant antagonism. It will be a somewhat boring relationship, with Serbian audiences lavishing extended applauses on the performances of the Zagreb Philharmonic Orchestra and Croatian audiences attending in droves plays by Serbian touring theatres, with Serbian entrepreneurs investing money in Croatian businesses, and with the Croatian minority in Serbia not being marginalized and discriminated against. The Croats need no longer fear being thrown into some kind of a new federation of the Balkan nations, and the Serbs need no longer be envious of Croatia's membership in the EU because being a member of the EU, burdened with many problems as the Union is nowadays, is a dubious honor. The Croats have come to realize that, regardless of what union of nations they are a constituent part of, cooperation with their neighbors is a must. And the Serbs have come to realize that Croatia is their window into the West. With time, the scars of war will heal and the stereotypes will lose its potency. Most of these stereotypes come from the detritus of history and often serve a contemporary political purpose. Both the Serbs and Croats are now free to come to terms with the past. There will be no need for stereotypes to either bolster or justify whatever political initiative. As Olivera Milosavljević, a renowned Serbian scholar once wrote, "A Croatia that is politically distant is the main precondition to establishing a future relationship based, among other things, on the healthy indifference our generation reserves for the first enemy of Serbia, the Bulgars." History tells us that we always got along splendidly with the Serbs when we did not depend politically on one another. We still, however, have to realize that not everything coming from across the eastern border is bad. There are many differences between the Serbs and the Croats. And they point to many valuable lessons we can learn from one another.

Who Does Nikola Tesla Belong To?

How to brand great individuals

The Serbs say that Nikola Tesla was one of the most remarkable scientists of the 20th century and the greatest Serb that ever lived. The Croats agree with the first statement but vehemently disagree with the latter. They think Nikola Tesla was one of the greatest Croats that ever lived. A string of public opinion surveys about Nikola Tesla have been conducted in Croatia during the last 20 years or so. The Croatian weekly magazine *Hrvatski Obzor*, in 1999, organized a poll to select the Croatian person of the century. The editors came up with a list of about 30 names. Nikola Tesla won by a large margin. In 2003 the weekly *Nacional* magazine conducted a similar poll, only this time the respondents had 100 names to choose from. In that poll Nikola Tesla came in second. In 2011 the leading Croatian agency for communications management Millennium conducted a poll to find out who the most important great men of Croatia were. Nikola Tesla won 83% of the votes,

Ruđer Bošković 63% and Miroslav Krleža 48%. Branimir Pofuk later broke down the numbers and said this about Nikola Tesla's 83% of the votes: "In every age group most respondents voted for Nikola Tesla. If we divide the respondents according to gender, place of residence, whatever, the vast majority of respondents in any given group voted for Nikola Tesla. Most of the highly educated respondents voted for Nikola Tesla; most of those who only finished primary school voted for Nikola Tesla. If we divide the respondents into groups according to this or that party membership, or those completely apolitical, again we have the same picture; most of the respondents in each group voted for Nikola Tesla. This is worthy of note since people in Serbia insist that Tesla was a Serb. I have to point out again, most people from Zagorje, Slavonia, Dalmatia, Podravina, all over, voted for Nikola Tesla. Granted, more people hailing from Tesla's home region, Lika, voted for him, in terms of percentages than those hailing from other parts of Croatia. If only Croatian politicians, or academics, were as united as regards various issues as the respondents regarding Nikola Tesla. But, it's a huge thing, for Croats, to agree at least on something for once. Besides, Tesla is too big for both the Croats and the Serbs. The man invented electricity, for crying out loud! He did not invent electricity for the Croats, or for the Serbs, he invented electricity for the whole humankind! Being shared between the Croats and the Serbs would be a bigger miracle than any of Tesla's inventions. But then again, as I discovered during my research for the book *Hrvatska i Susjedi* (Croatia and its Neighbors), there are Serbs who have no problem with admitting that Tesla was just as much a Croat as he was a Serb."

So, most Croats agree that Nikola Tesla is one of the greatest, if not the greatest, Croat to have ever lived. No one seems to be bothered with the fact that the Serbs perceive Tesla as their own, on account of his ethnicity and religion, nor by the fact that he left Yugoslavia and went to America, where he made a name for himself. In that sense he's more American than he is either Serbian or Croatian, because he left Croatia behind as a place unsuitable for his talents. There are some in Croatia who would gladly let Serbia have Nikola Tesla. They say since they want him so much and have him on their banknotes and since they've named a major airport after him, let them have it, no big deal. There were even some Croatian politicians in the 90s who had a problem with Nikola Tesla because of his Serbian ethnic origin. Luckily, the number of such bigots has steadily been decreasing and there are ever more of those that think Nikola Tesla should be perceived as one of the greatest Croats that ever lived. They don't see any point in perceiving Nikola Tesla as American or Serbian. That logic makes sense because Tesla was born in Croatia, he was educated in Croatia and spent his formative years in Croatia. In that respect Croatia generated Tesla's genius. True, he could not realize his potential at home and he went to the USA, but he cherished his homeland and was always ready to come to its aid. On the other hand, Nikola Tesla did not have much of a relationship with Serbia. He visited Serbia only once in his life and stayed there for only 31 hours. It doesn't really make sense attempting to appropriate Tesla because he transcends the constraints of time and space and his genius and universal humanism belongs to the legacy of the true prophets.

But, some Croatian and a larger number of Serbian officials do not seem to get that. On the 70th anniversary of Nikola Tesla's death in 2013 a formal event was organized at the New Yorker hotel, comprising an award ceremony and a two-day conference. The government of Serbia was a co-organizer of the event and the stars of the ceremony were the mayor of New York Bloomberg, the tennis player Novak Đoković and the then President of the United Nations General Assembly Vuk Jeremić. No Croats attended the event. Jeremić, a controversial figure on account of things not related to Nikola Tesla, in his speech about the success of an ordinary man from the Balkan Peninsula in the wide world, stated that Tesla "personifies some of the most recognizable traits of the Serbian national identity". Nobody deigned to mention where Tesla was born. It is notable that in most official documents his place of birth is either Austria-Hungary or Military Frontier. Only in a few places is Croatia given as an additional qualifier. In most sources Tesla's nationality is given as "Austrian". Most people tend to associate Nikola Tesla with that country that appropriates him most creatively. And at this point that country is not Croatia or Serbia, but the United States of America. This is understandable because a lot is known about Nikola Tesla's activities on the eastern seaboard of the United States and his earlier life remains shrouded in mystery. And we have no one but ourselves to blame for this sad state of affairs. If we are too lazy, or too incompetent to inform the world about our greats, then most people will accept at face value the information that is readily available, regardless of whether that information is inaccurate or provided in bad faith. Croatia doesn't seem to be keen on capitalizing on Nikola Tesla's legacy, not even when other countries take the lead in honoring Nikola Tesla's achievements. Saying that Nikola Tesla was a Croat means nothing if the claim is not backed up with books, documentaries, articles, YouTube videos, podcasts and so forth. If we do not give our Nikola Tesla to the world then other countries will give their Nikola Tesla to the world. And the fact that we have the accurate information and those other countries do not becomes completely irrelevant in the face of our indolent attitude.

For years Croatia did nothing to create a brand out of Nikola Tesla's name. In 2006 the first tentative steps in that direction were taken. On the 150th anniversary of Tesla's birth the Croatian Parliament declared the Year of Nikola Tesla and many celebratory events took place commemorating the anniversary. The most momentous event that year was the opening of the Nikola Tesla Memorial Centre in Smiljan, in the Lika region. It is a truly magnificent facility, offering something for everyone. The complex consists of the house and estate where Tesla was born, as well as the Church of St. Peter and Paul, a cemetery, stone monuments and benches made by architect Zdenko Kolacio, a monument by sculptor Mile Blažević, prototypes of Tesla's experimental station from Colorado Springs, turbines, a remote-control boat, a bridge, a multimedia center, a hi-tech playground... The location for the memorial centre wasn't picked at random – Tesla was born in the region of Lika and spent his formative years there. But unfortunately, only a few people are aware of the centre because no one has deemed it necessary to advertise its existence. There is only a small brown sign post on the road to Gospić pointing the way to the Nikola Tesla Memorial Centre. No doubt many foreign tourists on their way to the coast have asked themselves: "Now what has Croatia got to do with Nikola Tesla?" Again, we have only ourselves to blame.

As part of the celebrations commemorating the 150th anniversary of Nikola Tesla's birth his monument was erected in Zagreb, at the intersection between Preradović Street and Masaryk Street, a work of the most famous Croatian sculptor, Ivan Meštrović[6]. Tesla met Meštrović in 1924 and they became good friends. Meštrović considered Nikola Tesla and Ruđer Bošković the greatest Croats ever born. Tesla admired Meštrović as a sculptor of infinite genius. Tesla had refused many offers by globally renowned artists to paint his portrait or sculpt his bust. But Nikola Tesla did suggest to Mestrović to sculpt a monument to him, saying: "For the sake of our posterity and Slav nations I'd like to leave behind a bust sculpted by none other than the great Meštrović".

In 2014, at the initiative of the Nikola Tesla Association – Genius for the Future, the Croatian Parliament declared Nikola Tesla Day, that is to say, Science, Technology and

---

[6] The monument was originally built in 1956 and displayed in the park of the Ruđer Bošković Institute, alongside the monument to Ruđer Bošković. In 2006 it was taken from the park to the aforementioned location.

Innovation Day which is celebrated every year on Tesla's birthday, July 10. This sparked an initiative to erect Tesla's tower from Long Island in Zagreb, as a tourist attraction. In 2015, according to the decision of the Zagreb City Hall, the Technical Museum housing the cabinet where Tesla's inventions are demonstrated was renamed the Nikola Tesla Technical Museum. At the moment of writing there is a campaign in progress to start celebrating Nikola Tesla Day on a global level, in other words, a campaign urging the UN to designate an international day of Nikola Tesla. The first diplomatic moves have been taken and the former Secretary-General of the United Nations Ban Ki-Mun wholeheartedly supports the initiative.

Those in the business of branding know that the country which promotes a given historical figure with creativity and persistence – through films, documentaries, manifestations, products, museums – will profit the most. Austria, some people jokingly aver, is the world champion in branding through historical figures because it has convinced the whole world that Hitler was a German and Beethoven an Austrian! There is actually a lot of truth in the joke. Nikola Tesla was born in Croatia and is one of the greatest Croats who ever lived. The fact is indisputable and Croatia should really do its utmost to ram the fact home, promote Nikola Tesla, his name and his achievements as a Croat until the cows come home. Tesla's name is an asset of tremendous importance in today's globalised and high-tech world. Moreover, Croatia has an obligation towards Tesla to keep the memory of him, as a Croat, alive. Croatia, it has to be pointed out, officially recognised Tesla's genius while he was still alive. In 1896 Tesla became an honorary member of the Yugoslav Academy of Sciences and Arts. In 1926 he was awarded an honorary doctorate by the University of Zagreb (10 years later the University of Belgrade followed suit, as well as the Polytechnic School in Graz and the University of Paris 11 years later). In 1936, when a celebration was held at Banski Dvori commemorating Tesla's 80th birthday, Tesla sent a cable to the then leader of Croatia thanking him for the honor and stating that he was proud of both his Croatian homeland and heritage and Serbian ancestry.

Tesla loved Zagreb, as the capital of his homeland and had nothing but deep respect for the city. When he visited Zagreb, at the invitation of the then mayor of Zagreb, Milan Amruš, in 1892 he gave a speech in the Zagreb City Hall. At one point he said: "I consider it my duty, as a citizen of my country, to help Zagreb in any way I possibly can!" During his stay Tesla also gave a lecture to the representatives of the Zagreb City Assembly about the possibilities to electrify the capital. Other information about his stay in Zagreb is not known. He stayed in the capital of Croatia for three days, unencumbered by matters of protocol and free to do as he wished. From Zagreb the road took him to Varaždin and thence to Budapest. Three days after leaving Zagreb, in the evening hours on June 1, he arrived in Belgrade from Budapest by train, at the invitation of the Belgrade City Hall. Altogether he stayed in Belgrade 31 hours. Tesla's stay there was exactly the opposite of his time spent in Zagreb. Everything was pomp and circumstance. Already at the train station hundreds of people waited in welcome for him, including the Belgrade elites. The poet Jovan Jovanović Zmaj even wrote the following verses in honor of Tesla's visit to Belgrade:

Today Belgrade is a happy city
Shaking hands with him who's done Serbia proud
Revealing its joyous heart
To our Serbian hero ever so loud

The following day Tesla was received by the recently crowned King Aleksandar Obrenović and then the visit turned into a tiring protocol – meetings, receptions, toasts… Tesla's visit to Belgrade meant a lot for the Serbian leaders and members of the Serbian academic, scientific and religious communities. In a way it was a confirmation of his Serbian ancestry, especially because he had never been to Serbia before and had no relationship with either the country or its capital city. The Serbs simply decided to exploit the fact that Tesla was an Orthodox Christian and Croatian Serb for all it was worth. Tesla would never travel to Serbia again.

Croatia was lucky in the sense that Nikola Tesla remained loyal to it to the very end. Still, his ideas presented to the councilors in Zagreb were never realized, even though the then Mayor of Zagreb Milan Armuš was staunchly in favor of the electrification of the city. Lacking investors and good will, Zagreb had to wait to be electrified for 15 long years after that visit by Nikola Tesla. Only in the fall of 1907 was a thermal power station built, providing the city of Zagreb with electricity. Still, Tesla's words directed at the councilors had some effect; it gave a confidence boost to a number of

Croatian engineers who, following Tesla's instructions, built a hydroelectric power plant under the Skradinski buk waterfall on the Krka River. It was the first hydroelectric power plant powered by AC built in Europe and second in the world – the Skradinski buk power plant was put into operation only two days after the hydroelectric power plant at Niagara Falls, built by Nikola Tesla's patents, had been made operational. Thanks to the electricity received from the Skradinski buk hydroelectric power plant, Šibenik was the first city in the world with public electric lighting and with household use of alternating current. Even though the Niagara Falls hydroelectric power plant was the first of its kind in the world, the city of Buffalo only started receiving electricity from the plant one year after its construction, when the power lines had been built and the low voltage distribution network set up. Zagreb did not recognize Tesla's vision and did not take advantage of his good will and readiness to help, but Croatian engineers did justify the claim that Croatia is the homeland of the great Nikola Tesla.

Nation with Two States

Bosnia and Herzegovina in fact and imagination

The Croats are one of the rare peoples in the world who can say that they have two countries they can call their own – Croatia, where they are the only constituent nation, and Bosnia and Herzegovina, where they are one of the three constituent nations. The Bosnian Croats are well aware of that fact because for decades they have perceived the Republic of Croatia as their champion and savior, only to be abandoned and left to fend for themselves time and again – Croatian politicians always think it is better to kowtow to the international community and Sarajevo than to protect the interests of the Bosnian Croats. The Croats in the Republic in Croatia look down on Bosnia and Herzegovina. For them the country is an impoverished southern neighbor deeply scarred by the war, where food is exceptionally good. Some Croatian politicians perceive Bosnia and Herzegovina as an albatross around Croatia's neck. The perception is grounded more in fiction than in fact. The central tenet of the perception is the idea that there exists a powerful Bosnian Croat mafia hell bent of infiltrating the Croatian government for the purpose of building swimming pools in the backyards of their houses in Herzegovina and consequently emptying Croatia's Treasury coffers. It's pure nonsense, but a fair number of people of Croatia subscribe to it. At times one can feel an undercurrent of almost racial hatred towards Bosnian Croats in Croatian society. Unfortunately, this sentiment is not conducive to developing viable and constructive policies towards Bosnia and Herzegovina and plays a destructive role when it comes to taking political and economic advantage of the fact that Bosnia and Herzegovina belongs as much to the Croats as it does to the other two constituent nations.

Franjo Tuđman believed that Croatia should be deeply involved in all spheres of life of Bosnian Croats in Bosnia and Herzegovina and his policies were geared towards that goal. But, in 2000 the Croatian politicians completely washed their hands of the Bosnian Croats. For them it was more important to act in the interests of the international community and the Bosniaks than create policies beneficial for the Bosnian Croats and, by extension, Croatia too. Things changed slightly for the better when Ivo Josipović became President in 2010. However, too many opportunities regarding Bosnia and Herzegovina in general and Bosnian Croats in particular have been squandered so that, in my opinion, it is no longer possible for Croatia to play an important political, cultural and economic role in that part of the Balkan Peninsula. The accession of Croatia to the European Union and the Schengen borders separated the country further from Bosnia and Herzegovina and Bosnian Croats. Croatia is going to have – regardless of the public's insistence on the necessity of regional cooperation – ever more contacts with Slovenia, Austria and the Czech Republic and ever less with its eastern neighbors, because as a member state of the European Union Croatia finds itself divided from them by different laws, different standards and customs regulations. Croatia had excellent opportunities to become a major player in the Bosnian-Herzegovinian market but, as we have seen, it wasted all of its opportunities. Germany, Slovenia, Turkey and Serbia and a host of Arab countries are there instead... Some Croatian companies, to be sure, maintain a strong presence in the Bosnian-Herzegovinian market, but that's a far cry from what Croatia could have, and should have achieved, especially given the fact that Croatia's reputation in Bosnia and Herzegovina is far better than that of any other country in the region. Croatia should today enjoy the status of Bosnia and Herzegovina's main trading partner. But, unfortunately, Bosnia and Herzegovina is not a "Croatian" country, despite what its constitution says. It should be though, on account of its constitution, on account of the Dayton Agreement, on account its Croat population... For many Croats Bosnia and Herzegovina is a mystery because their perception is clouded by negative stereotypes and incomplete or downright fake news regarding what takes place on the other side of the border and informed by Bosnian sitcoms and the occasional tourist excursion to the country. Most Croats don't know what went on in Bosnia and Herzegovina during the war. The twenty years that passed after the end of the war have blunted memories and younger generations don't seem to care. It is safe to assume that precious few Croats are aware that, according to the numbers of refugees in relation to the total population of Bosnia and Herzegovina in 1991, the Croats suffered the most during the war. 61% of the Bosnian Croats were expelled from their homes. By way of comparison, 47% of the Bosniaks suffered the same fate. 800,000 Croats lived in Bosnia and Herzegovina before the war. Today, there are only 500,000. 92% of the Croats living, before the war, in what is today the Republic of Srpska, were expelled during the war from their homes. We are talking about ethnic cleansing on a staggering scale. The government of Bosnia and Herzegovina has done nothing to rebuild the homes of the Croatian refugees, nothing to enable the expelled unfortunates to return to their homes. By contrast, Croatia rebuilt each and every Serbian home that had been destroyed during the war and invited all the Serbian refugees back, giving them lavish pensions and other benefits... And the Croatian public is blissfully unaware of these things.

The myth that Franjo Tuđman wanted to dismember Bosnia and Herzegovina persists in many political circles around the world to this day, despite the fact that there exists not a shred of evidence supporting the fable. Many experts and self-styled upholders of Bosnia and Herzegovina's integrity from many different countries poured criticism and scorn on Tuđman for allegedly trying to carve up Bosnia and Herzegovina between Croatia and Serbia. Today, Bosnia and Herzegovina is a divided country, between the Serbs and the Muslims. And the experts and champions of Bosnia and Herzegovina's integrity who were so vocal in signaling virtue by demonizing Tuđman, the very man who saved Bihać from the fate suffered by Srebrenica, are conspicuous in their silence today. Many people are not aware of the fact that in 1994 an agreement was reached according to which Croatia and Bosnia and Herzegovina would function as a confederation of the two countries! That agreement was called the Washington Agreement and it called for the creation of the Federation of Bosnia and Herzegovina and a confederation between the Federation of Bosnia and Herzegovina and Croatia. The Washington Agreement has never been annulled. The Croats dissolved its republic in Bosnia and Herzegovina called Herzeg-Bosnia for the sake of the interests of the Muslim population of Bosnia and Herzegovina and thus put themselves at a strategic disadvantage in relation to both the Serbs and the Muslims. The Muslims repaid this gesture of good will by attacking the Croats during the war, and after the war by accusing Croatia of waging an aggressive war against Bosnia and Herzegovina. The Serbs, in the meantime, refused to violate, in any way, shape or form the sanctity of their territory in Bosnia and Herzegovina. They completely ethnically cleansed the territory and the international community rewarded them for a job well done by giving the territory the status of republic. In Croatia many people for some reason believe that the Bosnian Croats don't really want to live in Bosnia and Herzegovina and are trying to distance themselves from the other two constituent nations. Hard facts tell a different story. The Bosnian Croats, for example, insist that the city of Mostar be a single unified city but the Bosniaks are determined to divide the city – according to the Bosniaks one part of the city should be exclusively Muslim.

For that reason no elections have been held in the city of Mostar since 2008 – an achievement no other city in Europe can match. The situation is actually made possible because the international community, inexplicably, finds it unpalatable to stand up to the Bosnian Muslims.

Many people in Croatia are under the impression that the Bosnian Croat politicians cooperate closely with their Bosniak colleagues. But the reality is different. The Bosniak politicians have committed many serious transgressions against the Bosnian Croats that even the Serbian politicians in Banja Luka at one point cried foul.

The perception in Croatia is that doing business or engaging in political dialogue with Bosnia and Herzegovina is a costly exercise in futility. Not many people are aware the Bosnian Croats have given a lot more money to Croatia than Croatia has spent on protecting their political and economic interests. Bosnia and Herzegovina is Croatia's main trading partner. Croatia actually earns a lot of money from its trade with Bosnia and Herzegovina. Croatia exports a lot more than it imports in relation to Bosnia and Herzegovina. In 2011 alone (prior to the establishment of Schengen borders) Croatia's income from doing business with Bosnia and Herzegovina was 1.17 billion euros. Most of the money came from the capital Sarajevo and areas with predominantly Croatian populations.

Many Croats complain that hordes of tourists from Bosnia and Herzegovina descend on the Croatian coast every summer with the intention of spending as little money as possible. Maybe there is something to the complaint. It is not widely known, however, that Bosnia and Herzegovina receives many tourists from Croatia. 15% of the tourists who visit Mostar and Sarajevo are from Croatia. Croatia is a Catholic country and one would expect that most of the visitors to Međugorje come from Croatia. Not so. According to statistics, there are many more Italians, Americans, Irishmen, Poles, Spaniards… About a million people from all over the world visit this pilgrimage site, arguably the largest of its kind in this part of Europe. 65% of these visitors are highly educated. No Croatian tourist destination can match Međugorje. It has to be said that thanks to the visitors to Međugorje, the airports in Split and Dubrovnik serve ever more passengers every year.

Unfortunately, the Bosnian Croats no longer see Croatia as their promised land. The paradigm shifted with Croatia's accession to the European Union. Nowadays, most Bosnian Croats choose to emigrate to Western European countries. The situation is somewhat ironic because when Croatia entered the EU, the Bosnian Croats, as holders of dual citizenship, automatically became citizens of the European Union. The development should not surprise us. The Bosnian Croats are second-class citizens in Bosnia and Herzegovina and salaries and wages are higher in, say Germany or Ireland, than they are in Croatia.

Those among us with an optimistic streak may hold the opinion that the Bosnian Croats have a political trump card in the fact that Croatia is a member of the European Union. Unfortunately, Croatian politicians cannot be bothered with fighting for the interests of the Bosnian Croats in the corridors of power in Brussels. Both the Bosnian Serbs and Bosniaks outnumber the Bosnian Croats and the politicians representing these nations know that they can bully the Bosnian Croats till hell freezes over because the Croatian political elites from Zagreb simply do not want to waste time to support Croatian national interests in Bosnia and Herzegovina. The irony is even larger in light of the fact that Croatia shares a 932-kilometer border with Bosnia and Herzegovina and that the Bosnian Croats represent the only remaining political and economic advantage Croatia enjoys in that part of the world.

Međugorje as a World-Famous Brand

Appeal and uniqueness of a pilgrimage site in Herzegovina

In today's world of constant competition every city and tourist destination wants to become a globally recognised brand and to attract attention, tourists, investors and immigrants. Millions of euros are thus spent on promotion in an effort to beat the competition. But, only those destinations that have something unique, regardless of whether it is historical heritage, culture, architecture or popular events or their ability to launch relentless and viable marketing campaigns can become true global brands. To become a brand, a destination needs to have a lot to offer – accessibility, various attractions, quality accommodation are absolute musts but there also has to be something more, something truly unique, and something that can touch visitors on an emotional level. The most popular destination in Croatia is undoubtedly Dubrovnik. It is a truly global brand and the city constantly features on top ten or top five lists of most popular tourist destinations and has pride of place in many travel guides and similar publications. There are other popular tourist destinations in Croatia – Rovinj, Hvar, the Plitvice Lakes and Zagreb. Zadar has also become popular, ditto Split, Varaždin and the Istria region. There's potential in Opatija, but unfortunately we are not tapping into that potential. But these Croatian cities, beautiful and attractive as they are, cannot even begin to compare with one small village, a hamlet almost, in Bosnia and Herzegovina, that is a true global brand. And the funny thing about the village is that there is no marketing campaign worth the name underpinning its success. Millions of people from all over the world visit it every year. The tourist season lasts all year round there. Celebrities, presidents, prime ministers, princes and princesses are regular visitors; sometimes openly, sometimes incognito. The best-selling music artists perform for free there – like Jose Carreras and Andrea Bocelli. The village has fans and admirers in the US Congress. Most of the visitors travel there without any great expectations – they just want to return home spiritually rejuvenated and sporting a happier disposition. Of course, the name of the village is Međugorje. The village is in Bosnia and Herzegovina, situated almost on the Croatian border from the direction of Split. For the last 37 years the village has been considered by millions of people from all over the world as a pilgrimage site, a spiritual oasis and a source of spiritual comfort.

Most of us who are privileged to live within easy driving distance from Međugorje are not aware of the potency of the Međugorje phenomenon. It somehow seems to us that there is nothing extraordinary in the fact that people from all corners of the world, all races and nationalities visit Međugorje in search of spiritual rejuvenation and comfort. We only start to ponder the power of the story when we are on a tourist trip abroad and a native, trying to make conversation, surprises us with his or her in depth knowledge about Međugorje, even though the friendly native may not exactly be sure whether Međugorje is in Bosnia and Herzegovina or Croatia. There is an unbreakable connection between Međugorje and the Croatian nation and that bond was one of our trump cards in the early 90s when we were forced to defend ourselves from Serbian aggression and needed international attention and support. Vladimir Peter Goss writes about that in his book *Washintgonska fronta* (Washington Front).

In 1991 Croatian activists in the USA printed thousands of leaflets, contacted the press and congressmen and organized a rally in Washington in an effort to thwart the effects of the disinformation campaign about the war launched from Belgrade. The toil of the Croatian activists bore unexpected fruit when they were contacted by a businessman called Jack Arnissen, offering his help. When Arnissen introduced himself to the Croatian activists, he emphasized that he was an American Catholic of Norwegian ancestry and that he had been to Međugorje seven times. He also expressed his concern about what was happening in the former Yugoslavia at the time. He wasn't satisfied with the State Department's policies regarding the war in the former Yugoslavia and the dearth of reliable information about what was really taking place there. He was searching for verifiable information about the real situation in Croatia and

Bosnia and Herzegovina so that he could make his American friends aware of who was really attacking whom. He had heard about Serbian attacks on cities and villages near Zagreb but he admitted that he had no idea where Zagreb was because on his trips to Medugorje he had flown to Dubrovnik and thence ridden the bus to the pilgrimage site. In his mind, Dubrovnik was a suburb of sorts of Medugorje and he wanted to know everything about Serb attacks on that city too. For Arnissen Croatia was the Medugorje – Dubrovnik line, but still he felt compelled to help the Croats. He then realized that, at that point in time, there were about 6 million friends of Medugorje in the USA who had been there at least once, and 10 million of those who kept themselves regularly informed about the situation in Medugorje. And most of those people were in constant touch with one another. In Congress they were represented by the influential Christopher Smith and they had their "chapters" all over America. "If something happens to Medugorje we'll burn the White House down," said Arnissen jokingly to Goss and went to work.

We'll never know how many famous and less famous people were spurred by their awareness of Medugorje to help Croatia during its hour of need. But we do know that Medugorje has become a global brand that has for decades been transcending borders and inspiring people to do good. Many people have tried to find proof that miracles happen in the Medugorje phenomenon, some tried to dig up scandal. But, the Medugorje phenomenon has captured the hearts of millions of people all across the planet with its simplicity. It all happened quietly, like a spring shower, without any communication strategy, promotional or advertising campaigns. The message spread by word of mouth, from one media outlet to another, from country to country. The fates of many people testify to the power of Međugorje. The spiritual experiences of many people who have visited Međugorje serve as the most potent of recommendations. In this day and age everyone seems to be seeking spiritual rejuvenation, inner peace, other dimensions, health... There is no doubt that modern life is a constant source of stress and spiritual unease. And Međugorje gives inner peace, hope and consolation. There are precious few places on the planet that can offer what Međugorje offers. No spa, wellness complex or other exotic refuges from the rat race can compete with Međugorje. And a visit to Međugorje can inspire a change of life, a compulsion to jettison negativity and embrace positive emotions. Many people, among them a significant number of celebrities like the American actor Jim Caviezel, experienced that life altering force. Most visitors to Međugorje time their visit to this pilgrimage site to coincide with their vacationing on the Croatian coast. In that sense a lot of income generated by the Split and Dubrovnik airports comes directly from the pilgrims on their way to Međugorje.

We know how much effort, money and ability it takes to create a global brand out of a tourist destination, one that could attract millions of visitors, tourists... Sometimes the process of branding increases the popularity of a tourist destination in the short term but pretty quickly the novelty of it all wears off and tourists go elsewhere to find something better, or more attractive, or just different...

Međugorje is, obviously, an absolute value. It has become a global brand on account of something far deeper and more meaningful than marketing campaigns, of which there were none anyway. Međugorje doesn't need artificially created attention, or stardust, generated by the media or PR people. The village imposes another, completely different dynamic; one that is impossible to mimic or emulate. It tells to the world an important story about the power of faith. To all of us who are blessed to live in its vicinity it opens a window into the world and graces us with attention that is impossible to manufacture. We have to, however, be honest with ourselves and admit that we haven't really deserved this gift from God that Međugorje undoubtedly is. And all of us who live in the vicinity of that holy piece of Herzegovinian soil should treat it with far more respect than we do. Međugorje has grown out of a hamlet into a veritable city on account of Mary's apparitions alone. It is true that many people have gotten rich in Međugorje on more than 50 million pilgrims and visitors during the last 37 years. It is a fact that one can observe many things in Međugorje that are grounded in greed and commercialization. But visitors to Međugorje regularly also see spirituality, simplicity, honesty... The whole thing started in 1981 when Mary appeared. Nobody could predict then that the village would become one of the most visited places in Europe. It has to be said that the Communist authorities, with the willing help of the then bishop, struggled tooth and nail to suppress the news of Mary's apparitions and nip the whole thing in the bud. When they failed in that they accused the people of Međugorje of trying to manipulate the masses. That ploy ended in failure too. Millions of people recognize Međugorje for what it is. There is no manipulation there. If you ask any person from Međugorje about it he or she will tell you that they have absolutely no control of the phenomenon and that a higher, divine power pulls the strings. During the era of Communism the residents of Međugorje had a ready-made excuse for doing nothing as regards urbanizing the village and controlling its development. Now that excuse is gone and it is painfully obvious that the residents of Međugorje should face the challenges that the global fame of their village presents them with. They should take care of the development of the village's infrastructure, its architecture, quality of services... I am not trying to put the Franciscans, who manage wisely and constructively the pilgrimage site and serve the needs of millions of pilgrims who visit Međugorje, on the spot here. I am referring to the local authorities, Međugorje's residents and small businesses who earn money from the Međugorje phenomenon. Their actions and their behavior determine the impression the visitors take with them when they leave Međugorje. The residents of Međugorje are morally obligated to behave in a civilized way 24/7 so as to imprint a sense of religiosity on the emotional make-up of the visitors. The identity of Međugorje and the faith have to be a lifestyle, not something to be displayed for the visitors' sake. It would make much more sense for the residents of Međugorje to start perceiving their village less as a source of income and more as a source of spiritual strength. The Međugorje phenomenon is a gift from God, but it is also a huge responsibility and a moral obligation. And by accepting that responsibility the residents of Međugorje will justify the gift they received from God. Međugorje has to retain its identity and must not become a tourist destination. However, that doesn't mean that the village should not be urbanized and that services catering to millions of visitors should not be provided. Because the visitors are the promoters of Međugorje and Mary's presence there and potential advocates of the Croatian nation, if the Croats choose to earn that honor with their behavior! To truly grasp the potential of the Međugorje brand we have to ask ourselves the following question: What would Međugorje look like if it was located in Italy or the USA?

PART IV

Croats and Church

The Croats Celebrate the Patron Saint of Ireland and Ignore the Patron Saint of Croatia

Saint Joseph and Saint Patrick

In the month of March two widely known Catholic saints have their days – March 17 is Saint Patrick's Day and March 19 is Saint Joseph's Day. There is no doubt that there will be noisy and raucous celebrations in Zagreb on the former date and only a few special masses and maybe a few private parties thrown by Saint Joseph's namesakes on the latter. Most Croats immediately associate Saint Patrick's Day with Irish music, Irish dancing, gallons of beer, parades, shamrock and color green. One would be hard-pressed to find a person in Croatia who isn't aware of the myth that Saint Patrick gave Christianity to the Irish and expelled snakes from the island. By contrast, Saint Joseph is known in Croatia only as that carpenter guy who married the Virgin Mary and took care of Baby Jesus. And the funny thing about it all is that Saint Patrick is the patron saint of Ireland and Saint Joseph is the patron saint of Croatia! So what's going on here?

How come we know so much more about Saint Patrick than about our own patron saint? How come we ape the Irish on their national holiday? Some people say that the Irish tradition surrounding Saint Patrick is longer that the Croatian tradition regarding Saint Joseph and therefore it is only natural that Patrick is the more popular saint. Those people need to get their facts straight. The Croatian Parliament, during the session of July 9 and 10 in 1687 declared, by unanimous decision of all classes and ranks, Saint Joseph the patron saint of the Croatian kingdom. The Croats have always called the Blessed Virgin Mary the Queen of Croats so it made sense to choose her unassuming, unobtrusive and quiet fiancé Joseph, who gave shelter and protection to Baby Jesus when he needed it most, as their patron saint.

The Croatian bishops in 1972 at their meeting in Split upheld the decision of 1687 declaring that "the decision of 1687 is still valid because the Croatian Parliament did not refer to some abstract Croatian kingdom but to the Croatian people which has outlived every squabble over sovereignty..." In 2008, as a lasting reminder of that historic decision, the relief of Saint Joseph was placed above the entrance into the Croatian Parliament building, a work of sculptor Šime Vulas. In Ireland, on the other hand, Saint Patrick's Day was for centuries a religious holiday, celebrated more fervently by the Irish immigrants in America than by the residents of the Emerald Isle. Up until 1970 there was a law in Ireland banning pubs from opening on Saint Patrick's Day. Everything changed in 1995 when the Irish government launched a campaign to use Saint Patrick's Day to promote Irish tourism and pub culture. That meant turning Saint Patrick's Day into a three-ring circus and attracting binge drinkers from all over the world. The Croats never did anything remotely similar with Saint Joseph or any other Croatian saint. Every year, for the last twenty years or so, about a million people descend on Dublin to celebrate Paddy's Day. Millions more celebrate it in other countries. Big green hats are worn, potatoes and cabbage is everybody's favorite dish on that day, copious amounts of alcohol are consumed and even little kids recount the story of how Saint Patrick told the snakes to get lost. Rivers are dyed green in Chicago. The largest Saint Patrick's parade in the world is held in New York. There's a saying that goes: "We're all Irish on Paddy's Day." There is a lot of truth in the saying because Saint Patrick's Day has truly become a global event. In Zagreb too there are parades, gigs and parties on Paddy's day. And green outfits, and green beer. And more than 90 per cent of the Croats have no idea who the patron saint of Croatia is.

Some Croats, belonging to younger generations, may say that celebrating Saint Patrick's Day is cool, far cooler than celebrating some Croatian stuff. Nobody prevents the Croats from popularizing the patron saint of Croatia, organizing lavish celebrations in his honor and taking the saint out of the strictly religious sphere of existence. We can devise our own unique way of celebrating Saint Joseph, something different from the debauchery of Paddy's Day, something dignified and sophisticated and yet equally, or even more attractive. The usual counterargument in Croatia is that Saint Patrick spent a part of his life in Ireland (he wasn't actually Irish), and therefore the Irish are emotionally attached to him, whereas Saint Joseph is just our spokesperson in heaven, without any this-worldly connection to Croatia. The argument is flawed because there are many saints who were born in Croatia and many saints from other lands whose bones reside in our churches. And we don't celebrate any of them. Saint Jerome, most famous for translating the Bible, was born in Dalmatia. The martyr Nikola Tavelić is the first Croatian saint. The mummified remains of Saint Simeon, a man who held the newborn Jesus in his hands, rest in a silver chest in Zadar - the Chest of Saint Simeon. The chest is the most valuable work of medieval goldsmithing in Croatia. And almost nobody outside of Zadar is aware of that.

To be fair, we have celebrations on local levels, ones that even attract tourists. For example, the residents of Split proudly celebrate Saint Domnius, and Dubrovnik lives for the Feast of Saint Blaise. The event is on the UNESCO intangible cultural heritage list. But, Croatia has nothing comparable at the national level. There are those who criticize the Irish for commercializing their holiday. The line between commercialization and banalization is a thin one indeed. Still, commercializing saints is a sure way to make money and promote your values and way of life. The Irish have been very successful with their commercialization of Saint Patrick's Day. The fact that Paddy's Day is celebrated in Croatia, with all the accoutrements and behaviors native to Dublin, shows just how successful. And again, the Croats are not the only nation aping the Irish in that regard. Of course, there is nothing wrong with celebrating Saint Patrick's Day in Croatia, far from it. But it is peculiar to unhesitatingly embrace what is foreign and automatically jettison what is yours. And the Croats are the world champions in exactly that. I still remember one poll conducted in 2001 in a number of European countries. It was about how much people respected their own countries. One of the questions was: Which country do you admire the most? For the Croatian respondents Germany was number one and Croatia number seven! It would seem that Croats desperately want to be something or somebody else. Our politicians constantly behave as if they believe that they should be ruling a developed Western country like England, and it is therefore beneath them to concern themselves with problems of Croatian citizens. Walking down any major street in Croatia and reading the names of restaurants and cafes is like reading an English dictionary (with a lot of typos and grammar mistakes, regrettably). Whenever we listen to our politicians we hear hideously butchered English phrases. If we analyze some, well, most, of the recently organized tourist manifestations we cannot help but conclude that we're ignoring our own history for the sake of caricaturing that of other peoples. Tomislav Šola, our renowned cultural theoretician and curator, warns: "If the task of planning in relation to culture and heritage is allocated to amateurs among the politicians and entrepreneurs, the trap that I'd simply call the hick town syndrome is impossible to avoid: every value gets destroyed by a lack of expertise, knowledge and good taste. And thus, on every corner there are incarnations of Edward Teach, better known as Blackbeard in period clothing; only the clothing is not remotely accurate for early 18th century. In other places one can see French musketeers reenacting the French revolution or knights in ceremonial armor reenacting jousts. The people who organize such abominations have obviously never read a book in their lives. The road to hell of the cheesy tourist attractions is paved with abominable work of ambitious buffoons. The experience of others teaches us that trivializing tourist assets in order to earn a quick buck inevitably leads to the forfeiture of said assets." We should not become caricatures of ourselves or turn ourselves into bad copies of others. We should become more aware of our identity and proudly present our rich heritage to the world. There certainly are a lot of people around the globe envious of what we've got. To that we propose a toast in honor of Saint Patrick, if we have to celebrate Paddy's Day. We should not forget Saint Joseph Day though. He has been protecting the Croats for 330 years now and his national shrine is located in the Croatian city of four rivers – Karlovac.

The Greatest Dalmatian

Croatia's debt to Saint Jerome

In 2020 Croatia will take over the presidency of the Council of the European Union. Croatia could also find itself in the centre of attention of the Christian world in 2020 on account of one important jubilee. 2020 will mark the 1,600[th] anniversary of the death of one of the most important saints in the history of Christianity, a truly great man in the context of European civilization and Christian culture. He was born in Croatia and his name is Saint Jerome. We celebrate his day on September 30. On that day, in 420 AD Saint Jerome died and was buried under the main altar of the famous Basilica di Santa Maria Maggiore in Rome.

Saint Jerome is known all over the world. Many churches, monasteries, institutes, institutions, streets and squares bear his name. Saint Jerome was one of the most educated people of his time. He translated the Bible from Hebrew and Greek into Latin. It took him 15 years to complete the translation and up until recently the text was considered the official Latin translation of the Bible. Saint Jerome is, alongside Saint Ambrose, Saint Augustine, and Saint Gregory the Great, among the four great Western Church Fathers. At the Council of Trent he was declared Doctor of the Church (the highest possible title in the hierarchy of saints – there have only been 30 Doctors of the Church in the 2000-year history of the Church). Some historians consider him the first European thinker. His intellectual output is the bedrock of European culture because he enabled the use of Latin as the language of Western European cultural integration. He played a pivotal role in connecting the cultures of Greece and Rome with Western Europe and in popularizing the Biblical heritage. Almost all Renaissance and Baroque painters of high renown, like Rubens, Durer, El Greco, Van Dyke, to name just a few, painted their renditions of Saint Jerome. He was also the favorite motif of many Croatian artists. One of the most beautiful sculptures of Saint Jerome, created by Ivan Meštrović, stands in front of the Croatian Embassy in Washington (as a powerful statement of identity and marketing intent – unfortunately our diplomats are blissfully oblivious to the potency of the sculpture in said regards, as are the visitors to the embassy). The 1,600[th] anniversary of Saint Jerome's death is a historic opportunity for Croatia to present itself to the world as the homeland of that unsurpassed intellectual, philosopher, saint and thinker.

It is known that Saint Jerome was born, in the middle of the 4th century AD, somewhere in the Roman province of Dalmatia. It is also known that he spent the last 34 years of his life as a hermit and lived a life of penance in Bethlehem, the birthplace of Jesus. There is a lot of controversy surrounding Saint Jerome's place of birth. We know that he was born in the town of Stridon, but historians disagree about the exact location of the town. A whole myriad of places have been suggested as the location of the ancient town of Stridon, from what is today Šuica near Tomislavgrad to Štrigova in Međimurje. Even the father of the Croatian literature Marko Marulić wrote an essay in which he argued against the theory that Stridon had been located in Istria. Saint Jerome was not a Croat, because the Croats settled in Dalmatia about 200 years after he had been born. Most historians think he was a Roman or a Romanized Illyrian. Now, some people may find this confusing and pose this question: "Why would the Croats commemorate the 1,600[th] anniversary of the saint's death if he wasn't a Croat?" Those among them with some knowledge of history may point out the fact that according to the Cathedral Chapter of Zagreb, the first Croatian saint was Saint Nikola Tavelić from Šibenik. The argument is really irrelevant. The world recognizes great historical figures according to their place of birth. Therefore, if the place of birth of a historical figure is located in a modern country that did not exist at the time of his or her birth, that modern country automatically becomes the protector of the heritage and legacy of that historical figure. For example, the Roman Emperor Constantine, who officially established religious toleration for Christianity by the edict of Milan, was born in what is the modern city of Niš in Serbia. Due to that fact Serbia, in 2013, hosted a huge celebration commemorating the 1,700[th] anniversary of the edict. The pope himself almost attended the event. Apart from the place of birth there is nothing connecting Constantine to Serbia. The connection between Saint Jerome and Croatia, by contrast, transcends geography – Saint Jerome is an important part of Croatia's historical identity. Many churches in Croatia and Croatian communities all over the world dedicated in the honor of Saint Jerome (Maksimir in Zagreb, Rijeka, Šibenik, Slani and Herceg Novi, to name just a few locations), and Croatian cultural heritage testify to that fact. The Pontifical Croatian College of Saint Jerome in Rome, the most important Croatian institution in the Eternal City, was dedicated to the saint in the 15th century – at that time, on the left bank of the Tiber River, there was a small chapel and an inn at the site. Even the popes perceived the Croats as the protectors of Saint Jerome's legacy and for centuries it was believed that it had been Saint Jerome who had given the Glagolitic script to the Croats. Croatian Glagolitic priests ardently spread the belief and depicted Saint Jerome as their fellow countryman and father of their language with the aim of gaining credibility. And the aim was achieved. In 1248 Pope Innocent IV issued a letter in which he allowed the bishop of Senj to use the Glagolitic script and hold services in Old Slavic (which was pretty revolutionary at the time), thus upholding the bishop's earlier assertion that the people and clergy in Croatian dioceses perceived Saint Jerome as the originator of the Glagolitic script and the Croatian language. And so this saint, who was beyond reproach, became the protector of the Croatian identity in the face of constant pressures from Rome to impose Latin as the exclusive language of liturgy and theology and attempts to keep vernacular tongues out of the sphere of religion in an effort to nip the emergence of possible heresies in the bud. This tug of war between Rome and Croatian dioceses had been going on since the time of King Tomislav and Gregory of Nin. There is no doubt that Saint Jerome was widely perceived as a Croat in the Middle Ages. In Petris' Miscellany from 1468 Saint Jerome is referred to as Jerome the Croat. One anonymous Glagolitic priest wrote, in a manuscript that has survived to this day, in the 16th century: "Jerome is Dalmatian; he is the pride, honesty and glory and the bright crown of the Croatian language." Saint Jerome was identified with Dalmatia because he saw himself as a proud Dalmatian. He was also aware of his difficult personality. He often said: "Forgive me God for being Dalmatian!"

Even the learned Croatian humanists embraced Saint Jerome and his alleged influence on glagolitism as an integral part of the Croatian tradition and link with the rest of the Christian world. The learned minds in Europe also accepted Saint Jerome's ties with the Glagolitic script and Croatia. Europe was well aware of the Glagolitic script. For example, the Holy Roman Emperor and King of Bohemia Charles IV founded the Emmaus monastery in Prague in 1347 and he dedicated it to Saint Jerome, emphasizing in the charter, "I am dedicating the monastery to Saint Jerome so that he could be celebrated and praised in this kingdom as he is with his own people." Marko Marulić also accepted Saint Jerome as his fellow countryman, calling him a theological authority of the first order and the most influential saint. The perception of Saint Jerome as a Croatian saint started to fade with the Croatian National Revival. The leaders of the Croatian National Revival put a lot of stock on purity of Croatian bloodline and for them Saint Jerome simply did not have a pure Croatian pedigree. However, the cult of Saint Jerome could not be significantly diminished. It remained strong, especially in Dalmatia. In 1930 Tin Ujević wrote the following lines about Saint Jerome: "In Dalmatia... the masses, since time immemorial have revered him more than any other saint, and sent their prayers to him as the region's ambassador to the kingdom of heaven, but it is a sad fact that his life and his works, studied by a handful of erudites, haven't reach a wider readership. The public simply does not sense sufficiently the historical meaning of his thought in relation to the existing culture." This is a reference to the less known fact that Jerome did not only translate the Bible but also wrote commentaries about it. Many contemporary Bible scholars consider these commentaries exceptionally useful and surprisingly relevant in the context of theology, aesthetics and priesthood. Saint Jerome's work *De Viris Illustribus* (On Illustrious Men) a collection of biographies of 135 authors, is one of the earliest bibliographic works.

What Ujević said in 1930 is especially relevant today, on the threshold of the 1,600th anniversary of Saint Jerome's death. The Croatian clergy and the political leadership should understand that the history of Croatia does not begin in the 7th century when the tribes calling themselves Croat started lavishing their unwelcome attention on the settled communities of the Pannonian valley and the Adriatic coast. The secular and religious leaders of Croatia should understand that many different peoples lived in the territory of what is today Croatia and that modern Croats are the protectors of those people's legacy, heritage and, let's face it, genes. We should be aware of the totality of our roots and heritage because, if for no other reason than to honor, cherish, appreciate and celebrate our fellow Croat Saint Jerome.

Not that long ago a research team from the Massachusetts Institute of Technology came up with a list of 11,000 people who had left an enduring mark on human history in general and on the countries they had been born in in particular. There were two major historical figures on the list who were born in what is today Croatia before the 7th century: Saint Jerome and the Roman Emperor Diocletian. No one can dispute that the Croats are the inheritors and protectors of Diocletian's heritage and legacy – Diocletian was born and died in the province of Dalmatia.

Diocletian was one of the most important Roman emperors. Thanks largely to his modernizing reforms the Roman Empire did not collapse in the 3rd century AD. In 305 AD Diocletian abdicated the throne and moved into a huge palace built on the Adriatic shore in his native Dalmatia and lived there until his death in 312 AD. Diocletian obviously considered Dalmatia as an ideal place to live. After the imperial rule broke down in the western part of the empire in 476 AD, the Ostrogoths established their authority in the province. Diocletian's palace was abandoned until the 7th century when Croatian tribes started invading the region. Fleeing from the marauding Croats, many locals sought refuge behind the palace walls. The event marks the beginning of the development of the modern city of Split. From that point on the city steadily grew in size and population. Many other modern Croatian coastal towns developed along similar lines. The Croats settled in the region and established their own state, gradually accepting Roman culture from the urban, Romanized population and steadily adding to its size. Thus, the element of Greek and Roman antiquity is an important ingredient of the Croatian identity. Croatia would today look completely different without that heritage. Roman and Greek presence in the territory of modern-day Croatia created all the necessary cultural preconditions for the integration of our lands into the sphere of Western Europe and, in the long run, established the foundations for the development of the classical features of material culture, especially in the context of urban development, architecture and art. Still, despite all his accomplishments, Diocletian is not exactly a popular historical figure in Croatia – his persecutions of Christians are neither forgotten nor forgiven. However, everyone agrees that he played a pivotal role in shaping the history of Croatia and it is safe to say we still live in the shadow of his legacy. So, it is unlikely that the Croats will commemorate on a grand and lavish scale anything Diocletian did any time soon simply because they don't perceive him as their own. On the other hand, most Croats perceive Saint Jerome as a full-blooded Croat, despite what the champions of the Croatian National Revival had to say on the matter. And the 1,600[th] anniversary of his death is just around the corner.

The Centuries-Long Alliance between the Vatican and the Croats

Pragmatism or spiritual connection

We all know how much help Croatia received from Pope John Paul II. Croatia was one of the few countries he took a deep liking to. He made three official visits to Croatia (and he chose the country as the destination for his 100ᵗʰ trip). Benedict XVI, unlike John Paul II, did not like to travel much, but he did visit Croatia during his pontificate. It is worth mentioning that Croatian was among the seven languages he gave his farewell speech in. We often hear that the Croats have a special relationship with the Vatican, dating back to John IV and Pope Agatho, when the Croats became the first Slavic people to convert to Christianity.

In 879 Pope John VIII recognized the ruler of Croatia, Branimir, as the Duke of the Croats and the independence of the Croatian polity. At that time the right to rule derived directly from the Pope's approval. In that respect no medieval ruler could hope to stay on the throne without, at least to an extent, honoring the Vatican's wishes. The papacy, depending on the situation on the ground, often found it politically expedient to push Croatian rulers into the orbit of the Byzantine Empire. King Zvonimir managed to break away from Byzantium and strengthened his political ties with the Vatican. Pope Gregory VII sent a crown and royal insignia to Zvonimir's coronation in 1075. Gregory VII also sent a letter in which he stated that any attack on Croatia would be considered an attack on the Holy See. King Dmitar Zvonimir promised in return that he would always be loyal to the Pope, protect the poor, orphans and widows, oppose slavery and rule justly. The promise and Zvonimir's benevolent rule led to the creation of the Baška tablet, which serves as record of Zvonimir's donation of a plot of land to the Benedictine monastery in Baška on the island of Krk.

The Holy See respected Croatian rulers and tried to help them as much as possible. However, some popes resented the idea of an autonomous Croatian national Church. Matters came to a head during the reign of King Tomislav when the Croatian Bishop Gregory tried to establish the city of Nin as the ecclesiastical capital of Croatia. The Holy See opposed the initiative and successfully subordinated Bishop Gregory to the Latin archdiocese of Split. Many popes were irritated by the use of the Glagolitic script in church services in Croatia. The Holy See tried to ban the use of the Glagolitic script in church services in Croatia, stating that the script represented a remnant of Byzantine influences, but the attempts were unsuccessful. Pope John X allowed the use of the Glagolitic script to lower clergy and Innocent IV extended the permission to bishops as well. These developments enabled the preservation and further development of the Glagolitic script. Later popes used Croatian Glagolitic priests as their link with the Eastern Orthodox Church. Croatia was the first polity where church services were held in the vernacular in the Christian world. It is worth noting that the vernacular completely replaced Latin as the language of liturgy at the Second Vatican Council in 1962.

The relationship between the Vatican and Croatia became even closer during the centuries of the Ottoman invasions of Europe, when Croatia was Europe's first line of defense against Ottoman aggression. Pope Leo X (1513 – 1521) called Croatia the bulwark of Christendom and did everything in his power to assist the Croats in their fight against the Ottomans. In 1519 the Croatian Ban and Bishop Petar Berislavić, who had received substantial financial aid from the pope, advanced into Bosnia and defeated an Ottoman army near Jajce. The pope, following Berislavić's military victory over the Ottomans, sent an emissary to the ban with a message that he, as Pope, would never allow Croatia, the bulwark of Christendom, to fall to the Ottomans. In recognition of Berislavić's ability as commander and his successes on the field of battle, Pope Leo X appointed Berislavić Cardinal. Unfortunately, Berislavić was killed in an ambush by Ottoman soldiers in 1520 before he had learned of the honor the pope had bestowed on him. Juraj Utišinović Martinušević, a Croatian nobleman, ecclesiastic and Hungarian politician suffered a similar fate. Pope Julius

III named him Cardinal in 1551, but Martinušević was killed in battle before having a chance to wear a red cloak. There is an interesting parallel between the two Croatian heroes and Josip Uhač, a notable papal diplomat who died in Rome in 1998, just one day before Pope John Paul II announced the names of the newly named cardinals. Josip Uhač's name was on the list.

Pope Innocent X (1644 – 1655) and Pope Clement XI (1700 – 1721) staunchly supported Croatia in its struggle against the Ottoman Empire. The latter Pope was especially fond of Dalmatia. The story of how Pius II (1458 – 1464) tried to help Croatia is especially interesting. In 1463, Bosnia fell to the Ottomans and the Bosnian Queen Katarina fled to Rome. Pius II was deeply shaken by the loss of Bosnia and disgusted with the refusal of the great European powers to send help to the beleaguered Croats who were defending Europe, for all intents and purposes, alone. He raised an army and planned to disembark the troops in Dubrovnik and then march on Bosnia. The campaign ended before it even started because, unfortunately, Pius II died before the armada set sail from Ancona.

Croatia was oftentimes a collateral victim of deals the Holy See made with Venice, and later on with Austria and with Hungary. The unfavorable political situation Croatia was in started to improve when Ban Josip Jelačić secured the support of Pope Pius IX and the Austrian emperor for elevating the Diocese of Zagreb to archdiocese and metropolitan see. The First Vatican Council, at which Bishop Strossmayer gave a great speech, was held during Pius IX's pontificate. Strossmayer was good friends with the pope but that did not stop him from opposing the concept of papal infallibility. Strossmayer wasn't the only Croat who spoke his mind unafraid of the consequences in the Vatican. The Dominican priest Andrija Jamometić sharply criticized Pope Sixtus IV (1471 – 1484), accusing him of being responsible for a number of scandals in the Curia and of nepotism and immorality. The Bishop of Split Mark Antony de Dominis was one of the greatest minds on the continent in the late 16th and early 17th centuries. He was a renowned scientist and philosopher. In his book *De Republica Ecclesiastica* he criticized the policies of the Holy See and as a result he was declared a heretic by the Church. Unperturbed he simply converted to Protestantism and continued his career in England, where he taught at Cambridge and Oxford. James I made him Dean of Windsor and Master of the Savoy Hospital in London. In 1621 his friend Alessandro Ludovisi was elected Pope and took the name Gregory XV. Mark Antony de Dominis returned to Rome and lived on a pension granted him by his friend the pope. Gregory XV died in 1623 and soon after de Dominis quarreled with the Inquisition and was duly imprisoned at Castel Sant'Angelo where he died one year later. A few months after his death, on the order of the Inquisition, his body was dug out and publically burned, with his books, in Campo de Fiori, the very spot where Giordano Bruno had been burned alive 20 years previously.

The Holy See never had any serious problems with the Croats, despite a few hiccups along the way. But, many popes focused their attention on Bosnia, where they tried, by any means necessary, to stop the spread of heresies. Pope Innocent III (1198 – 1216) sent his emissary to Ban Kulin in Bosnia, unhappy with the ban's policy of tolerance towards heretics. Prompted by the emissary, Ban Kulin gathered the nobility and a large number of commoners in Bilino Polje where together they swore allegiance to the Catholic faith. Pope Nicholas IV (1288 – 1292), a Franciscan friar, sent Franciscan friars into Bosnia as inquisitors in 1291 with the aim of strengthening Catholicism in the face of the Bosnian Bogomils (also known as patarenes). The event marks the beginning of constant presence of Franciscan friars in Bosnia and Herzegovina that lasts to this day.

During the course of history thirteen Croatian archbishops were named, on account of their loyalty to Rome and high standing at home, cardinals by various popes, which enabled them to take part in conclaves and even be elected as pope themselves. The first Croatian to be named Cardinal was Demetrije, the Bishop of Zagreb and Archbishop of Esztergom. He died in 1387. The first archbishop of Zagreb, Haulik, was also named Cardinal. Alojzije Stepinac's heroic display of defiance towards his Communist prosecutors and persecutors and his subsequent martyrdom at the hands of the Yugoslav Communist authorities did not go unnoticed in the Vatican. Every archbishop of Zagreb after the death of Alojzije Stepinac has been named Cardinal. In 1994 that honor was also given to the Archbishop of Vrhbosna Vinko Puljić.

Rome became home to many Croats throughout history. The hermit Jerome from Dalmatia requested from the pope to build an inn in Rome for Croatian pilgrims and refugees fleeing from the Ottomans. In 1453 the pope agreed and gave the Church of Saint Marina and its grounds to the Croats. Shortly after that the Croats built a hospital and sanctuary at the location and dedicated the structures to Saint Jerome. At the site today stands the famous Pontifical Croatian College of St. Jerome, one of the more important Croatian institutions outside Croatia.

Many Croats worked in the service of the Holy See. For example, Ruđer Bošković, at the request of Pope Benedict XIV in 1742 created plans to repair the apse and the dome of Saint Peter's Basilica in Rome and measured the meridian arch between Rome and Rimini, which resulted in the first accurate map of the Papal States. Giorgio Baglivi, a native of Dubrovnik and one of the most renowned Croatian physicians of all time, was the personal doctor of two popes – Innocent XII and Clement XI. Pope Paul III employed the great Croatian miniaturist Julije Klović to illustrate his books. The Dominican friar and Archbishop of Zagreb, and later a beatus, Augustin Kažotić, also left his mark in Rome. He was considered the best orator of his time and he closely collaborated with Pope John XXII. Pope Martin V and Pope Eugene IV had enormous confidence in Ivan Stojković, a native of Dubrovnik and professor at the University of Paris. Because of his outstanding oratorical prowess he was one of the most appreciated speakers at two councils – the one in Pavia and Sienna and the one in Basel. In 1968 Pope Paul VI named the Archbishop of Zagreb, Cardinal Franjo Šeper, Prefect of the Congregation for the Doctrine of the Faith, which is one of the most important duties in the Vatican.

Šeper continued in that post during the pontificate of John Paul I and that of John Paul II. He retired in 1981 and died shortly after. Franjo Šeper was succeeded by Cardinal Ratzinger, the future Pope Benedict XVI.

For a time Croatia was the only European Catholic country outside the EU. John Paul II and Benedict XVI, logically, supported Croatia's bid to join the Union. The nature of the future relations between the Holy See and Croatia and the intensity of the support of the Vatican's diplomacy for Croatia will, in large measure, depend on the relationship of the Croatian government with the Church and the role of Croatia in the ecumenical processes regarding the Orthodox Church. History teaches us that the relationship between Croatia and the Vatican was always just as much cordial as it was pragmatic.

Pope John Paul II's Promotion of Croatia

Croats – the first Slavic people to convert to Christianity

We usually perceive saints as entities existing outside the constraints of time, as ethereal specters watching over us. On the other hand, and somewhat contradictorily, we perceive them also as historical figures that lived many centuries ago, people from bygone eras who cannot really understand our prayers – the entreaties being grounded, as they are, in modernity and the needs our age imposes on us. Pope John Paul II is a different kind of saint. He was canonized in 2014 and we celebrate his holiday on October 22. Finally we have a saint who lived and walked among us, who was a vocal advocate of Croatia's independence, who actively encouraged finding a peaceful solution to the Yugoslav problem… Three times he visited Croatia. His speeches given in the Croatian tongue still resonate loudly. Among the prize possessions of many Croats are photographs of family members taken with him. John Paul II loved Croatia and untiringly championed the country's causes. There is no reason to doubt his continued loyalty to and unceasing support for Croatia in heaven. Wojtyla introduced Croatia to the world. As a fellow Slav, he understood our collective soul and took a liking to it. He was a charismatic leader, great orator and media darling. His almost fanatical struggle for peace, prosperity and justice earned him the world's respect. He used the potency of that respect to help nations and social groupings in need, raising awareness of their plight and problems and promoting their values... As soon as he was elected Pope in 1978 he took up the Croatian cause. At that time the world did not know much about Croatia because the nation was hidden behind the cloak of Communist Yugoslavia where national identities were outlawed.

Not enough has been written about the importance of Pope John Paul II's support for Croatia, especially in light of the fact that during his twenty-seven-year pontificate he devoted more than 780 messages, letters and speeches to the Croats. He often talked or wrote about Croatian identity, religion, history, present and future. There is no doubt that John Paul II played an important role in the establishment of Croatia as a viable political player in the international arena. The Polish science magazine *Poznańskie Studia Slawistyczne* kindly asked me to analyze Wojtyla's writings and speeches about Croatia and the Croats so as to determine how the pope perceived the Croats and how he presented them, and their country, to the world. Fairly quickly I came to the conclusion that he understood our identity better than any other political or religious figure that ever lived. He was also one of the staunchest, and most successful, promoters of

Croatia. Unlike the current pope, Francis, who is focused on the individual and social groups as opposed to nations and their unique features, John Paul II took care to focus his attention both on the individual and identity of nations. The identity and history of the Croats were frequent motifs in his speeches and writings. He regularly talked about the Croats as the first Slavic people to convert to Christianity, praised them as a reliable ally of the Holy See and drew attention to the fact that early Croatian leaders had striven to detach themselves from the influence of the Byzantine Empire and turn to Rome. John Paul II recognised that the Croats remained loyal to the Vatican in the face of numerous challenges throughout history. He emphasized how much the Croats had suffered during the course of their history and how many sacrifices they had made for the safety of Europe. It is worth noting that John Paul II never hesitated to present the Croats as victims of both Communism and Nazism. He considered the Archbishop of Zagreb Blessed Alojzije Stepinac the ultimate symbol of the suffering inflicted on the Croatian nation by the Communists, Fascists and Nazis.

John Paul II, a Pole, was fond of comparing the Poles to the Croats. One of the things the Croats share with the Poles is piety and devotion to the Mother of God. John Paul II liked to present the Croats as a people with a rich cultural heritage and tradition but also as a nation of emigrants. It is worth noting that he perceived Croatia as a link connecting the East and the West, a meeting point of different cultures and religions. He liked to say that Croatia was a beautiful country of proud people.

His links with Croatia predate the beginning of his pontificate. In 1976 the then Archbishop of Zagreb Franjo Kuharić informed the future pope, at that time serving as the Archbishop of Krakow, of the commencement of the celebrations of the 1,300th anniversary of Christianity in Croatia. Cardinal Wojtyla responded with a congratulatory letter, in which he referred to the Croats as brothers and pointed out that the histories of both nations had often intertwined, mentioning specifically the names of their common rulers, and the holy brothers, apostles Cyril and Methodius. That same year Cardinal Wojtya sent a letter to Cardinal Franjo Šeper, who, in the capacity of Papal Emissary in Solin presided over the celebrations commemorating the 1,000th anniversary of the first known church dedicated to the Virgin Mary in Croatia, built during the reign of Queen Jelena. In that letter, dated July 21, 1976, the future pope mentioned the similarities between the Croats and the Poles and the role of women in the histories of both nations (queens Jelena and Dabrowka). In the same letter he referred to the Mother of God as the Queen of the Croats and the Queen of the Poles and mentioned two shrines – the one in Solin and the one in Częstochowa. Two years later and a few months before Wojtyla would become Pope John Paul II, Franjo Kuharić visited Krakow. Together with Wojtyla he led a pilgrimage to the Marian shrine Pyekari and he delivered a sermon in Croatian. According to eyewitness accounts, the event solidified the future pope's affinity for the Croats.

John Paul II's first speech in the Croatian language, in which he talked about Croatian identity, was given on April 30,

1979, in St. Peter's Basilica in Rome, where the pope held a Mass with the Croatian bishops and pilgrims, celebrating the 1,100[th] anniversary of the correspondence between Duke Branimir and Pope John VIII and the blessing that the pope had sent to Duke Branimir and the Croatian people in 879. In that speech, dedicated to the centuries-long ties between Croatia and the Holy See, the pope emphasized the similarities between the Poles and the Croats and referred to "White Croatia" as the ancestral home of the Croats and his homeland. Fifteen days after the celebrations commemorating the anniversary in Rome the pope sent a letter to the Archbishop Kuharić and Catholics in Croatia. The letter was read out in Croatian churches during the commemorative activities in relation to the anniversary. In the letter the pope again mentioned the fact that the Croats had always been staunch allies of the Holy See and emphasized the role of Duke Branimir: "There is no doubt that by his brave deed Duke Branimir, choosing to side with Rome and the West, during the time of the schism between the Eastern and Western Churches, ensured that the reality of the Croats would be a Catholic one."

Addressing the fact that the Croats had always been loyal to Rome, the future pope wrote "that it is wondrous and remarkable that the Croats stayed true to the faith while confronted with numerous invaders and troubles."

The National Eucharistic Congress was held on September 8 and 9, 1984, in Marija Bistrica, marking the end of the celebration of the 1,300[th] anniversary of Christianity in Croatia. On the occasion of the Congress Pope John Paul II read out a message to Croatian Catholics on Vatican Radio and then sent a letter, which was read to the participants of the Congress. In the letter, amongst other things, the pope stated: "At the beginning of the 7th century, your ancestors from the Carpathian region of White Croatia – not that far from my home town – settled in the territory that is today your beautiful country and came into contact with Christianity, a religion well entrenched in the area since the time of the apostles. That land, watered with the blood of martyrs from Solin, Istria, Sisak and many others, became the homeland of your people. By accepting baptism and embracing the only apostolic, Roman Catholic rite, the Croats also came into contact with Western Roman culture and became an integral part of Christian Europe which, at that time, was in the process of being formed into a spiritual and cultural whole…"

In addition to the above, the pope pointed out a number of features of Croatian identity: loyalty to the Mother of God, turbulent history marked by suffering…

In a special letter to the youth of Croatia, read out during the celebration of the International Youth Year in the Zagreb Cathedral on October 27, 1985, Pope John Paul II again reminded them that "the Croats received Christianity thirteen centuries ago, the first among the Slavic peoples to do so". He also addressed the youth of Croatia directly: "You, young Catholics, because you live at the meeting point between the East and the West and are in contact with different peoples and cultures in Yugoslavia (...) have a special duty to develop a dialogue with Christians of other denominations, with Muslims and non-believers but you always have to remain aware of your religious, cultural and national identity."

Talking to the youth of the Archdiocese of Zadar during the Holy Mass in Rome on December 14, 1985, John Paul II mentioned Pope Sixtus V, describing him as "the great benefactor of the Croats". On October 21, when visiting the Pontifical Croatian College of Saint Jerome in Rome the pope talked about a saint the Croats consider their own because he was born in Dalmatia – Saint Jerome. In his sermon the pope called him "your fellow countryman, a great Dalmatian, a paragon of piety and servitude to God."

The three visits John Paul II made to Croatia – in 1994, 1998 and 2003, were important in the context of promoting the country, especially in the Catholic world. It has to be kept in mind that popes had never been in the habit of visiting one country three times in a relatively short period of time. Viewed from that perspective, the fact that John Paul II visited Croatia three times during the course of nine years is extraordinary indeed. Each visit the pope made to Croatia was reported by the media all over the world and Croatia was seen, for the most part, in a positive context. During his third visit John Paul II openly said that Croatia should become a member of the European Union, pointing out that the country's rich heritage would strengthen the Union, both as an administrative and territorial whole and in the context of the Union's cultural and spiritual reality. During the previous two visits the pope called on the Croats to be forgiving and open toward other nations. After his first visit to Croatia, John Paul II, during his general audience in Rome on September 14, 1994, described Croatian Christian identity, pointing out all key connecting points between the Croats and the Holy See. On that occasion, amongst other things, he said: "The Croats were the first Slavic people that came into contact with Christianity; missionaries from Rome were responsible for the evangelization of the Croatian people and the process started in the 7th century. The beneficent influence of Saint Cyril and Saint Methodius, the apostles of the Slavs, was present in the evangelization process. The Croatian people early on established a relationship based on firm unity with the Holy See, and that relationship grew gradually stronger over the centuries. Pope John X corresponded with the first Croatian king, Tomislav, calling his subjects 'the dearest sons of the Holy Roman Church'. During the Ottoman invasions of Europe, Leo X described the Croats as the bulwark of Christendom. That description has found its true meaning in the history of the faith and holiness which the Croatian people always knew how to realize and have been proving steadily throughout the nine centuries of the existence of the Zagreb Church."

In October 1998 in Marija Bistrica, during his second visit to Croatia, Pope John Paul II beatified Cardinal Alojzije Stepinac, who "by serving God and the people" during World War II and the postwar Communist dictatorship became the symbol of righteousness and martyrdom. The pope beatified Alojzije Stepinac despite a chorus of protests of those who, for their own political gains, were fond of accusing Stepinac of being a nationalist and a Fascist on account of his position at the helm of the Church in Croatia during the period of the Ustasha regime. The pope's beatification of Stepinac went a long way toward clarifying that era of Croatian history and showing to all the world that Stepinac had been a martyr who died fighting for the downtrodden and for the dignity of every individual. When John Paul returned from Croatia he analyzed his visit during his general audience in the Vatican on October 7, 1998. He said the following about Stepinac and the history of Croatia in general: "His deeds and his fate are the embodiment of the tragedy that afflicted Europe during this century, marked by the great evils of Fascism, Nazism and Communism."

Reading the pope's speeches dedicated to the Croats, and his messages sent to Croatia, one cannot avoid concluding that John Paul II understood Croatian identity and was one of the most staunchest and successful promoters of that identity among the world leaders. We can learn a lot from him about how we should present ourselves to the Christian world.

A Catholic Country Led by Atheists

Can a Catholic be an able politician?

86% of the citizens of Croatia consider themselves Catholics – says the last census from 2011. That particular statistic is not surprising because everyone knows that Croatia is a Catholic country. The former papal nuncio to Croatia Lozano, in an interview given on Vatican Radio in 2004, described Croatia as "one of the most Catholic countries in Europe", adding that "I am not aware of any other country where the public accepts so readily the opinions of the Church, even as regards purely social issues". He concluded the thought by saying that "politicians in Croatia have to keep that in mind during the election". Is it not strange, then, that from the moment it declared independence to 2015, a period of 25 years, Croatia had not had a practicing Catholic at its helm? The first Croatian President Franjo Tuđman respected religious institutions but, as a former member of the Communist party, Partisan guerilla fighter and general of the YPA, he only became a Catholic towards the very end of his life, with the wholehearted support of Cardinal Franjo Kuharić. The second president, Stjepan Mesić, refused to have anything to do with religion as such and vocally criticized the Catholic Church at every opportunity. The third president, Ivo Josipović, treated the Catholic Church with respect but the man is a committed agnostic. This sequence of, for all intents and purposes, non-Catholics was broken when Kolinda Grabar Kitarović was elected President in 2015. The situation with the prime ministers is similar to that regarding the presidents. To be sure, Ivo Sanader was upheld, at the beginning of his term of office as a paragon of patriotism and Catholics values, but if only half of the things he was accused of during his trial for corruption are true then he can hardly be considered a disciple of the faith.

So, Croatia is obviously a strange country in relation to the religious sentiments, or lack thereof, of its leaders as opposed to those of the majority of the population. There are four possible reasons for this dichotomy. Maybe the Catholic majority is so open-minded and tolerant that nobody really cares who believes what, even when it comes to the leaders of the country. Or do true Catholics perceive politics as a dirty occupation and so the people have to choose the lesser of two evils when they elect their leaders? Or could it be that Croatia is Catholic only on paper and that there are not that many true Catholics in the country, people who actually follow the teachings of Christ as opposed to declaring themselves Catholics out of habit, or to satisfy their need to follow tradition, or maybe because they think it is trendy to be a Catholic these days? It is also possible that people are genuinely wary of "Catholic politicians", afraid that bishops could gain too much political clout through them. Vladimir Šeks once said: "...most of our Catholics are not prepared to grant any religion, including the Catholic one, more of a say in the political arena."

And what if all four reasons are valid? Then, if the Catholic majority is so tolerant and open-minded as to elect an agnostic as President and an atheist as Prime Minister, all those who claimed, after the referendum on the definition of marriage in 2013, that the Catholic majority consisted of intolerant and backward people who should be institutionally reformed in the name of democracy, are actually completely out of touch with reality. Taking into account the total number of voters, and the total number of those who rarely abstain from voting, it is hard to believe that Croatian society is split down the middle along some imaginary political fault lines. Those who vote for presidents are the same people who vote in referendums. Had only those who voted "against" in the referendum voted in the elections of 2009, Josipović would not have been elected President. The same holds true for the parliamentary elections when the SDP won.

A number of priests have openly talked about their concern that there are not that many true Catholics in Croatia. They think that only about 30% of professed Catholics are true Catholics who lead their lives according to the teachings of Jesus. The rest, according to the priests, are those who celebrate Christmas and Easter out of habit, to keep the tradition alive so to speak, and those who declare themselves Catholics for cultural and similar reasons. Many people believe, and rightly so in my opinion, that most Croatian politicians are corrupt. Therefore, most Croats tend to steer clear of politics. The Croatian academic Ivan Supek said that politicians do not possess enough intelligence and honesty but possess an exceeding amount of lust for power. And he was right on the money. However, honest people with a moral compass should not eschew politics simply because it is at this point in time populated by venal people. The last three popes themselves insisted that quality people should enter politics and that it is their duty, as believers in Jesus Christ, to do so. "There is an ever growing need for politicians who are believers and those who are trustworthy, who will fight for the common good as opposed to their own venal gains," said Pope Benedict XVI during his visit to the Czech Republic in the fall of 2009. In the same speech he put modern politicians on the spot, saying: "It is not enough to look honest, one has to be honest!" Pope Francis also, in 2013, affirmed that those in power have to be humble and caring and that ordinary people, especially if they are Catholics, cannot afford to be disinterested in politics. He added that politicians have to love their people, because having power means serving the people. "Everybody who accepts a position in the government has to ask themselves these questions: 'Do I love my nation so that I can serve it better? Am I humble, do I know how to listen; do I respect other people's opinions so that I can lead my people on the right path?' If they do not ask themselves these questions, they will not be able to do their jobs properly!" said Pope Francis unambiguously.

The high standards the popes insist on may seem unattainable to us, especially in this age of spin, manipulation, exclusivity, tribalism and tendency to insult the intelligence of one's constituents. Most of the politicians in Croatia (believers and non-believers alike) perceive the country in bipolar terms. For them, the citizens of Croatia belong to one of the following two groups – those who agree with them and those who don't. The only relevant fact to our politicians is whether a given person is affiliated with one or the other camp. Those in their camp are good, and all the others are bad. If somebody, hitherto vilified, from the other camp, defects to their camp then they'll praise that person till Judgment Day. It's toxic tribalism at its worse. Crooks in one's own camp are considered able and competent people. Those outside one's own camp are always potential targets of persecution and prosecution. Self-interest is oftentimes the only relevant value in politics. No wonder then that in that environment there is no room for Christian and humanitarian values. To be sure, the Christianity card is often played in support of this or that populist agenda and for the purpose of staying in power. Polls confirm Vladimir Šeks' statement mentioned in a preceding paragraph. Catholics don't like priests who hold political speeches from the altar. For them, churches are refuges of spirituality, not rostrums. This doesn't mean, however, that Christianity and the Church should be banished from public life. The Italian philosopher Marcello Pera, who considers himself a liberal and agnostic, in his book *Why We Should Call Ourselves Christians* claims that Christianity is of paramount importance in the social life of Europe because he thinks that the causes of the current problems in Europe are groundless liberalism, absence of common identity (if Christianity is removed from the equation) and ethics devoid of truth. The political creators of the European Union, Robert Schuman, a Frenchman, Konrad Adenauer, a German and Alcide de Gasperi, an Italian, were well aware of the dangers Pera warns of. After World War II the three politicians played an instrumental part in the rapprochement of the European peoples and creation of European unity. Unfortunately, the Europe they strove for remains incomplete. Many intellectuals agree that politics would benefit greatly from an influx of spirituality and moral values because democracy entails a lot more than simply following rules; true democracy comes from embracing those values that inspire democratic processes such as human rights and common good... If there's no consensus as regards those values, democracy loses its meaning and ethical principles are relativized. And Christianity is that element in Western society that staunchly insists on human rights and common good. Spirituality in politics can only be an added value, never a burden... "People believe in God because they do not have faith in themselves. History teaches us that they are quite right in that, because we haven't proven ourselves worthy," wrote the Peruvian Nobel laureate Mario Vargas Llosa in his book *Notes on the Death of Culture: Essays on Spectacle and Society*. Llosa claims that a free society cannot be only neutral, secular. It needs "deep spiritualities", it needs to be religious because the functioning of society is not dependent only on good laws but also on the awareness of the critical mass of the population that it is "good" that there are laws, that it is "good" to have a moral compass. Without that foundation any point of law is a dead letter, any law is essentially meaningless. The destructivity of human behavior, immorality, dishonesty in relation to human relationships cannot be curbed by any decree but only by some other-worldly power, something people are afraid of and respect on some deeper level. If this life is all there is, and there is nothing and nobody to hold us responsible for our actions after we die, then decrees and limitations have absolutely no purpose or meaning. Therefore, it is logical to conclude that those who truly follow the teachings of Jesus Christ should take more responsibility for their lives. Of course, that is seldom the case. Some assertive Christians often express their disapproval of atheists by claiming that the worst dictators and mass murderers of the 20th century were atheists who had no fear of God or man, like Mao Zedong, Stalin or Pol Pot. However, we must not forget that people like Mussolini, Franco and Pavelić declared themselves as Catholics. A wise man once said that he would rather live in a country full of honest atheists than in a country full of crooked Christians. From a theological standpoint, the assertion is correct. Llosa too holds that religion, if lost in a culture of spectacle, tends to become a three-ring circus, especially when religion morph with the profane and loses their purity and authenticity: "There where religion is trivialized, reduced to a spectacle, partying, then it is religion itself that becomes the main pillar of undeterred capitalism and is the main agent of the current crisis." We often see the separation of form and substance and Christianity, ever more often, is evaluated according to the public image of a given priest or bishop, and not according to the teachings of Jesus Christ.

In this day and age it is hard to be a politician with sincere religious beliefs. For example, the former British Prime Minister Tony Blair (a social democrat!) refused to talk about his religious beliefs during his term of office, even though rumors about his devotion to God abounded. Today he admits that he was afraid to speak openly about his religion while he was Prime Minister for fear of being perceived as somebody heading to the funny farm. But he also says that without his belief in God he would not have been able to overcome the most difficult moments of his career. He raised his four children as Catholics, even though he converted from Anglicanism to Catholicism after he left Downing Street. He feared that converting to Catholicism while he was still in office would create unnecessary political problems in the country because of the close connection between the Church of England and the state. It was a valid concern and in that regard it is worth mentioning that the prime ministers of Britain commended bishops to the Queen, until Blair's successor, Gordon Brown, discontinued the tradition.

Even the USA, where 25% of the population is Catholic, had a Catholic president and recently a Catholic vice president, Joe Biden. John Kennedy's story shows that it is possible to be a practicing Catholic and committed liberal. During the election campaign, it was often acerbically suggested to him that if elected President his loyalties would be torn between the Catholic doctrine and the American Constitution. Kennedy always replied that he would immediately resign if it ever came to that. He was convinced that his Catholic faith could only help him to be a better leader, more responsible president and serve his country conscientiously. Jesus Christ was Kennedy's inspiration, especially in the context of Jesus' advice to all of us that we should consider all people our brothers and to always help those less fortunate and disenfranchised to "do unto others as you would have them do unto you" and to "render unto Caesar the things that are Caesar's, and unto God the things that are God".

Honoring these principles Pope Francis started a media revolution and became a role model to many politicians. It is somewhat ironic that many politicians who declare themselves Christian are unaware of all the good advice the Bible – a book millennia old – has to offer. We hope and pray that there will be more true as opposed to false Catholicism in Croatian politics, regardless of whether a given politician is a believer or not.

PART V

Homeland and Diaspora

Unrealized Dream of the Croatian Diaspora

Croatian emigrants as a valuable asset of the Republic of Croatia

At the beginning of the 90s, when Croatia broke away from Yugoslavia, there was a lot of talk about unity of all Croats and return of emigrants. There was hope for a better, prosperous future in the air. Nobody could predict, and nobody dared predict, that twenty years later the relations between Croatia and the Croatian diaspora would be strained almost to a breaking point and that hundreds of thousands of people would have left Croatia in search of a better life abroad, many of them vowing never to return. We remember with nostalgia the optimism that pervaded every facet of life during the early days of Croatian independence; "emigrants from far and wide, from New Zealand to Chile are now going to return to Croatia, they are going to invest millions of dollars in Croatia, we are witnessing the dawn of Croatian unity that will surely result in the creation of a new social elite, willing and able to position Croatia alongside the successful Western nations," people enthusiastically argued everywhere. Some even predicted that all the projects regarding the preservation of Croatian identity, hitherto the sole preserve of the Church (because every other institution in the country was led by Communists) and conducted through hundreds of Croatian Catholic missions, clubs and associations all over the world would be given to the ever grateful Croatian government, adding a new diplomatic dimension to the endeavor. It is painfully obvious today that none of that happened.

The first Croatian President Franjo Tuđman considered it his duty to include Croatian emigrants into all structures of government. It was a wise move. The emigrants brought a spirit of democracy, patriotism and Western work ethic into the political and social fabric, scarred by a half century of Communist rule, of the newly independent Croatia. During those days the Ministry of Return Migration and Immigration existed and the Croatian diaspora had 12 representatives in the Croatian Parliament. And the representation was well deserved. The Croatian diaspora played an instrumental part in the creation and defense of Croatia. A large number of Croatian emigrants took out loans in foreign banks and sent the money to Croatia. Many of them returned and joined the Croatian army or helped in other ways. Unfortunately, there were many dishonest and immoral people in positions of power and influence in Croatia who took advantage of the goodwill of the Croatian diaspora to enrich themselves or promote their interests, or both. Millions of dollars sent to Croatia were stolen or embezzled. It often happened that money sent to buy medical supplies, weapons and other things essential for the defense of the country simply disappeared. But, these acts of blatant thievery did not diminish the love of the Croatian diaspora for Croatia... However, all over the world questions were being raised, inquiries launched. All to no avail. To this day nobody seems to know who stole the money!

In 2000, when the SDP came to power, the Croatian diaspora was vilified in the media, now controlled by the new government. Ostensibly, the Croatian diaspora's sentiments were too rightist for the SDP's taste. Many politicians in the new government were former Communists and they saw the Croatian diaspora as a class enemy... The situation turned very ugly quite soon. The media space was saturated with ideological diatribes given by former Communists against the Croatian diaspora. The aim of this ruthless propaganda campaign organized along, more or less, Stalinist lines, was to deny the diaspora representation in the Croatian parliament. All the help the Croatian diaspora gave to Croatia during and after the war was ignored as irrelevant. Ditto all the potential in terms of expertise and contacts that the diaspora was always ready to put into the service of Croatia. In true Communist fashion, the former Communists resented and envied the success, ability, experience and knowledge of Croatian emigrants. And, of course, by purging all progressive, Western influences from the structures of government, the former Communists, incompetent as they were, protected their own jobs and positions. Unsurprisingly, the Croatian diaspora felt betrayed and cheated. Many people from the diaspora resignedly stated that they had fought for a different Croatia. A significant number of those who returned to Croatia couldn't function in the Croatian version of capitalism with Communist mentality. They packed their bags and emigrated again. The dream of Croatian unity had turned into a nightmare.

Most of our politicians, with the exception of Tuđman and his government, did not even try to tap into the potential of the Croatian diaspora. There is no doubt that Croatia is rightly considered a country of emigration. There are about 4 million Croats and their direct descendants living all over the globe. And not all of them are guest-workers or manual laborers who have forgotten Croatian without ever properly learning the language of the host country, as has often been insinuated in Croatia. Not all of them are rabid right-wing fanatics either... Actually, many of them are American congressmen, Chilean academics, bishops and authors, Argentinean landowners, British businessmen, Australian bankers, German hoteliers... The second- and third-generation Croatian immigrants should not be forgotten here either. They are familiar both with the mentality of the Croats and that of the people of their country, they are native speakers of at least two languages, they have been educated at prestigious universities, they are connected with the ruling, academic and scientific elites in their countries and they love Croatia and, at least to an extent, consider themselves Croatian... How many of these remarkable and able individuals have gotten a chance to represent Croatia as, for example, ambassadors or consuls? How many of these scientists and academics are involved with the

Croatian institutions whose job is to lead the country on its path of economic recovery? How many of these businessmen have we convinced that it is a good idea to invest money in Croatia? The answer is none. We hope that foreign institutions will give us non-refundable grants with no strings attached and we spend a lot of time and effort, unsuccessfully more often than not, to induce them to do so but we ignore Croatian businessmen, and those of Croatian ancestry who regularly invest incredible sums of money all over the world are ready and willing to invest in Croatia only if we could give them guarantees that the money will not be embezzled. Nevertheless, many Croatian immigrants invest money in the absence of such guarantees, out of sheer patriotism. Many more send money to their relatives in Croatia on a regular basis.

We take pride in the fact that tourism is the country's main source of income. But not many Croats are aware that Croatia's second largest source of income is the Croatian diaspora. In 2012 the Croatian diaspora sent more than 2.5 billion dollars. According to one analysis made by the Croatian World Congress in Germany, the Croatian diaspora, in the first 20 years of Croatia's independence, sent about 100 billion euros to Croatia. That is almost six national budgets. Add to that millions more sent by Croatian immigrants to their relatives in Bosnia and Herzegovina. What nation on the face of this planet would not bend over backwards to tap into such wealth? The Israelis, Poles, Irish have realized long ago that their immigrants all over the world represent a huge demographic, financial and lobbying potential. Croatia's neighboring countries have ministries devoted to maintaining viable relations with its diasporas... And we are doing everything humanly possible to keep our immigrants from all over the world at bay. We have wasted a golden historic opportunity. Many feasible processes have been discontinued, many mistakes have been made. But, there is still hope. Not all is lost. We can still change our ways. Croatian unity is not a lost cause. However, if something is not done soon then all will be lost. Globalization and the development of communications technologies give us the second chance. We just have to utilize them. If we are willing to learn how.

Between Assimilation and Return to the Homeland

Destroying stereotypes about the Croatian diaspora

Anyone from Croatia who visits any given expatriate community is astonished by how much the immigrants and their children and grandchildren love the homeland and are interested in what is happening there. The homeland is best loved from afar, as one Croatian poet once said. Croatian immigrants are emotionally tied to the homeland and no amount of work, or time spent abroad, or miles separating them physically from Croatia can diminish that connection. They care about their native land and are prepared to do everything they can to improve the quality of life in Croatia. On the other hand, it is a fact that years, oftentimes decades of living abroad have modified their perception of Croatia. Many Croatian immigrants thus idolize the homeland beyond measure. And they set themselves up for disappointment because the news reports from the homeland are seldom good, dominated as they are with stories of ideological quarrels, economic hardship and a sense of pessimism. Their homeland is not what they thought it would become when independence was declared in the early 1990s. Moreover, many of the immigrants have not managed to assimilate fully into their host societies and the time spent abroad, successful financially but disastrous from a social perspective, has made them alien to their relatives and countrymen at home. They have become lost in a limbo between the two worlds. In fairness, it is not easy to become assimilated and at the same time retain one's traditions, customs, habits... Many Croatian immigrants in Australia solved the conundrum by fiercely, and for decades, resisting assimilation by existing as a society apart, clinging desperately to their language, traditions and way of life. Definitely not a recipe for happiness, the pursuit of which, ironically, led them to Australia in the first place. Oftentimes the picture of the homeland they carried in their mind's eye became the prism through which they viewed the new reality around them. And we know that most of them left Croatia out of either political or economic necessity, or an unfortunate combination of the two. That's why they are always thirsty for good news from home. But Croatia has gone through many breathtaking changes since they left the country behind. Some changes were for the better, and others for the worse. I remember one anecdote told to me by a friend. She was born in Australia to Croatian parents but relocated to Croatia in the late 1990s. She explained to me how her parents adored Croatia and had sent large amounts of money to various Croatian institutions during the war to give their contribution to the defense against the Serbian aggressor. Still, when she told them about her decision to relocate to Croatia they tried to dissuade her, saying that "you'd have a hard time setting yourself up because the spirit of Communism in politics and society is still very much alive and the economic situation is bleak". She argued that Croatia was now a modern Central European country where she could easily get a job with a large multinational company. The parents were adamant – they loved Croatia with every fiber of their being but still considered it not good enough for their daughter. The young Australian woman found a job with an American corporation in Zagreb and since has made a successful and lucrative career in Croatia. Her parents still daydream about their ideal Croatia. Recently she told me that she was enjoying life but that she worked twice as hard as she had done in Sydney and that the results were not half as good. "We're wasting too much time on trivialities. Unfortunately the state apparatus is not a service, as it should be, but a parasite. And, the Croatian mentality compels us to focus on other people instead of on ourselves. Such a waste of time and energy!" she said.

The creation of the Republic of Croatia had a two-fold effect on Croatian immigrants. On the one hand, it was a justification of their struggle in their host country to preserve their identity and traditions and a vindication of their decades-long travails to explain to their co-workers and neighbors the realities of life under the Yugoslav Communist regime. The Australian Croats, when Croatia declared independence, breathed a collective sigh of relief – finally they had their own state, their own national institutions that could now legally promote everything people used to go to jail for in Yugoslavia. This newly emerged optimism also encouraged many immigrants who had assimilated into the host country's society. Croats of all walks of life strove, together, to help the homeland in its hour of need. The Australian Croats, inspired by that wave of optimism, built the grandiose new building of the Croatian embassy in Canberra. On the other hand, the forces motivating Croatian immigrants to stick together, like the campaign of assassinations launched by the Yugoslav Secret Service for example, disappeared practically overnight. After Croatia proclaimed independence, many Croatian immigrants felt like their mission had been completed and found themselves searching for new causes to fight for, for a new raison d'être. The Croatian Catholic missions, which up to that point had been the hubs around which Croatian immigrants coalesced, started to redefine their role, hoping that the newly formed institutions of the Republic of Croatia would assume the leading role in dealing with the Croatian diaspora through diplomatic and consular representatives so that the Church could focus on ecclesiastical matters. But Croatian diplomacy dropped the ball, and keeps dropping it. Instead of building on the foundations set by the Church, Croatian diplomacy cannot even hope to organize an event abroad involving the Croatia diaspora without the active support of the Church.

We have to admit to ourselves that we really do not understand the Croatian diaspora. During the Communist regime in Yugoslavia state propaganda depicted the Croatian emigrants as demons from the deepest pits of hell. Maybe the Croats in Croatia could not be bothered to understand their fellow Croats who lived abroad, even though it's hard to find a Croatian family without a relative working in one of the countries of the West. Only after the first multiparty elections in Croatia did we realize that another Croatia existed outside our borders and that the Croatian emigrants were not fascists that needed to be eliminated as enemies of Yugoslavia as the leadership of the Yugoslav federation had insisted. The Croatian emigrants feel underappreciated by their fellow Croats at home, and rightly so. We are all aware how much they helped Croatia financially and in a myriad of other ways when the outcome of the Croatian War of Independence hung in the balance, with the odds stacked overwhelmingly in favor of Serbian imperialism. But, many Croats conveniently continue to ignore the Croatian diaspora's intellectual potential. Maybe they feel threatened by it.

One of the common stereotypes is that all those who emigrated were not able enough to make it in the former Yugoslavia. The stereotype, if anything, seems to confirm the concluding sentence of the preceding paragraph because cold facts clearly show that some of the most able Croatian intellectuals were forced into exile because their mindset was deemed anti-Yugoslav by the authorities. And so they achieved renown and recognition abroad. Needless to say, their host countries benefited greatly from the fruits of their labor, and not Yugoslavia, or Croatia, for that matter. Croats have a better reputation abroad than people belonging to any other immigrant group. That is because Croatian emigrants, generally speaking, are true cosmopolitans, unlike the Croats, also generally speaking, in Croatia. Our politicians, when visiting Western countries, can see for themselves how valuable the achievements of Croatian immigrants are to those countries. They thrive in their new environments. They only stagnated at home. Second-generation Croatian immigrants, luckily for them, have no experience of cumbersome and parasitic bureaucracy, rampant corruption, addiction to politicizing everything and anti-entrepreneurial atmosphere. And for that reason most of their attempts to invest in Croatia or start a business have failed, because they are seen, more often than not, as dangerous competitors. Croatian immigrants who want to invest money in Croatia come from a completely different business environment and have no time for declaratory statements the likes of "the government will regulate". They demand efficiency and results, not meaningless activity. Of course, besides money Croatian immigrants offer their know-how and expertise necessary for viable economic strategies on a global level. Also, their business practices are grounded in a responsible attitude towards entrepreneurship and managing economic resources and in that regard Croatia can benefit greatly from their work ethic and experience. Every successful country in the world has such people at the helm of a number of ministries, especially those dealing with investments, development and economy. I guess the incompetent Croatian ministers and those responsible for the economic well-being of the country are too cool for school.

By the same token, we shouldn't think that Croatian immigrants are embodiments of everything that is good in the Croatian national character. There is envy and strife in the Croatian diaspora just as there is at home. And it is exactly this Croatian syndrome that prevents them from being more organized, united and therefore that much stronger and able to realize their potential to the fullest extent possible. The Australian Croats have still not managed to place their representative in the Federal Parliament in Canberra. Australia is a true multicultural country, with almost 200 ethnic communities where federal and local authorities provide direct support to many immigrant organizations. The Croatian community is among those communities who receive very little support because they do not have an official representative organization. So it is clear that the Croatian diaspora also has problems, and the Republic of Croatia should not ignore these issues. For example, a significant number young Croats, successful professionals belonging to the second- or third Croatian immigrants, barely speak Croatian and have very little or no interest in the traditions of the homeland of their parents. They don't even consider themselves Croatian. The trend is worrying, especially because many respected physicians, lawyers, scientists and businessmen of Croatian ancestry do not declare themselves as Croatian in their professional environments. Obviously these highly successful and smart people do not see their Croatian heritage as an added value and maybe in the context of their chances of promotion or advancement they see it as a liability. The younger generations have grown weary of having Croatian traditions, language and customs shoved down their throats by their parents and grandparents. Confronted with the realities of consumerism and globalization, education costs and loans they have to pay off, they find it easy to jettison the burden of their parents' woeful past all the better to meet the challenges of the modern world. We have to be realistic and admit it to ourselves that people populating the Croatian immigrant communities are a dying breed. However, maybe successful people in America or Australia of Croatian ancestry do not speak Croatian, but we can keep their inner yearning for their roots alive by providing quality content in the media and new media about Croatia, that is to say, by using the entertainment, music and news industries to foster pride in being Croatian. Establishing ties with the education systems abroad, for the purpose of promoting the Croatian language, history and culture is also a good strategy.

Croatia is not a country with a long democratic tradition. Since the invention of nationalism in the 19th century the Croats lived in the Hapsburg Empire, later called the Austro-Hungarian Empire, which was an absolutist monarchy, dissolved after the end of World War I; after that it was the Kingdom of Serbs, Croats and Slovenes, later renamed the Kingdom of Yugoslavia, also an absolutist monarchy and ruled by a Serbian dynasty. That unfortunate union disintegrated in 1941 when the Croatian Fascists established the Independent State of Croatia, sponsored by Mussolini and allied to Fascist Italy and Nazi Germany. The experiment came to a bloody end in 1945 and the Croats had to endure half a century of living under a brutal Communist dictatorship. Democratic traditions simply were not given a chance to develop. On the other hand, Croatian immigrants had to adapt to the political systems of their host countries, most of them democratic. We shouldn't forget that Croats started emigrating in large numbers from what was then the Austro-Hungarian Empire in the second half of the 19th century. It is no wonder then that Croatian immigrants and those of Croatian ancestry abroad simply can't understand the apparent inability of both the Croatian politicians and population at large to understand democracy, adopt democratic practices and agree on any issue of high national importance. Croatian immigrants expect Croatia to live up to its stated system of government; they expect both the government and people to agree that the country suffers from a lack of viable democratic processes and a weak economy. Everyone in Croatia agrees that the country has problems but there is no agreement as to what the problems exactly are. It is ironic that all the dictators that ruled over the Croats during the last 200 years were able to detect problems and solve them. To be sure, sometimes that meant killing hundreds of thousands of people, like Tito, a figure still revered in Croatia, did. The Croatian diaspora expects the Croats in the homeland to grow out of the frame of mind of the Russians serfs, exemplified by the serfs' favored locution: "The Tsar will give!" The Croatian immigrants want to see more self-sufficiency in Croatia, less reliance on the impotent government because relying on something that is impotent makes no sense, more professionalism, more patriotism and less insularity. The Croatian diaspora is acutely aware of the inadequacy of Croatian politicians, especially when compared to those of the developed and successful countries. The verdict on the Croatian politicians is that much more damning in light of the fact that the leaders of the Western world are not exactly paragons of intellectual excellence and morality. The Croatian diaspora, it is safe to say, sees Croatia as a failed state. And we cannot blame the Croatian immigrants for holding such a view. They love Croatia and are worried, rightly so, about its future. The modern state of Croatia was forged in blood and suffering, and the Croatian nation endured terrible hardships in its history. Now that we have our own country, many Croatian immigrants say, it is criminally irresponsible to have inadequate people at its helm, and equally irresponsible of the Croatian population in the homeland to adopt an ambivalent attitude towards the idea of democracy. And this is the source of the rift between the Croatian diaspora and the Croats living in Croatia. This schism has to be repaired as soon as possible. The Croatian diaspora has to understand that a democratic frame of mind cannot be adopted collectively overnight, and it is up to them to do more to educate the Croats in Croatia about democracy. On the other hand, the leaders of Croatia have to wake up to their inability to face the challenges of the 21st century and find people who are capable of doing that. And many such people can be found abroad, in the Croatian diaspora. In this sense, this terrible split between the two parts of the Croatian nation – the one at home and the other in the diaspora – is a blessing in disguise, a historic opportunity to bring the two parts together for the purpose of making Croatia successful and promoting national interests.

Why They See Croatia as a Promised Land

Croatia and the descendants of Croatian immigrants

The media space in Croatia is inundated with stories about how young people are leaving the country in droves in search of a better life abroad. These stories create an impression that life in Croatia is bleak and futile to the point of agony. On the other hand, not many people in Croatia are aware of the fact that many descendants of Croatian immigrants, born, raised and educated in the West, have been relocating to Croatia for years. On the one hand, we have thousands of people from Croatia relocating to Ireland, Canada and Germany, and on the other, there's a steady stream of highly skilled, educated and experienced professionals of Croatian ancestry relocating to Croatia from Canada, the USA, Australia and the UK. Do they see something in Croatia we don't? It's a logical question. I recently discussed this, for want of a better word, phenomenon, with Adrian Beljo, a young expat from Canada, who works as the Director of the Center for

International Cooperation at the Edward Bernays College of Communication Management in Zagreb. He relocated to Croatia with his family in the early 1990s and has never regretted the move, despite having to grapple with many illogicalities inherent in the Croatian bureaucratic and administrative apparatuses. During the conversation it occurred to us that we should conduct a poll among second-and-third generation Croatian immigrants and among foreigners who have relocated to Croatia. And so we interviewed 21 expats (15 of those were young professionals of Croatian ancestry from the USA, Canada, Australia, Argentina, Germany, the UK, Sweden and South Africa and 6 foreigners with no ancestral links to Croatia from the USA, the UK, Ireland and Australia). The idea was to see how they perceive Croatia. The results were published in the Proceedings of the 2nd Croatian diaspora Congress, held in Šibenik in the summer of 2017.

We decided to interview young people who had relocated to the land of their parents and grandparents after completing their education abroad. It was a novel approach, because similar surveys in the past had always been focused on the perceptions of first generation Croatian immigrants. Their views and perceptions regarding the homeland differ widely from those of second-generation Croatian immigrants. That's not surprising. Those of Croatian ancestry born abroad do not share the emotional baggage relating to the homeland with their parents. They do not even understand it. And how could they? Their reality is that of the country they were born in. And that was why we decided to get their perspective in our survey.

The survey showed that second-generation Croatian immigrants' perception of Croatia is not informed by any given emotional factor. They are able to contrast and compare Croatia with their countries of birth objectively. All of the respondents decided to relocate to Croatia not because they were emotionally drawn to Croatia but because they concluded that by moving to Croatia they could improve the quality of their lives. That emotional detachment makes them the perfect observers of Croatia and its people. That said, the survey also showed that the connection of the respondents of Croatian ancestry is deeper than that of the expats who had no ancestral ties to Croatia.

We didn't just ask the respondents yes-or-no questions, we actually talked to them. The aim was to find to whether their decision to relocate to Croatia was informed more by emotions or by rational reasoning. A number of respondents who relocated to Croatia in the 90s didn't have much say in the matter because it was their parents' decision to return to Croatia. Not surprisingly, these respondents think that their parents were guided solely by their emotions. Those respondents of Croatian ancestry who relocated after the 90s were old enough to make their own decisions. According to them, emotions were not a factor in the equation. They analyzed everything rationally and decided that it made perfect sense to move to Croatia. We received the same answers from the foreigners.

- After the war I started vacationing in Croatia. I couldn't help but consider the option of moving here. Such a beautiful country. So I started, sort of, leaning in that direction. After graduating from college in Toronto I applied for a postgraduate program at the University of Zagreb and started exploring the option of setting up a business here, pretty much the same thing my family had been doing in Canada since 1988. The situation was promising but I still wasn't 100 per cent sure whether I want to relocate for good to Croatia. That changed when I met my future wife in Zagreb in 2005. (Mike, Canada)

- My parents were on about, constantly, how we should move to Croatia. It kind of made sense what they were saying. So, one day I decide to relocate to Croatia, and they were appalled, telling me time was not yet ripe for that. Still, I reckoned I could make a name for myself in Croatia practicing my profession because I'm good at it. Besides, I'm bilingual. I travelled to Croatia, got a job in a big bank. It's great living in Europe. (Josip, Australia)

- I was born in Philadelphia. Had somebody told me that one day I'd be living in Croatia I would have laughed at them. Anyway, I found myself traveling to Croatia, almost by accident. It didn't take me long to realize that Croatia was the ideal country to live and raise a family in. Zagreb is perfect. Croatia's great, despite some problems with the economy. (Joseph, USA)

Then we asked the respondents about what the advantages of living and working in Croatia were. The majority of the respondents listed, among other things, the Croatian way of life, low crime rate and pristine environment. Some respondents also pointed out the free education system and universal healthcare, low living costs, business opportunities and similar things.

- I've got more free time here than I did back in Oz. (Pavo, Australia)

- Compared to the weather in Canada, the weather here is absolutely amazing. Family values are important here, and there's no crime. It's a safe place for kids. (Paul, Canada)

- The pace of life is humane. Working hours are shorter, annual leaves longer. In Canada I commuted one and a half hours to work. Here, it's 10 minutes by bicycle. (Anna, Canada)

- Croatia is a safe country. Child care services are excellent. Life is less stressful than in most other countries, and people actually have time for socializing. (Marija, Canada)

- Life's different here than back stateside. There, it's all about work and long hours. The Croats know how to take it easy. This lifestyle makes it easier to make friends. (Romana, USA)

- Pristine environment. It's like living in a national park. (Ivan, USA)

- Low living costs in comparison to other European cities. Low education costs. (Stjepan, South Africa)

could actually come in handy to anyone who wants to come up with a strategy for creating a recognizable brand out of Croatia.

- Good and affordable child care system (kindergartens and schools), safe environment for children. (Marija, Canada)

- Humane pace of life. (Ana, Canada)

- Croatia is an ideal place to live, on account of its natural beauty, quality of life, climate, geographical position. However, starting a business is difficult. (Paul, Canada)

- In comparison to other European states, Croatia is a land of great business opportunities, because in those other countries the market is saturated. (Pavo, Australia)

- One can actually become friends with his or her colleagues. In the West that is impossible. (Mark, UK)

- All major European capitals are only an hour or two away by plane. And Croatia has retained its authenticity, which is a rare quality today in the world. (Joseph, USA)

- One can work here and still enjoy life, which is impossible in other places. (Ivan, USA)

- Security and relatively low living costs. (Stjepan, RSA)

- Most of my friends in Canada are also second-generation Croats. Simply put, I'm living their dream. If somebody gave them a business opportunity, even for three times less money, they'd be here in a heartbeat. (Mike, Canada)

- In this globalization age it doesn't really matter where your office is. You can be located in Zagreb and still work for any given corporation. For this reason the location you choose has to offer everything you and your family needs as regards leisure time. Croatia is a great place to live in that regard. (Markus, Austria)

- Croatia is safe, beautiful and socially conscious. The food is healthy and traditional values, some of which I've heard about from my parents, are still cherished. In Australia they're long gone. (Vida, Australia)

It is obvious that these expats, well educated, well read and well traveled young professionals with connections all over the world, can be the best promoters of Croatia and the country's new link with the world. Their perception of Croatia is accurate and devoid of any emotional attachment and undue exaggerations. Ironically, Croats tend to scoff at the very features of Croatia other people see as advantages. For the average Croat the grass is always greener on the other side. Until they actually travel to the other side and realize that it is not green at all.

PART VI

Made in Croatia

Sea and Water

Croatia's trump cards at the European table

It seems that for some reason Croatia is simply not able to use it advantages. The country is situated in the very heart of Central Europe, its geopolitical position between the West and the East is ideal, and its Adriatic coast is more than 1,000 kilometers long. Croatia connects the Mediterranean with the rest of the continent. Its cultural heritage is vast and the environment pristine. Croatia has so much prime arable land that it could feed the whole of Europe. It has so many tourist attractions that we could earn from tourism more than any other country in Europe. There are countless forests in the country, and good furniture designers too... Croatia could be the main manufacturer of high quality furniture in Europe, surpassing even Italy and the Scandinavian countries. Recently it was announced that there are vast oil deposits in Croatia – we just have to locate them... Many people say that if Croatia was populated by Germans or Americans it would be one of the most successful countries in the world. There's a lot of truth in that assertion. Croatia is a country of great potential and greater opportunities. Many developed and successful countries have been casting envious glances at all the advantages Croatia possesses for decades. But, it would seem that the Croatia is cursed because the Croats are not able to use those advantages to develop the country, improve their quality of life and put the country on the business map of Europe.

The list of Croatian advantages is inexhaustible. However, if we had to pick the two most important Croatian assets, the two aces up our sleeve, trump cards that give us a marked advantage in relation to other European countries, what would those assets be? It was exactly this question that students of the Zagreb School of Economics and Management posed to the globally renowned marketing expert Philip Kotler in 2016 when he gave a lecture in Zagreb. This celebrated American expert has helped many countries and corporations worldwide to utilize their advantages, keep ahead of their competitors and create successful brands. In his books he regularly points out that the process of marketing a product starts before the product is even created, because marketing is actually a search for great ideas and products people need and are willing to pay money for without even being aware of it. He also advises that corporations doing business in countries like Croatia should specialize in providing services and manufacturing products for which demand exists not only locally but globally as well. He adds that in that particular regard developing a country from a marketing standpoint is crucial. Kotler claims that every country has to develop a recognizable identity, recognize its advantages and invest money into utilizing these advantages... When the question about the two most important Croatian advantages was posed we were all ears, eagerly anticipating the professor's answer. Kotler was lost in thought for a few moments and then authoritatively said: "Global advantages of Croatia are: sea and water."

He did not tell us anything knew really; he merely confirmed what many of our experts had been saying for decades and showed how informed he was as regards our country.

Fresh water is a resource without which life on earth cannot thrive. There is an ever growing number of experts predicting that wars will be fought over fresh water in the near future, just as wars are fought today over oil. 97% of the planet's water reserves, however, lie in the seas and oceans and is not drinkable, not without expensive desalinization processes anyway. Two thirds of the remaining 3% is stored in ice sheets and the snows of the Arctic and Antarctica. The remaining one third is unevenly distributed. 1.2 billion people today lack adequate access to drinking water. The United Nations has grimly predicted that in 50 years time about half the world population will not have access to enough drinkable water needed for a normal existence. And where is Croatia in that bleak picture of the future? Croatia possesses an incredible 32,818 cubic meters of renewable reserves of drinkable water annually per inhabitant, which means that Croatia is the third richest country in drinkable water in Europe, after Norway and Iceland. In the context of the whole planet Croatia is among the top 30 most water-abundant countries. It is a very advantageous position, given the fact that there are 230 countries currently in the world. To put all these numbers into context it has to be said that 1,000 cubic meters of drinkable water a year per person is considered the minimal amount needed for survival. So, thirty times less than every Croat has access to. Incredible as it may sound, about 25 countries in the world do not even have access to the mentioned bare minimum of drinkable water. Most of those countries are on the continent of Africa, but a fair few countries in the Mediterranean and Middle East will not have enough drinkable water in the near future. In the long terms that could cause mass migrations into Croatia and present a threat to our national security... Croatia has enough renewable reserves of drinkable water and should not be affected by the looming crisis of diminishing reserves of drinkable water. The fresh water issue will, undoubtedly translate into a major ecological, economic and security concern in the future. In that sense, it is of paramount importance for Croatia to manage its fresh water reserves properly – they must not be sold, polluted or, for want of a better term, embezzled. As Anđelko Brezovački points out in his book *Mitovi i činjenice o pitkoj vodi* (Myths and Facts about Drinkable Water) "we can safely say that drinkable water will be the most important Croatian resource in the 21st century, a treasure that has been taken for granted but an asset that could very well determine the country's geopolitical position, its economic development and its image in the world." Many Croats are not aware of how important fresh water is, and will become for the future of the country and most households use much more water than realistically needed. Not many people in Croatia think, despite all the evidence, that the planet will run out of drinkable water any time soon. In Spain, for example, many riverbeds where once water flowed all year round are dry. It is high time our politicians realized that drinkable water has already become a powerful political tool. Turkey has been trading fresh water for modern technologies with Israel for quite some time now and Arab countries offer oil for water… The Croatian state institutions, at this point in time, are not doing nearly enough to take advantage of the fact that we have fresh water to spare.

Cold numbers irrefutably show that Croatia is not managing its reserves of fresh water in an efficient manner. Households use about 38% per cent of available fresh water, industrial facilities and factories about 60% and only 0.9% is used for irrigation. To put the numbers into a clearer perspective; the average expenditure in the EU is as follows: 14% is used in cities, industry uses 10% and agriculture accounts for 30% of water expenditure. About 32% of fresh water is used to generate electricity and for cooling. It is painfully obvious that Croatia is in need of a viable strategy regarding fresh water management. In the absence of such a strategy, our valuable reserves of freshwater will remain a neat little statistic today and an asset in foreign hands tomorrow.

The Adriatic Sea is our gateway to the Mediterranean and as such forms an integral part of our national identity. The Croatian coast is more than 1,000 kilometers long, with more than 1,000 islands scattered more or less evenly along the coastline. The sea is clean, rich in fish and the weather during the summer months pleasantly warm, making the whole of the Croatian coast a paradise for swimming, diving, sunbathing, hiking, biking, resting, exploring, rowing or just enjoying being alive in that pristine environment. Croatia should have become a tourist superpower ages ago. And yet, every year we fear that an unfortunate spell of rainy weather could financially ruin the season. The glorious days of large Croatian merchant and war fleets are long gone and have completely faded from the collective consciousness of the Croats. The Croatian fishing fleet is something we ought to be proud of. Our falkuša, a traditional fishing sailboat, participated in the celebrations of the 200th anniversary of the Kingdom of Norway held in Oslo in 2014. The Norwegians honored that boat from Komiža with the distinction of being the most beautiful historic boat in the world and it led the procession, alongside two Viking dragon-ships, of 300 historic ships from all over the world during the main ceremony. And boats like the pasara boats from Mali Lošinj and Krk, the trupa and lađa vessels from the Neretva, the gajeta fishing boats from Mljet, the Dubrovnik galleons, the Adriatic bracera cargo vessels, the Omiš pirate ships should have been included in the procession... Some people may find it strange, and rightly so, that once we were a maritime power in the Adriatic and Mediterranean to be reckoned with and today we depend on the ferries of *Jadrolinija*, a state-owned shipping company. The fact that there are more than 1,000 islands and islets off the coast of Croatia is, paradoxically, becoming a burden for the state. There are no modern motorways connecting Dubrovnik to the rest of the country.

In light of that fact, it is no wonder that maritime links connecting the islands to one another are virtually non-existent and those connecting the islands to the coast completely inadequate. That means that the islands, a potential source of wealth, prosperity and influence for the country, are left to wither on the vine. The Adriatic Sea has always been our gateway into the world. Ever since the Croats settled in the region, the lure of the sea produced many Croat adventurers, cosmopolites and world travelers. The trends arriving with the returning Croatian ships and visiting foreign vessels altered the way of life of the Croats. The sea made us inhabitants of the village of the once wide world, but at the same time it lured away many of our people to distant shores, where their descendants live and prosper to this day. Once upon a time the Adriatic Sea was one of our diplomatic trump cards, an asset in the hands of our traders. Once upon a time Dubrovnik fleets ruled the waves. In Yugoslavia that glorious tradition was followed by: *Croatia Line, Tankerska plovidba Zadar, Atlantska plovidba Dubrovnik, Split Jadroplov, Lošinjska plovidba...* At the tail end of the 80s, the ships of these companies comprised a fleet of about 200 merchant vessels. Today no one in Croatia knows how many of that number are still in usable condition. The Croatian merchant fleet, both by number of vessels and by tonnage, has never been smaller. Still, we derive some consolation from the fact that Croatian seamen are sought after in today's labor market. Many Croatian seamen have had successful careers working as officers and captains on foreign ships. At home, their skills, ability and experience are not appreciated at all. Instead of exporting large quantities of quality fish, we export seamen. Two large ports, once of crucial importance for the SFRY – Rijeka and Ploče – have become backwaters, simply because there are no viable road or rail links with the mainland of Croatia. Once upon a time, not so long ago, as the popular song goes, generations of Croats lived off fishing, and their catch was regularly served in the imperial courts of Europe. Today only Japan buys our fish, and we export modest quantities through the Cromaris company from Rovinj and the Adriatic Queen company from Postira. Inexplicably, we allow our neighbors to fish in our waters, with the result that Italian fishermen catch more than 150,000 tons of fish a year while Croatian fishermen catch only 35,000 tons.

Our shipyards, once our pride and joy, now resemble ship graveyards. It is painfully clear that calling Croatia a maritime country is unrealistically optimistic. Those responsible for our economy have obviously no intention of taking advantage of the fortuitous geographical position of Croatia, knowledge and experience of our seafarers and seamen and turning the Adriatic Sea into the economic heart of the Mediterranean basin. They perceive the coastal region as a place to buy or build houses in with embezzled money and our sea not as the asset that Kotler talked about but as a burden, because the ruinous state of our fishing industry and merchant fleet threatens to expose their incompetence and provoke inquiries into the source of their miraculously acquired wealth.

The sea ain't water, say the Dalmatians. To the inhabitants of the inland regions of Croatia water is both the sea and what comes out of the tap. Despite this difference in the perception of water, the sooner we all realize that both kinds of liquid are the country's major assets, the better.

Do Croats Have Wine?

How much is "Made in Croatia" worth?

Would you rather buy a TV with a "Made in Japan" label or a "Made in Turkey" label, assuming that the price and quality of both sets are roughly equal? Like most consumers you'd probably go for the Japanese one. Chances are you'd buy the Japanese set even if it was more expensive than the Turkish one because you have more confidence in Japanese television sets than in Turkish ones. Based on the same psychology buyers all over the world have a preference for German cars, Swiss watches, Italian pasta and French fashion items. And when it comes to choosing wine, furniture or any other product, the same psychology applies. People don't like to analyze too much the quality of any given product they're looking to buy. The determining factors in deciding to buy this or that product are past experience with a given brand and the image of the manufacturer and the country of origin. There are just too many products of any given type on the market and the amount of information that's out there regarding all those products is really prohibitive. People have to trust their gut feeling, informed by the two factors mentioned above. Many countries, especially successful ones, have become aware of that trend among consumers and invest serious amounts of money into managing their identity and image for the purpose of securing an advantage for their producers and manufacturers in the world market. Not only managers nowadays deal with the issue, but social scientists as well, who have coined the term *the country of origin concept.* It is all very simple though. The social scientists merely recognize that consumers all over the world would rather buy a product made by an established manufacturer and coming from a country with a good image and even pay more money for it than for a product of similar quality made by a relatively unknown manufacturer, especially if the manufacturer is located in a country with an unrecognizable image or not so good a reputation. Again, image and reputation, regardless of whether the former is grounded in reality or not and latter deserved or not, count for everything these days. Thus most people still believe that the Bentley and the Mini are British cars, even though they are manufactured by German companies.

Connecting a product to the image of its country of origin can lead to positive or negative generalizations which in turn can lead to forming uninformed opinions about everything coming from the country in question. For example, most Croats believe that Chinese products are cheap and of extremely low quality, despite the fact that China has been making high quality products for years.

Uninformed opinions can also lead to undeserved positive perceptions. Those countries which were quick on the uptake prepared the ground in time for the phenomenon and thus secured an advantage for their products in the world market. For example, many French and Italian fashion and cosmetics products and foodstuffs are attractive to most people simply on the strength of the fact that they originate in France and Italy. It's the same thing with Colombian coffee, Swiss watches, Persian rugs, computers from the USA... On the other hand, there are excellent products on the market, manufactured in less attractive countries that are widely perceived as mediocre, or even bad. For example, many excellent products come from Slovakia these days but the manufacturers refrain from putting "Made in Slovakia" labels on them. Instead they opt for "Made in the EU" labels. It is generally accepted that any piece of furniture manufactured in Scandinavia is of the highest quality, or that wine and fish from Chile taste better than wine and fish from some other country... Many products of the highest quality are manufactured in many countries throughout the world but, for some reason, positive stereotypes simply don't get attached to them. Unfortunately for those countries and products, stereotypes, positive or negative, true or not, have become the gauge of quality. It used to be possible for countries to become synonymous with certain products quite by accident. That doesn't happen anymore. In this day and age, manufacturing a quality product doesn't mean much if a positive image is not attached to the country of origin of that product. A country needs to enjoy a positive image in the world for a number of reasons and one of them is to give to its manufacturers and companies a fighting chance in the global market. In today's globalised world countries cannot afford not to spend a lot of time and effort on strategies for developing a positive image of themselves.

Many companies are fond of outsourcing production processes to countries where labor is cheaper than in the home country. Ironically, the country of origin is no longer the country of manufacture. But the "made in" labels are not changed accordingly. Usually, and falsely, the country of origin is cited as the country where the head office of the company is located. Many companies from the West have long outsourced their production processes to Asia and Eastern Europe. At first the consumers didn't seem to care. But now the perception of the consumers seems to be shifting; they don't have as much confidence in products the manufacture of which has been outsourced as before. For example, buyers are getting leery of supposedly French products sporting "Made in the Philippines" labels or German cars which are actually manufactured in Slovakia. It is considered in many business circles that it makes sense to move production processes from a country with a weaker image to a country with a stronger image. The logic is not foolproof though. If consumers, for example, want to buy a Croatian product, it is important to them that the product indeed originates in Croatia. In that sense a "Made in Germany" label doesn't mean that much. It can only annoy the buyer into requesting his or her money back.

As we have seen, reputation counts for a lot. People would always rather buy French perfumes than those from other countries, ditto German cars, Japanese electronic equipment or Italian clothing items. However, the sales of other products from those countries suffer as a result of the aforementioned products' stellar reputation. For example, Italians make excellent computers but due to the country's image as the manufacturer of high quality clothing items it is difficult for Italian makers of IT equipment to sell their products in desired quantities. German clothing manufacturers, such as Hugo Boss, find it prudent not to emphasize the fact that they are German – one would always rather buy an Italian clothing item. Until recently, Turkish soap operas and popular Swedish movies were considered oxymorons. Art too suffers from perceptions informed by stereotypes. However, it is obvious from the two examples that perceptions based on stereotypes can change, and always will change if enough effort is exerted towards that goal. Even Japanese products were considered inferior 50 or so years ago and today they are a byword for quality. The Japanese have put a lot of money and effort into promoting their country and their products and today they are reaping the rewards. Until recently it appeared perfectly logical to buy Slovenian-made skis because Slovenia is a mountainous country. But today, after the incredible successes of the Croatian alpine skier Janica Kostelić, most people would gladly buy Croatian-made skis, if there were a company in the country manufacturing them, regardless of the fact that Croatia is widely considered a Mediterranean country. In that regard, products that can be directly associated with the identity, geography and traditions of their country of origin enjoy a distinct advantage on the global market. For example, some twenty years ago nobody knew that Croatia was a producer of olive oil. Today, olive oil produced in Istria and Dalmatia is considered hands down the best in Europe. A few years ago I was served olive oil in one luxurious restaurant in London; the waitress enthusiastically explained that the olive oil was the best in Europe, coming from a beautiful, only recently discovered region close to Italy, located in the new member state of the European Union – Croatia. Keeping a straight face I asked her: "Do you by any chance serve wines from Croatia?" She gave me a funny look, obviously dumbfounded by the question. After a few seconds she recovered her professional composure and said: "I'm not sure that Croats make wine."

Obviously the Croatian producers of olive oil are better at marketing than the Croatian wine makers are. Or maybe the competition in wine making is fiercer…Anyway, it seems more natural that quality olive oil, rather than wine, is associated with a beautiful Mediterranean country with a thousand islands… It takes a lot more effort to establish a reputation of an industrial product to the point where the country of origin factor can boost sales. Unfortunately, Croatia does not have a group of products that could be called Croatian and competitive in the global market. The ships built in the Croatian shipyards used to be that product, but they're long gone and the shipyards appear like something straight out of a post apocalyptical movie. There is some potential in the food industry, but the country of origin factor works only in the region, not in any wider European or global context.

Quality products and brands can, in time, become an important communications channel and also a symbol of a country's identity, that is, powerful ambassadors of the national image. That promotional synergy is apparent whenever a product is marked with a design (one would be hard-pressed to find a Swiss product without a white cross on red background somewhere on it, or an Italian product without some kind of a design based on the three colors – green, white and red). The packaging of any given Croatian product, unfortunately, is not distinguishable in that particular regard. It is as though we are ashamed of being Croatian. Many producers and manufacturers of commercial brands are trying to conquer the global market with a nationally neutral approach – the aim is to be perceived as a global brand not connected to any country. Labels denoting the country of origin, on such products, do not exist. However, many studies clearly show that the strategy is wrong. It is important for consumers to know what the country of origin of a given product is. Brands that are nationally and regionally conscious, so to speak, are more successful in the global market than rootless brands. Buyers want to know where a given fruit or vegetable was grown, and how something they are going to keep in their house was manufactured. Products without origin are deemed as dodgy. This is confirmed by the experiences of some multinational companies that tried, unsuccessfully, to internationalize themselves, only to return under the national flag again (British Airways, for example). Connecting a product to its country of origin is often the more lucrative option if the image of the country is positive. In that case the country of origin in and of itself is a solid market value that already exists in the collective consciousness of the consumers because it has a form and shape. In that sense products draw on the value of that "brand umbrella" and at the same time contribute to its strength.

It is clear that the country of origin factor is not an absolute value. Images of countries change. Production processes change. Companies change. There are often, within a given industry, differences in the qualities of products of different manufacturers in the same country. And consumers are aware of these differences, regardless of whether the image of the country is positive or negative. On the other hand, the potency of stereotypes, image and perception is stronger than ever. Croatia should learn from the best and create the necessary synergy between the manufacturers and the state and at the same time work on improving the country's image (as an economic power to be reckoned with, not just a tourist country) and creating viable marketing strategies. Before that happens, Croatia's promotional and marketing efforts for products wrapped in the Austrian or Italian colors will not bear much fruit. Also, low quality Croatian products in distinctive red and white checkered packaging that seem to be all the rage these days when everyone's eagerly anticipating the start of the World Cup, are not going to improve the country's image or ever be truly competitive in the global market. No Croatian product will ever be competitive in the global market as long as "Made in Croatia" labels keep provoking the question: "Croatia? Who are these guys?" If we want the country of origin factor to work in our favor we have to roll up our sleeves and start doing some serious work. If we continue to follow the path of least resistance then we'll inevitably end up hiding behind the "Made in EU" label. That won't do us much good, because the consumers will ask – where exactly from the EU? And we all know how big and diverse the continent is.

Why Brand Croatia? How to Brand Croatia?

Problems with identity and image

One would be hard-pressed to find a person who does not associate the Netherlands, a country situated below sea level, with the term "low country" and also with the picturesque canals of Amsterdam, endless fields of tulips, windmills, the famous painter Rembrandt, clogs, tolerance, liberal attitude towards soft drugs and prostitution... By the same token, most people associate Denmark with bicycles (Copenhagen alone has 400 km of bicycle lanes), outstanding design, Lego bricks, the Vikings, Hans Christian Andersen and his fairytales *The Little Mermaid* and *The Ugly Duckling*... Almost everyone knows that the Danes are the happiest nation on the planet, that they know how to enjoy the moment and the warmth of the family home (hygge), that they live in harmony with nature, that Denmark is a healthy welfare state and that their foreign policies are geared towards promoting and keeping peace. What associations does Switzerland evoke? Most people would immediately say the Alps, chocolate, cheeses, banks, watches, neutrality... Not for nothing do the precise and trustworthy Swiss safekeep the money of many rich and powerful people and protect the pope.

There is no doubt that Denmark, the Netherlands and Switzerland are successful brands, reaping the benefits of their positive image – earning vast sums of money, imposing trends on other countries and enjoying the respect of the modern world.

Why did I pick those three countries? Because – this may come as a surprise to many Croats – all three are smaller in size than Croatia and because Croatia can learn a lot from their example. Denmark, the Netherlands and Switzerland are not afraid of telling their stories to the world, they are proud of their respective identities, histories, cultures, ways of life... Any given feature of Denmark, Switzerland and the Netherlands is immediately recognizable all over the world. Not only have they informed the world about their values, but they have also incited us to discover them for ourselves. No self-respecting Dane, Dutchman or Swiss, would ever dream of saying that the small size of his or her country precludes it from being successful and influential globally. By contrast, almost all Croats are fond of hiding their inadequacies and those of the country's leaders behind the excuse that Croatia is simply too small in size to be a major player either regionally or globally. Denmark, the Netherlands and Switzerland are influential on a global scale and make a lot of money on their respective identities and images! They recognize the value of branding and behave like the global brands they are.

It is universally known that a country's image plays an ever more important role in international relations. The image of a given country actually determines that country's status in the political arena and that status in turn determines the state of that country's economy – by attracting or repelling tourists, foreign investors, buyers of its products and invitations to participate in international forums and/or associations... Any country that aspires to be successful today has to manage its image and identity and engage in the branding process for the purpose of getting noticed globally, keeping ahead of the competition, neutralizing negative perceptions about itself, and imposing its values on other countries.

In this day and age countries can ill afford not to bother to promote their values. Foreign investors rarely invest their money in countries that do not have a positive reputation and tourists would rather travel to destinations that are aggressively advertised in the media than to those that exist below the radar in that particular regard. There's not that much that separates the countries in the developed world in terms of tourist attractions, investment opportunities, standards of living or cultural heritage. Small wonder then that tourists, investors and expats choose destinations that are more recognizable than others. In that context, those countries that have become brands have a distinct advantage over those that have failed in that endeavor or haven't even made the attempt. Also, those countries that don't deem it worthwhile to try to become a brand run the risk of being "branded" by others. Of course, it is in the interest of no country to depict its potential competitor in glowing terms. Therefore, those countries that fail to become brands will more often than not be perceived by the world public on the basis of disinformation and lies spread by other countries, global institutions or individuals. In simple terms, if a country is not a brand, it means it's fair game and the hunting season never ends. The accepted term in learned circles for that kind of branding is "outside branding".

A country is a successful brand if people around the world immediately associate it with positive things and are aware of its advantages, its culture, its contribution to the community of nations, its great men; when it has become a popular tourist destination, when its way of life is imitated and its cuisine universally praised…

Croatia is a European tourist brand. Almost everyone who has heard about Croatia knows that Croatia has the cleanest sea in Europe, magnificent beaches, an indented coastline and beautiful islands. On the other hand, not many people know that Croatia has a rich cultural heritage. A fair few people know that we fought a war for our independence in the 1990s and that we languished under Communist rule for half a century. Sports fans around the world respect our national football team and know that many a Croatian professional athlete is a holder of many gold, silver and bronze medals. On the other hand, there are a significant number of people in Europe who don't know that Croatia has actually joined the European Union. And they don't care one way or another. They don't know anything about Croatia apart from the fact that it is a beautiful country; they don't know anything about Croatian products; they have never read a book written by a Croatian author; they don't know anything about the Croatian way of life; they don't know what makes us different from the other nations on the Balkan Peninsula. There are also many people, including renowned intellectuals, who are misinformed about the Croatian War of Independence and know close to nothing about the origins of the wars that devastated the region in the first half of the 1990s. The situation would be funny if it wasn't actually tragic for Croatia. Important facts about Croatia are obscured, facts that could, and should determine the country's image abroad. For example, precious few people in Europe know that a number of Serbian politicians active today were directly involved in Serbia's attack on Croatia in the early 1990s; even fewer know that Blessed Alojzije Stepinac saved a large number of Jews and Serbs during World War II and worked actively against Ante Pavelić and his government sponsored first by Mussolini and later by Hitler; nobody in Europe seems to have heard of Marko Marulić, one of the most popular writers in Europe of the 15th and 16th centuries, or of Ruđer Bošković, whom those few who know a lot about Croatian history call "the precursor to Einstein"; nobody seems to know, or care, that Europe, as the former powerhouse of the world, owes a huge debt of gratitude to many Croatian greats. Unfortunately, the common perception in Europe, and in the world, is that Croatia is a small and insignificant country. It is worth noting, however, that many foreigners who got to know Croatia, its history and cultural heritage fell in love with the country and became the country's promoters. It is important to point out that these promoters of Croatia found out the story of Croatia on their own thanks to a fortuitous set of circumstances. We didn't do anything to attract them to Croatia and we are doing close to nothing in that regard today. Croatia is a popular tourist destination but we cannot earn the world's respect simply on account of that. Croatia has to be strong politically and economically and it has to promote its values and cultural heritage – Croatia has to become a brand that encompasses everything from economy, politics, culture, science and gastronomy to art. We deserve to be a brand more than most other European countries that are brands. We just don't know how to promote ourselves.

Many Croats will say that Croatia is a young country without any money to promote its values and so become a brand, like Denmark or the Netherlands. That's nonsense. Croatia declared its independence and was internationally recognised more than 20 years ago. Croatia has been a member of the European Union for more than four years now. But, we haven't introduced ourselves to the world yet and have missed countless opportunities to do so. There is really no excuse because the technology today allows us to promote whatever we want to promote, on any given level, and reach billons of people, almost instantly. A country doesn't have to be big or rich to utilize the new media or to gear its traditional media outlets towards promoting its values. Therefore, every country in the world can become a brand. It's just a matter of putting in the hours and creating content – promotional, documentary, whatever. As far as the argument that our geopolitical circumstances are unfavorable – the opposite is actually true. Croatia is both a Mediterranean and Central European country. Nowhere in Europe can one find so much diversity, uniqueness and so many cultural monuments from all historical periods in so small an area. Croatia lies at the crossroads of many cultures, religions and national identities. The serendipity of Croatia's geographical location is reflected in the country's rich cultural heritage, gastronomy and especially in the Croatian way of life, which is so addictive to everyone who has experienced it. Our creative industries are not being used to the fullest extent of their potential, our unique UNESCO world heritage sites remain shrouded in obscurity and a whole myriad of Croatian greats who played pivotal roles in making Europe great are unknown both within Croatian borders and outside of them, which is especially lamentable because with a modicum of effort on our part their lives could be immortalized by Hollywood and their accomplishments an inspiration for all mankind.

Croats have a tendency to sell themselves short, to disrespect what God has given them and to deny their own potential and that of the country as a whole. The only Croatian government that promoted the country on a strategic level was that of President Franjo Tuđman back in 1994 – and it was limited to the tourist industry. No Croatian government since has seen it proper to manage the country's identity and image in a sustained and viable fashion. Even though we have more than 40 governmental agencies, we do not have a single institution tasked with strategic management of our brand and with promoting our values, advantages, economy, science, language, athletes, the Croatian diaspora... That's especially regrettable in light of the fact that every successful country does have institutions for promoting its values and establishing its identity and image, effectively its brand, on a global scale. Of course, amateurs, no matter how high in the political hierarchy they operate, cannot do justice to the task, only highly skilled and experienced professionals can. The politicians and decision makers in successful countries are aware of that, those in Croatia, unfortunately, are not. Simon Anholt, a leading British expert on nation branding, claims that countries can reap many rewards from successful nation branding; according to him successful nation branding means that schools, colleges and universities should promote their courses to students and researchers at home and abroad, the tourist board should promote the country to holidaymakers and business travellers, the investment promotion agency should promote the country to foreign companies and investors, the cultural institute should build cultural relations with other countries and promote the country's cultural and educational products and services, the country's exporters should promote their products and services abroad, the Ministry of Foreign Affairs should present its policies to overseas publics in the best possible light, and sometimes attempt to manage the national reputation as a whole. For some reason the Croatian leaders simply cannot grasp how important nation branding is. Why that is so is beyond my powers of comprehension.

When it comes to nation branding, different countries use different strategies. In practical terms, however, they all boil down to pretty much the same thing. Wally Olins, who participated in the successful attempts of many nations to brand themselves, identifies seven steps in the process of nation branding: 1) Set up working groups, 2) Perception of the nation, 3) Evaluate strength and weaknesses, 4) Central idea creation, 5) Visualization, 6) Message coordination, and 7) Launch liaison system.

Many countries developed their national brands by implementing the seven steps. Serbia, for example, set up a working group, gathered many entrepreneurs, businessmen and artists, commissioned research regarding the country's image abroad and invited tenders for creating a new national identity. At that point petty political rivalries retarded the process and the whole thing was dropped amidst a lot of acrimony. Slovenia, on the other hand, implemented the seven steps and created a new national identity as a modern European country existing in harmony with nature, adhering to the principle of sustainable development, belonging to Western civilization, having a rich cultural heritage and populated by industrious people. By contrast, Croatia made one lukewarm attempt at nation branding and soon gave up.

If Croatia ever decides to try again, the first step in the process will have to be reaching a consensus regarding who we are, what we really want and how we want to be perceived abroad. The renowned scholars Kotler and Gertner advise that a country that wishes to become a brand has to carry out a SWOT analysis first in order to determine what its main strategic advantages, weaknesses, opportunities and threats are. The second step, according to the scholarly duo, is to choose particular sectors, persons, natural features and historic events which could serve as a foundation for the process of nation branding. Simply put, the idea is to focus on everything that reflects our good sides, our uniqueness and those features that many people abroad may find interesting or entertaining, or both. After that's done, a common denominator has to be established, a framework to put all of the above within. Anholt favors a simpler approach. He suggests that everything starts with determining how most citizens perceive the state and finding out how that perception in turn determines their actions in relation to the state – do they actually believe in the state; do they invest their money in the economy; do they believe that the state is essentially there for them? The next step is to determine how the citizens should perceive the state and how that differs from how they actually perceive it. Finally, a democratic, effective and reliable process should be set up to transform the existing brand into the desired one.

Croatia has not been able, since its inception as an independent, democratic republic in the early 1990s, to gather together its leading intellectuals, creative people, communications experts, businessmen and politicians for the purpose of reaching a consensus about what values Croatia as a brand should contain and promote, what we are good at and what we want to be recognizable in the world by. Those who know us well say that our biggest advantages are the natural beauty of the country, natural diversity, favorable geopolitical position – at the crossroads of cultures and civilizations – rich cultural heritage, a huge number of talented and creative people, hospitability, openness, colorful traditions, a leisurely way of life with plenty of socializing, a rich culinary scene, a sense of fashion and style (we gave the tie to the world and everyone can see that Croatian women are among the best dressed women in Europe)…

Many people are envious of our food, clean water, favorable climate, safe streets and way of life. We have all the ingredients necessary to create a powerful national brand – we just have to get rid of Croatian Envy, stop destroying our society by identifying with defunct ideologies of Communism and Fascism, improve our self-esteem and drop the annoying habit of trying to imitate what we see in Hollywood films and American and British reality TV shows.

The Fragility of Croatia's Tourist Brand

Communicating with the world and Croatia's new image

It would be hard to find one of the more influential global media outlets that hasn't lately praised Croatia, its natural beauties and cultural heritage. Croatia, its islands and cities are regularly on top 5 or top 10 lists of most attractive tourist destinations in the world. Naturally, we bask in those accolades and think that everyone perceives us in a highly favorable light – we are happy with what we think is the country's image abroad. However, on closer inspection we see that the situation is not all that rosy. On the one hand, the country's image abroad is not based solely on the beauty of the Adriatic Sea but also on many other features that shed a less favorable light on our homeland, and on the other, we cannot fail to realize how important a role image plays in the global political and economic arena. The fact that Croatia (tourism notwithstanding) is doing virtually nothing in relation to the strategic management of its own identity and image is truly horrifying and does not bode well for the future of the country.

Thousands of studies and hundreds of books have been written that prove that consumers would always rather buy products made in a country with a good and positive image than those made in a country with a bad image, or an unrecognizable one. The studies and books also show that countries possessing the potency of charisma and power of appeal are the main political players in the world today, regardless of the size of their territory or armed forces. Image is all-important in today's world – a good image attracts tourists, a bad one repels them; a good image attracts talented expats, a bad one repels them; a good image attracts foreign investments, a bad one repels them; a good image induces international institutions to reach decisions that are in many ways beneficial to the country. The leaders of the USA became aware of the necessity of managing the country's image all the way back in 1938. Thus, the expansion of the economy and the armed forces was paralleled by a marked improvement in the image of the USA through popular culture. Hollywood is just as important for the USA's standing in the world as are its economy and armed forces. During the last 20 years many less developed countries have started investing steadily in nation branding with the aim of attracting the world's attention and achieving their political and economic goals. These countries engage the services of experienced professionals, establish cultural institutes, invest in public diplomacy, launch media campaigns, work on synergies between their products and national identity in order to make the product competitive in the world market... It has been proven that national pride fosters a positive attitude of the citizens towards the state and its institutions and is conducive to a healthy social atmosphere. Therefore, a country that is not aware of its own identity can easily become a victim of outside branding and malicious caricaturizations. For example, Kazakhstan, all around the world, is perceived as a horrible country, a joke, and all on account of the movie Borat. A country that, for whatever reason, is not able to use its national identity as an added value – as France has done with its fashion industry, Switzerland with its watches and Japan with consumer electronics – jeopardizes the health of its economy. And those countries with a positive image, like Germany or the United Kingdom, never cease to invest in nation branding because the profits of a positive image far outweigh the investment.

Croatia is a European and global tourist brand, after a fashion. Too many people still perceive Croatia through a prism of war and communism and believe the country is a good tourist destination only insofar as people on a low budget are concerned. And nobody seems to be aware of Croatia's rich cultural heritage, scientific achievements and history. We can gauge the real value of Croatia as a brand based on credible indices determined by analyses of how well state institutions function, what the country has to offer and measurable economic indicators. The indices clearly show that tourism is one of the main factors in relation to nation branding. However, no country has become a super-brand without globally popular products, high quality of life, attractive value systems, viable political institutions, rich cultural heritage, foreign investments, educated work force, authenticity etc. So, it is meaningless to regard the country only as a tourist brand without taking account of other parameters. It is equally pointless to promote the country as a tourist brand without considering its economic, political, investment and other potential. Tourists, consumers and investors carefully analyze the above mentioned parameters before deciding where to travel, what products to buy and where to invest money. For example, Simon Anholt's *Nation Brand Index* classifies countries on the basis of six parameters – tourism, exports, governance, immigration and investment, culture and people.

FutureBrand: Country Brand Index measures perceptions of country brand strength based on the following criteria: value system, quality of life, business opportunities, cultural heritage and tourism. The index puts Croatia in 44th place. During the last seven years the position of Croatia fluctuated between 40th place (2011) and 49th place (2010). Maybe we can find some consolation in the fact that the *Country Brand Index* mentions only Croatia out of the countries created by the break-up of Yugoslavia in its latest report. The other countries did not make the top 75 list. In 2012 that often cited index put Croatia in 9th place in the category of natural beauty. What is worrying though is that the natural beauty category is the only category featuring Croatia high in the ratings. This clearly shows us that we haven't done much to promote and take advantage of our other advantages and that our only trump card remains the bequest of the Slavic tribes that settled in what is today modern Croatia in the 7th century AD. It is as though all those Croats who defended and created Europe throughout the centuries never existed. History aside, we are very proud of the successes of our tourism industry but we are not actually aware that our tourist offer is not competitive at all in the categories like "value for money" attractions, quality of accommodation, shopping opportunities, availability of top brands, night life; even our gastronomy is relatively unknown.

According to the *Country Brand Index* the most successful brands among countries are: Japan, Switzerland and Germany. The key advantages of Japan are technology and innovation, rich culture, gastronomy and brands such as Toyota, Panasonic, Toshiba and Sony. Switzerland draws attention with natural beauty, safety, way of life, political and economic stability and brands like Rolex, Nestle, Toblerone, Lindt and Swatch. Germany has earned its title thanks to technology, infrastructure, business opportunities, living standard and cultural offer, with its automobile industry as an added value. *FutureBrand Index* predicts which countries will become brands in the future based on analyzing how viable governments and state institutions are, levels of foreign investment, quality of human resources, trends of economic growth, business environment, and global influence through cultural heritage. According to *FutureBrand Index,* the future belongs to China, the United Arab Emirates, South Korea, Israel and Qatar. Croatia, according to the same index, is stagnating.

Bloom Consulting, a consulting firm specialized in nation branding, ranks Croatia in 28th place as regards the fields of tourism and economy at this moment in time. As a tourist brand the consulting firm placed Croatia between 19th and 29th places in the world in the last seven years, depending on the year. The lowest place Croatia held among European countries only was 12th, which is very high given the economic might and tourist appeal of many countries in Europe. That said, *Bloom Consulting* ranks us low in the business category (investments and business) – Croatia is in 88th place in the world. Serbia is right behind us, in 91st place.

Brand Finance is an independent branded business valuation consultancy. It calculates the total value of a given nation-brand. According to its calculations, the value of Croatia as a brand diminishes by the year. In 2010 Croatia was in 53rd place in the world and was evaluated as one of the three biggest "winners" that year, with an estimated total value of $25 billion. Five years later, in 2015, Croatia held 76th place, with an estimated value of $32 billion and was evaluated as of the three biggest losers. Last year we improved our standing a bit and took 74th place. The consultancy firm estimated the value of the Croatian brand at $33 billion. By way of comparison, the value of Coca Cola is twice that amount. According to *Brand Finance* Serbia is moving up in the world. In 2016 it improved its standing by 5 places in relation to the previous year and is currently in front of Croatia. The value of the Serbian brand is equal to that of the Croatian brand, but Croatia has a more positive rating tendency. Slovenia holds 61st place in the same table and the estimated value of its brand is $53 billion dollars. That makes Slovenia the most valuable brand in the territory of the former Yugoslavia. This should not surprise us because

Slovenia is the only country in the region that has been systematically managing its identity and image and that has implemented all the steps of the nation branding process. While Croatia promotes itself exclusively as a tourist destination, Slovenia defined, in 2007 on the eve of taking up the presidency of the EU Council, its brand under the slogan *I feel Slovenia* and thus also defined its identity and means of communicating Slovenia as a brand, that is to say, means of communicating its policies, economy, tourism, art, culture, science and sports. Slovenia's brand also emphasizes the country's connectedness with nature and commitment to the concept of sustainable development. The Slovenes have succeeded in establishing the identity of Slovenia as a small European boutique country which lives in harmony with nature and promotes human values. *The Good Country Index* explains on its website that it "tries to measure how much each country on Earth contributes to the planet and to the human race, relative to its size (measured in GDP)". According to the index for 2016, Slovenia holds 28th place while Croatia is in 40th place. The index also ranks countries according to subcategories. For example, in the culture subcategory Slovenia is ranked 16th, while Croatia is ranked 35th. The situation is clear. Slovenia has been systematically improving its image in the world. The Slovenes actually started the nation branding process in 1986, while Yugoslavia was still in existence. To be sure, for a while the process was based on the trial and error principle but the Slovenes never ignored global trends.

Croatia started systematically promoting itself as an attractive tourist destination relatively early, in 1992. The promotional campaign helped us to distance ourselves from the rest of the countries in the region. However, Croatia never seriously attempted to engage in nation branding. In 2000 President Mesić formed a work group tasked with creating Croatia's nation brand. The group came up with a few lackluster suggestions. The members of the group then congratulated themselves on a job well done, picked up their hefty paychecks and disbanded the group. Every prime minister since then has said that Croatia needs to create a nation brand, but nothing has ever been done in that regard. Serbia, by contrast, performed better. At the end of 2016, at the initiative of the Serbian government, the Council for the Promotion of Serbia was formed. Its task was to develop a national strategy for promoting Serbia. The first head of the Council was the renowned manager Milka Forcan and later the director of the Belgrade Philharmonic Orchestra Ivan Tasovac. The members of the Council were respectable experts from various fields. Unfortunately for Serbia, the work of the Council soon got bogged down in a quagmire of controversy and recrimination and the Council was disbanded. Serbia also issued an open international tender for the creation of "strategies of branding Serbia". At the time of the writing of this essay the results of the tender are still not known. However, it is obvious that our neighbor to the east is aware of the importance of nation branding, regardless of the fact that its institutions are not capable of doing justice to the task.

The process of nation branding entails a lot more than coming up with a catchy slogan, filming short promotional videos and sending nice photographs to exhibitions abroad.

337

The process is about having a clearly defined vision and communicating, on a strategic level, with the world. It requires persistence, creativity and originality; qualities that can ensure recognisability and positive perception. Today, similar products, or services, from different countries are roughly the same in terms of quality and price. Therefore, nation branding, or product branding for that matter, is based on highlighting unique features of a given product or country. Naturally, the emphasis is always on the strengths of a given product or country so as to make it more competitive.

Tourism is Croatia's trump card. However, in order to create a viable nation brand in global terms, other segments of development have to be strong as well. Countries aspiring to become leading brands globally have to have more aces up their sleeve than just one. Every aspect of the nation branding process has to be grounded in excellence. Dysfunctional national institutions, economic instability, low standard of living and low quality products are factors that preclude a country from becoming a brand. One does not have to be a genius to understand that individuals, companies and corporations perceive a given country through the prism of a myriad of that country's characteristics. Therefore, tourists will flock to, companies will invest money into and corporations will maintain their presence in those countries that are innovative, open and responsible, that exhibit uniqueness and a can-do attitude, that offer quality in tourism, economy and politics, countries that know how to communicate their history and culture, protect the environment and are attractive to expats.

In the context of everything above, it is clear that Croatia does not have a vision of its own future. And that is the cause of all of the country's current economic, social and political woes. Most successful countries started their journey to prosperity by clearly defining their economic and political objectives and deciding what products to promote and what they wanted to be identified with. Since Croatia does not have a vision of its future it is impossible to come up with a coherent strategy for managing the country's identity simply because the lack of vision prevents the country from having an identity in the first place. And a coherent strategy means all state institutions, from the Croatian National Tourist Board to all the ministries, cultural institutions and the Croatian Chamber of Commerce following the same plan and working in concert for the purpose of making the nation branding process work. As it is, the left hand has no idea what the right hand is doing. It's a perfect breeding ground for incompetence and negligence. No wonder then that people abroad don't really know anything about Croatia, and no wonder that that knowledge gap is filled with disinformation by those who hate Croatia or perceive it as a potential enemy or competitor. Another problem is that Croatia does not have a central state institution, as most other countries do, notably Sweden, tasked with coordinating promotional campaigns with a global reach and communication of all the various institutions and ministries with the world.

Public diplomacy is one of the most powerful modern communications channels today as opposed to what we may call classic diplomacy. The latter breed of diplomacy is simply too cumbersome, slow and ineffective in today's information age. It is no longer enough to pull foreign officials or diplomats by the sleeve trying to sell something, steal something, beg for something or borrow something. The new paradigm calls for reaching the whole population of the planet. Public diplomacy, therefore, utilizes the most sophisticated means of communication, culture, creative industries, scientists, academics, film, music... Public diplomacy is still in its infancy in Croatia. That's why Croatia is often a victim of propaganda or malicious disinformation campaigns. We simply do not put enough effort into educating the world about us. Inexplicably, there are only a couple of books about the Croatian War of Independence, based on archival material and documentary evidence, published in the English speaking world. And these two books are the sum of the country's efforts to promote the truth about the war. At the same time, there are hundreds of books out there, written mostly by Serbian authors, that demonize Croatia and the Croatian Armed Forces without any shred of evidence, based on pure propaganda. Also, the Internet is awash with content proselytizing nonsense about Croatian history (with particular emphasis on lies about the Croatian War of Independence), culture and national mentality. It seems that nobody in Croatia knows how to utilize the traditional media and new media to promote Croatian history and culture.

Croatia has to start building its soft power, just like the Republic of Ragusa did, because that is the only way to swim with the big sharks and not getting eaten by them eventually. Natural beauty, rich cultural heritage, hospitable people, openness and geopolitical position at the crossroads of Central Europe, the Balkan Peninsula and the Mediterranean should be our trump cards. Of course, economic stability, viable state institutions, adherence to democratic principles and content population are the preconditions to successfully utilizing the trump cards to win the game.

The time is ripe for a new identity and image of Croatia. For that to happen we have to agree on where our place in Europe realistically is. There is absolutely no reason why Croatia should not become a country of content and proud citizens, a safe country with formidably efficient diplomats who are globally respected and members of various international boards, committees and institutions, a country led by likable, competent, intelligent and honest politicians. A country whose development is grounded in knowledge, ecology, modern technologies and creativity, a country that is a mecca for talented expats, a country that is an elite tourist destination. By the same token, there is no reason why products labeled "Made in Croatia" should not be more popular than similar products with other labels. Croatia has the wherewithal to become a country globally known by its natural beauty, its excellence, able and cordial people, a country jealously guarding its authenticity, natural environment and rich cultural heritage. A country free of envy and avarice, a country where competence is rewarded and appreciated. A country that starts global trends in design, fashion, architecture, art, music... Croatia can become a European super-brand. The best thing about that prospect is that it can achieve that status without compromising its roots and traditional values. We just have to get to work already.

Innovative and Creative Croatia

Challenges facing Croatia in the future

Ever more countries are trying to present themselves to the world through innovation and creativity. Some countries, like Sweden, communicate innovativeness as an integral part of their national identity. The British, in 2012, launched the GREAT Britain campaign, pointing out to the world everything the country has to offer and all the benefits it has bestowed on Western civilization, especially highlighting the fact that the UK is a global leader in the creative industries such as music, fashion, design and film. It is safe to say that creativity and innovativeness are the best means of communicating a country's creative and intellectual spirit. Natural beauty does not define a country on its own. Nor does cultural heritage. Natural beauty and cultural heritage are inherited values... Many Croatian historical figures can rightly be considered as leviathans of science, literature, politics, art, military prowess and many other fields of human endeavor. These great people are all dead now, and we cannot inherit their genius. Every generation has to produce its own great men, or suffer the consequences. The world's respect does not derive from having beautiful beaches within one's borders, or great men in one's history. Countries that foster and reward creativity and innovativeness attract talented immigrants, wise investors, demanding and therefore rich tourists. Creativity and innovativeness directly translate into profit and development! That's why countries that devise new values in creative ways and sell ideas prosper, and those countries that exploit and pawn what they have inherited stagnate. There are already indices out there that measure contributions of countries to the world, that is, whether the existence of a given country makes the world a better place or not. Innovativeness is a measurable quality and it cannot be faked. In that sense, a country either possesses the quality of innovativeness or it doesn't. The most innovative countries in the world are locked in fierce competition with one another. According to one study conducted in 2007 by Cornell University, INSEAD and the World Intellectual Property Organization, the most innovative countries in the world are: Switzerland, Great Britain, Sweden, Finland, the Netherlands, USA, Singapore, Denmark, Luxembourg and China. Similar studies conducted by other institutions also put Japan, Germany, Canada and some other countries on the list. It is obvious that a country does not have to be large in size to be innovative. Switzerland, the Netherlands and Denmark are actually smaller than Croatia. What is the secret of their success? The answer is a no-brainer – if a country fosters talent, creativity and competence and rewards ideas and innovations then two things will happen;

talented people will stay and prosper in the country, many talented people will immigrate to the country, making it even more innovative. However, implementing the solution is more complicated than it may at first appear to be – it entails developing complex national strategies, significantly improving state institutions, creating a viable business environment and developing infrastructures.

Croatia, as we all know, is a country of incredible natural beauty and rich cultural heritage. But is it a creative and innovative country? From a global perspective, absolutely not. To be sure, Croatia is a safe country with a high standard of living, attractive tourist offer, pristine environment and natural diversity. So far so good, people may say. But, it costs a lot of money to start a company in Croatia – plus it's also prohibitively time-consuming, the economy is not stable, state institutions are not efficient, politicians are not competent... Therefore, no one in their right mind perceives Croatia as a creative and innovative country. Paradoxically enough, most people around the world perceive Croats as creative and innovative people. One would be hard-pressed to find a country in which Croats have not made their creative and innovative mark; as scientists, innovators, artists, entrepreneurs and adventurers. Croatia has been a wellspring of excellence for centuries. No country as small as Croatia has given so many great men to Europe, men who have improved the state of the world in all fields of human endeavor. Unfortunately, we don't use the achievements of these great men to promote our country in the here and now. Maybe we feel we don't need to because many talented, creative and innovative Croats who have left

Croatia thrive abroad and achieve sterling results in their chosen fields of study or endeavor. Every successful institution, company and corporation in the world likes to hire Croatian professionals. Croatian professionals are seen as well educated, flexible, reliable, innovative and creative. Leading scientific institutions are always on a head hunt for Croatian professionals and regularly bestow awards and accolades on them. Croatian artists are renowned the world over. It is a sad fact that these talented and highly creative people cannot get a job in Croatia, not even in some obscure state institution with really low job requirements in relation to ability, expertise and work ethic. This begs the question: How come talented people cannot get a job in Croatia? Maybe the answer lies in the fact that envy, jealousy and lack of respect for excellence are inherent traits of the Croatian mentality. It is very hard for creative and innovative people to succeed in Croatia. Too many sacrifices are required and in most cases making a deal with the devil is unavoidable, the devil being this or that political party. Everything seems to be about politics in Croatia. The situation is exactly the opposite in innovative and creative countries, where everything is about competence and the pursuit of excellence. This year gives us two examples that confirm everything said above. Tomislav Mihaljević, MD, was named CEO of one of the most prestigious clinics in the USA, the one in Cleveland. Currently he is the CEO of a modern hospital in Abu Dhabi and he'll start in his new job next year. Of course, he was educated as a medical doctor in Croatia. Biljana Cerin, the director of the Croatian company *Ostendo Consulting*, was elected as a member of the board of directors of the largest world organization for information security, (ISC)^2. The organization has 125 members and is the leading company for information security in the world.

Sometimes even the fog of political war in Croatia cannot obscure originality and innovativeness of Croatian citizens. The Croatian automobile maker Mate Rimac and his company Rimac automobile from Sveta Nedjelja were granted an investment of 30,000,000 euros from the Chinese Camel Group. Mate Rimac will use the money to increase the manufacturing capacity of his line of fast sport cars in Croatia. The company already employs experts from 14 countries and now Rimac will employ even more people and become a player to be reckoned with in the highly competitive automotive industry, especially in the electric cars segment. Rimac has already conquered the global market by constructing the fastest electric car in the world, *Concept One*. The car literally left the competition in the dust, with its 4 sets of electric motors, 1,088 horse power, top speed of 355 kilometers an hour and the ability to reach a speed of 100 km an hour in only 2.6 seconds. The car's range on one battery charge is 499 kilometers. At the prestigious 86th Geneva Motor Show, in March of last year, Rimac introduced his electrical supercar and attracted interested investors who couldn't really believe that a young man from Croatia had produced a car superior to all the other cars currently on the market in the same category. Thanks to this tenacious young man, who was born in the town of Livno in Bosnia and Herzegovina, Croatia could gain its own recognizable automobile industry. Mate Rimac will launch a number of other products based on the technology he developed. One product already launched, the Greyp electric bicycle, is available in about a dozen countries around the world.

Damir Sabol is another creative, innovative and tenacious individual who is living the Croatian dream. He first made a name for himself with his company *Iskon*. Under his leadership the company became huge. At that point he sold it to German T-com to be free to pursue other business ventures. Sabol's application for solving mathematical problems *PhotoMath* instantly became a worldwide success. Only seven days after the application was launched it had more than 6 million downloads. At one point it was more popular than the ubiquitous *Facebook messenger*. The application solves math problems simply by pointing the phone camera at them. Immediately after the application was launched Sabol was contacted by one American publishing house specializing in school books. Sabol sees a lot of potential in the application in relation to the use of modern technologies in learning in Croatia. It has to be said that the potential of such application is limitless. Back in 2001 the Croatian corporation VipNet launched the M-Parking application. The app enables people to pay for parking services by sending a text message. The app was launched only a few months after GPRS, the basis for the M-Parking service, came to life in 2000. The Zagreb parking company was the first in the world to embrace that model of parking payment by phone. Today it is used all over the world.

Croatian innovators regularly win top prizes and awards in world competitions. This summer Croatian innovators won a staggering nine awards at *Japan Design and Invention Expo* held in Tokyo. It is especially heartwarming to see an invention created by a Croatian inventor in practical use worldwide. For example, Ivan Mrvoš, a student at the Faculty of Electrical Engineering, Mechanical Engineering and Naval Architecture at the University of Split, invented a solar-powered bench. That innovation, in use in front of the building of the rectorate of the University of Zagreb and all over Croatia and soon all over the world too, is a comfortable bench featuring four sockets for charging cellphones and tablets, a wi-fi hotspot, sensors for air quality, temperature and noise and at night doubles as a street lamp. It can function for ten days in darkness and it has a high impact resistance.

There are many talented students like Rimac, Sabol and Mrvoš, say those in the know at Croatian universities. They just need a chance to shine. And the Croatian government and institutions should do everything humanly possible to keep those talented young people in Croatia. It is true that we live in a globalised world and that many people spend time abroad to study and hone their skills. That's inevitable. But the tragedy of Croatia is that many people leave for good with their families. And who can blame them? Abroad they can make something of their lives, a prospect denied them in Croatia. The Croatian government is currently doing nothing to prevent the coming demographic breakdown of Croatia. If the politicians persist in their ineptitude, the brain drain will continue and Croatia will stagnate out of all relevance...

A huge number of Croatian scientists have made a name for themselves in many countries around the world. Igor Rudan, PhD, is a full professor of International Health and Molecular Medicine and Director of the Centre for Global Health Research at the University of Edinburgh. Last year he became the first Croat elected as a Fellow of the Royal Society of Edinburgh. He is one of the most influential and cited scientists in the world and the Thomson Reuters corporation as well as the American Institute for Scientific Information put him among the leading scientific minds of the world. He has collaborated with the UN and the World health Organization and he is responsible for a decrease in the global infant mortality rate and ongoing efforts to improve global health.

Igor Štagljar, PhD, made a revolutionary discovery in Toronto of a bad molecule that accelerates the proliferation of tumor cells. The discovery means that he is very close to finding a cure for lung cancer. Marin Soljačić, who's been already dubbed "the young Tesla" by the media, is one of the three winners of the prestigious Blavatnik Awards, which are given to the best young scientists under the age of 42. The fact that MIT nominated Soljačić for the award is a testimony to how much he is appreciated globally. Soljačič's field of study is wireless transfer of energy. He caught the world's attention in 2007 when he conducted an experiment in which he wirelessly transferred energy. His concept, called WiTricity has been deservedly called revolutionary invention by many people. Thanks to him, it seems that we'll soon be able to throw away all those annoying cables and wires needed to charge our laptops, cell phones and house appliances.

Iva Tolić, PhD, is a biophysicist known for her efforts to discover immunity to ageing. The science journal *Cell* put her in the top 40 biologists in the world. She has spent nine years in Germany where she was the leader of a research team at the Max Planck Institute of Molecular Cell Biology and Genetics in Dresden. After that experience of living abroad she decided to return to Croatia. She is of the opinion that viable scientific research can be done in Croatia and that in today's globalised world it isn't about where something is done but how it's done. Tolić has identified the first potentially immortal organism, fission yeast found in African millet beer which gets rejuvenated after each cell division cycle. This discovery could revolutionize the way we treat Alzheimer's disease or Parkinson's disease, and many types of cancer as well. Vernesa Smolčić, PhD, from the Faculty of Science at the University of Zagreb is the first Croatian scientist who was granted 1.5 million euros from the European Research Council for the purpose of researching the growth of stellar mass and growth of the mass of supermassive black holes. Vernesa is also a co-author of an article published in *The Astrophysical Journal* in which she and her colleagues show a reconstruction of the evolution of galaxies in the early universe. For their reconstruction the authors used the data gleaned from various satellites and telescopes and solved the mystery of the history of early and dead galaxies. The story was published in 2014 at the same time in the USA, Denmark, Germany and Croatia.

Speaking of astronomy, it is not well known that our Višnjan Science and Education Center is one of the most famous such centers in the world. It is a true Croatian brand created by Korado Korlević, an amateur astronomer who is one of the top discoverers of minor planets in the world. Thanks to his expertise, knowledge and tenacity and financial support from prestigious scientific institutions from around the world, Višnjan, a small village in Istria has become globally famous. Many vastly richer observatories are envious of Korlević's discoveries and many renowned institutes from around the world are on a constant head hunt for the graduates of the Višnjan School of Astronomy.

There is no doubt that there are many creative people in Croatia. The successes and achievements of our designers, architects, artists, writers and other successful individuals testify to that. This summer, *Grey*, one of the leading global marketing companies, became the majority shareholder of the Croatian creative agency *Bruketa & Žinić*. Thanks to the creative achievements of the creative agency, Zagreb was immediately chosen, alongside Stockholm and Düsseldorf, as a European creative centre of the Grey global network. The designers from Zagreb started collaborating with their colleagues in Milan, Moscow and New York and the newly named *Bruketa&Žinić&Grey* agency expanded the range of its services by recruiting a Croatian digital team for the purpose of forming the core of the new digital shopper hub which will help brands all across Europe through digital communication activities. The *Bruketa&Žinić OM* agency was started back in 1995 by Davor Bruketa and Nikola Žinić, who were college students at the time. Since then the agency has attained the renown on account of being the second most efficient independent advertising agency in the world and winning 450 international awards, which makes it one of the most awarded agencies in Southeast Europe. And all these successes came as a result of hard work and determination to succeed. Sandro Dujmenović and Marko Hrastovec are another pair of Croatian designers that have made their mark in the world. Last year the most famous museum in the world, the Louvre in Paris, changed its visual identity by choosing a new primary typeface authored by the mentioned Croatian duo. Their design was chosen over hundreds of others, made by some of the best design studios in the world.

We always brag about the cultural, artistic and architectural achievements of members of the Croatian diaspora. But, ever more people and companies from Croatia participate in global projects. The 3LHD architectural studio from Zagreb, which designed the magnificent Lone hotel in Rovinj, was given an attractive assignment in China. There, the studio's architects designed one of the most luxurious hotels in China – *LN Garden Resort* in the city of Nansha, at the mouth of the Zhujiang River (Pearl River) in southern China. The Croatian *Lotus Architecti* studio, headed by the architect Maja Bručić, is engaged, in partnership with the Spanish *Barcelona Housing System* company and the global WElink company, in one of the biggest architectural projects in the USA – building a new residential neighborhood in Chicago on U.S. Steel's South Works site, spreading over 12 hectares. The project is worth $4 billion and the Croatian architects will do the most attractive part of the job – architecture and design.

Our hotels, youth hostels, vacation homes, villas and apartments, designed by Croatian designers, attract ever more attention from specialized magazines from all over the world and win ever more awards for architecture and design.

Croatian designer furniture is becoming ever more popular in the world. And winning ever more design awards. Furniture makers like *Prostoria, Dizzconcept* and *Era grupa* employ creative designers and constantly introduce innovations in the design and manufacturing process. In that way they are making this branch of industry more competitive in the global market and show that Croats know how to design and make furniture as opposed to merely felling down trees and selling the logs to Italy or Scandinavia. The mentioned companies and also the *Regular Company* studio from Zagreb attracted a lot of attention at the *Salone Satellite* manifestation in Milan last spring. There is a whole plethora of successful and ever more famous furniture design companies, large and small, in Croatia. Most of them have the potential to become huge on a global level with just a little financial and logistic support from the government.

The successes of Croatian musicians abroad are truly fascinating. The 20-year-old student at the Zagreb Academy of Music Ivan Krpan, a pianist, in 2017 won the first prize at the prestigious Ferruccio Busoni International Piano Festival in Bolzano in Italy. There is no doubt that he is a worthy successor of our globally renowned pianist Ivo Pogorelić. There are others too. The world has also recognised the talent of one of the greatest Croatian classical musicians, the pianist and composer Matej Meštrović. Last spring, *Solopiano.com*, a famous website dedicated to classical music, described Matej's debut album *My Face Music Box* as the best classical music album of all time. His second album, featuring covers of Vivaldi's *The Four Seasons*, performed by Matej and two guest musicians, Matija Dedić and Hakan Ali Toker, won two silver medals at the Global Music Awards competition. We feel proud when foreigners praise the popular Croatia duo 2Cellos. I would be amiss if I didn't mention here our great pianist Maksim Mrvica, who is very popular all over the world, especially in Japan. Goran Višnjić is a household name all over the world. The playwright Tena Štivičić won the 2015 Susan Smith Blackburn prize, the oldest and largest prize awarded to women playwrights writing in the English language. The Croatian actress Zrinka Cvitešić took the London theatre scene by storm and is on her way to Hollywood. Many Croatian filmmakers, comic book artists, designers and artists have achieved global renown... The Croatian creative industries are ever more recognizable in the world... Thousands of awards and prizes won by Croats testify to that. There are hundreds, if not thousands of other creative and innovative Croats I could mention here but then this essay would be thousands of pages long. Still, those few I have mentioned clearly show that Croatia is an inexhaustible pool of talent in all walks of life. And it really should be instantly recognizable as such all over the world. At the moment, however, most people abroad associate the terms "talent" and "Croatia" exclusively with Croatian athletes.

Talented people, their ideas, projects and visions show us that there is a smart and innovative Croatia out there (Smart and innovative Croatia is the slogan of our largest corporate foundation – the Adris Foundation, which is committed to rewarding excellence). We are aware of the fact that when it comes to creativity and innovativeness Croatia has a lot of potential and the ability to realize that potential. We can be proud of that. The individuals I have mentioned above, by their own example, prove that the sky is the limit if one is prepared to work hard and follow his or her star no matter what, that the Croatian spirit is dashing and unbreakable and that no obstacle, no matter how daunting, can ever be an excuse to give up. And, again, there are many more talented people in Croatia equally committed to following their stars and pursuing excellence. But let us not fool ourselves. Luck also plays a determining role in one's success and failure. For that reason the factor of luck in the equation of success (or rather failure) should be minimized as much as possible. Therefore, state institutions should encourage and reward excellence. Young creative, talented and innovative people should be helped in their pursuit of excellence and upheld as role models for younger generations. The Croatian media space is awash with old stars, Croatian, Serbian and Bosnian of show business that have never been successful outside of Yugoslavia and politicians clinging to the practice of falsifying history for the purpose of glorifying the Communist party, which they, or their parents, used to be members of. It is as though the state run media in Croatia is desperately trying to cling to the defunct ideology of unity of all Slav peoples through venerating those who used to sing praises to Comrade Tito or to those who put Croatian patriots in jail on his behalf. Yugoslavia is dead and we should not sacrifice our talented, creative and innovative people at the altar of that failed state. The time we live in presents us with challenges only young, talented and creative individuals can help us overcome. They keep the faith in our own potential, values, knowledge and creativity alive, they are our beacon of hope. They can lead Croatia into the 21st century and make Croatia successful in today's globalised world. They, their stories and achievements should be the focus of media attention, and not our politicians whose only goal is to destroy Croatian society in loving memory of their Communist role models. Even if our politicians were not the despicable characters that they are, they couldn't do that much to improve the image of Croatia abroad. Not even politicians in the most powerful countries in the world are capable of that. For that reason, Croatian state institutions, if they care about Croatia's future and image in the world, should start recognizing those with a vision and willingness to realize that vision for the benefit of all Croats. They should also start rewarding excellence and work toward keeping talented people in Croatia. Only innovativeness and creativity can generate profit, create jobs and increase exports. The creative industries put countries on the map nowadays. In that sense, only a Croatia that is innovative and creative can attract talented and educated people. The more talented and educated people we have in Croatia, the more secure the future of the country. It is high time the world started recognizing Croatian creativity and inventiveness instead of marveling only at our coast which we did not toil for but simply inherited. The world should appreciate Croatia on account of what we have created more than on account of the country's natural beauty. In conclusion I'd like to paraphrase the renowned Croatian designer Boris Ljubičić – it's time we showed the world that what is Croatian is different, good, beautiful, worldly and yet always Croatian!

Croatian Sports Gene

Power of sport in the context of promoting Croatia

There are not that many countries in the world where sport is an integral and indelible part of the national identity and image. Croatia is one such country. Most people, in all corners of the world, have heard about some, or all successful Croatian athletes and therefore the image of the country is shaped, in large measure, by the successes of Croatian individual athletes, clubs and national teams. The Croatian national identity, by the same token, is forged in the collective emotional charge born out of successful, or sometimes less so, performances of Croatian athletes. Whenever a Croatian team or athlete competes in any given international competition, the whole nation is on the edge of their seats or on their feet, passionately invoking all the gods that ever existed to lead the team or athlete to victory. In this particular sense it is important to mention that Croatia, despite the fact that there is no concerted and systematic effort by the state to promote and encourage sporting talent and financially support sporting associations, sports clubs and national teams, is an inexhaustible well of talented and successful athletes. Obviously, there is something in the national gene pool that makes Croats good at sports. There is not a sport in which we do not have talented and successful athletes. Croatia is a small country and the government is not interested in developing the sports industry and supporting young talented aspiring athletes. In that sense all those numerous successes of Croatian athletes and teams constitute a true sporting miracle.

The list of Croatian sports stars is seemingly inexhaustible. Let's see, for example, how successful Croatia has been in sports during the last 20 years – since 1998, when the Croatian national football team won third place in the World Cup in France. The celebrated Croatian tennis player Goran Ivanišević, leaning towards the end of his career, won the Wimbledon singles title in 2001. Janica Kostelić reigned supreme in alpine skiing for years – five time world champion, overall world cup winner three times, winner of three gold medals and one silver medal at the Olympic Games in Salt Lake City in 2002 and winner of one gold medal and one silver medal at the Olympic Games in 2006 in Torino. Thanks to these successes, Zagreb hosts the Snow Queen race – men's and women's slalom – as part of the World Cup skiing circuit. The event is one of the most popular races of the circuit because the track is located only 20 minutes' drive away from the city center. The high jumper Blanka Vlašić won the world championship in 2007 again in 2009. She also won the gold medal at the World Indoor Championship in 2008 and again in 2010 and 2011.

The Croatian handball national team won the World Cup in 2003 and the gold medal at the Olympic Games in Athens in 2004. The Croatian water polo national team won the gold medal at the 2012 Olympics, the World Cup in 2007 and the European Championships in 2010. The alpine skier Ivica Kostelić won the combined World Cup title in 2011 and 2012. The discus thrower Sandra Perković won the gold medal at the Olympic Games in London in 2012 and again at the Olympic Games in 2016 in Rio de Janeiro. She is a two-time world champion – 2013 in Moscow and 2017 in London and four-time European champion. She also won the IAAF Diamond League 6 years in a row – from 2012 to 2017. Giovanni Cernogoraz won the Olympic gold medal in men's trap at the 2012 Summer Olympic Games in London. 2014 was marked by Marin Čilić's victory at US Open. Croatian athletes and teams won 10 medals at the Olympic Games in Rio de Janeiro in 2016, five of them gold. The successes of the Croatian athletes and teams at the Olympic Games in Rio de Janeiro in 2016 placed the country in 17th place of the most successful sporting nations per capita…

Luka Modrić has won 4 Champion League titles with Real Madrid – in the 2013/14, 2015/16, 2016/17 and 2017/18 seasons. In 2015, he made the FIFA FIFPro World 11. For four consecutive years he was in the UEFA Champions League Squad of the Season and in 2017 he received the Golden Ball Award as the best player at the 2017 Club World Cup. And then, in 2018 at the World Cup in Russia, he won the 2018 FIFA World Cup Golden Ball Award for the best player of the tournament. Also, he was named the UEFA Men's Player of the Year for 2017-18, edging out Cristiano

Ronaldo and Mohamed Salah, the leading candidates for the award. And finally, in the fall of 2018 FIFA named him the best player of the year. Modrić is arguably one of the greatest Croatian athletes of all time and definitely the best Croatian football player in the history of the sport. Nations larger in territory and more developed than Croatia can only dream of having such sporting successes.

Many world media outlets, like the BBC for example, wonder what the secret of the Croatian successes in sport is and what the world can learn from the Croats. *The Independent* has also tried to discover the secret. It is clear that the world is fascinated, in the context of sport, by our small nation and its ability to dream big and make the dreams happen. *The Independent* wrote that Croatia should serve as a role model to many nations in the world because talent, hard work, unity and a healthy dose of luck could launch a country on a path to success.

After the group phase at the World Cup in Russia, in which the Croatian national team had defeated all three rivals, including the mighty Argentina by three goals to nil, the German *Bild* magazine wrote that the "Croatia is the greatest sports country in the world". The article in the German magazine goes on to assert that Croatia has earned the status of the greatest sports nation in the world by its successes in various sports – water polo, tennis, handball and many others. The author of the article then points out the fact that Croatia is a small country with a population of 4.2 million, just slightly over than the population of Berlin (3.2 million). Only two days after the publication of the article, Marin Čilić defeated Novak Đoković in the final at Queens Club while Borna Čorić won the tournament in Halle, defeating the "undefeatable" Roger Federer. As a result of the defeat Roger Federer lost his world number one ranking.

It is not surprising that the most common association with Croatia, after natural beauty, tourism and the odd cultural monument, is sport. In 1998, when Croatia won third place at the World Cup in France and Davor Šuker, the side's principal striker, won the Golden Boot Award, everyone around the world, including the remotest of places, knew about Croatia, Davor Šuker and the checkered jerseys. The World Cup in France in 1998 was the first World Cup tournament Croatia as an independent state participated in. When the tournament started, many people considered the Croatian side, managed by the redoubtable Miroslav Ćiro Blažević, an underdog. When the Croatian national team reached the semifinal stage, having displayed marvelous football skills in the previous five games, everyone knew different. And everyone, at that time, respected not only the Croatian national football team but the nation as a whole. The World Cup in France in 1998 received more media coverage than any previous World Cup tournament. Croatian checkered jerseys were selling like crazy all over the world. The players comprising the Croatian national team became household names and media darlings all over the globe. At home, they were national heroes. When the team returned to Croatia, the players were greeted by about 80,000 fans. The summer of '98 was the summer of Croatia. Football fans around the world were enchanted by Miroslav Blažević's charisma, the team's eye-pleasing but still highly effective style of football and likeable Croatian supporters who travelled to France. Sports editors and sports correspondents from the largest world TV stations and newspapers were on a mission to score an interview with a Croatian player. In the absence of that, any story about Croatia was printable and any TV segment featuring Croatia desirable. All of a sudden, media space was awash with stories about the political situation in Croatia, tourism, Croatian history, culture... The world was thirsty for all things Croatian, courtesy of the Croatian national football team. People abroad stopped perceiving Croatia in terms of the disturbing imagery of the recently ended war. Suddenly, Croatia was not "that war-torn country" anymore, but "that great footballing nation". The success of the Croatian national football team, it is not unreasonable to claim, created Croatia's tourism industry as we know it today. Football, in today's world, is a continuation of politics by other means.

Fast-forward five World Cup tournaments and the Croatian national team was again pushing Croatia into the global limelight. There's are two slight, but at the same time rather significant differences between the World Cup in Russia 2018 and that in France in 1998 in the context of the Croatian national team. The first difference is that in Russia the Croatian national team made it to the final. The second difference is that back in 1998 the world wasn't nearly as globalised as it is today. The new media did not exist, broadband technologies were in their infancy and things like Facebook and Twitter were unimaginable. Therefore, Croatia benefited from the success of the Croatian national team in 2018 exponentially more than from the success of the national team in 1998.

As soon as the Croatian national team beat the host country Russia and qualified for the semifinals, all major TV stations around the globe started airing reports about the Croatian national football team and Croatia. More important still, a huge number of content regarding Croatia and the success of its national football team was uploaded to YouTube. Billions of people were exposed 24/7 first to stories and opinions, all of them positive, about the manager Zlatko Dalić and his prodigious charges, and shortly thereafter to stories, also all of them positive, about Croatia and the Croatian President Kolinda Grabar Kitarović who travelled to Russia to support, wearing a Croatian jersey, the national team. The whole thing immediately reached global proportions. Far more people around the world rooted for Croatia in the final game than for its nemesis, France (Croatia also lost the semifinal game against France in 1998). And billions of people around the world learned more about Croatia in the last week of the World Cup in Russia than they had in their whole lives previously. They learned about our values, way of life, history, tourism. Croatia was, for the first time in its history, presented to the world in all its glory. The Croatian footballers, with their skill, determination, professionalism, bravery and humility did more in a month in terms of promoting the true nature of Croatia than the Croatian diplomacy, tourist industry and academic community combined since the country gained independence in 1991. For a month being a Croat was arguably the most beautiful thing in the world. Social networks were awash with comments glorifying Croats and Croatia. The German *Bild* magazine wrote: "A raging fire burns in the eyes of the Croatian football players, fueling their desire and determination to win." The story continued to state that the Croatian footballers' thirst for victory was otherworldly, their demeanor authentic and that they were humble in victory and gracious in defeat.

Millions of football fans, from Alaska to New Zealand, from Tierra del Fuego to the north-easternmost reaches of Russia, typed the word "Croatia" into Google, trying to find out as much as they could about the country that had reached the final of the World Cup. Everyone working in the promotion industry knows how hard it is to catch and hold people's attention. There's a sea of information out there and people are bombarded with advertisements every second. The Croatian national team managed to pull off that task with flying colors. The Croatian football players actually motivated millions of people across the globe to educate themselves about Croatia.

According to some estimates, more stories about Croatia were published in 12 hours following the quarter final victory over Russia than in three years previously. By the end of the tournament more content had been aired and posted about Croatia than during the 28 years of the country's existence. Again, the Croatian national team generated more interest about Croatia than all other Croatian athletes, politicians, business men, tourist workers and all others combined.

The Croatian national team in Russia created one of the most beautiful stories of Croatian sport and of Croatian history, one that will never die or be forgotten, as long as there are people in the world. The success of the Croatian national team transcends the confines of sport. It is a watershed moment of seismic proportions. Nothing will ever be the same in Croatia and never again will the image of Croatia abroad be held hostage by venal and malicious people, both foreign and homegrown.

The Croatian footballers showed, by their own example, the true meaning of perseverance, hard work, discipline, genuine patriotism, humility and responsibility... This Croatian sporting fairytale enchanted the whole world. It's a modern story of David and Goliath. Most punters wrote off Croatia before the Argentina game, and then again before the Russia game. Almost everybody did that before the England game – the experts on ESPN and ITV with scorn bordering on disdain. The Croatian national team shut them all up and made them eat their words, inspiring millions of people around the world in the process. Everyone talked about the fighting spirit, courage and tenacity of the Croatian football players. And many projected those traits onto Croatian society as a whole and identified with our small and inspiring country, especially before the matches against Argentina, Russia, England and finally France (the game Croatia lost due to a few, masterfully exploited by the French team, to be sure, oversights by the referee). Practically overnight Croatia gained valuable and influential friends from the world of show business, politics, economy... Millions of people around the world were inspired by the dream the Croatian national team was living. Small wonder, because all of those inspired by the story of the Croatian national team in Russia actually took the time to learn about the life-stories of the Croatian players. And most of those stories read like scripts for Hollywood films – coming of age during the Croatian War of Independence, training during air-raid alerts, living in constant fear of being blown to bits by a missile or a shell but still chasing the dream of becoming a professional football player. Truly, this is the stuff of legend. The Croatian football players serve as role models to all those who dare to dream of and aspire to greatness, regardless of their current circumstances. They show us all that dedication, commitment, faith, unity, patriotism and adherence to moral values is a sure recipe for successes, in all walks of life.

The media coverage and exposure Croatia got as a result of the Croatian national team's successes would cost billions of euros to duplicate. However, the point is really moot because there exists nothing of the same magnitude that would provoke enough interest on which such coverage and exposure could be based. Therefore, what the Croatian football players did in terms of promoting the country is truly priceless. It has to be pointed out that underscoring the phenomenon of the Croatian national team and everything its success entails is the game of football itself. Only football can stop the world from turning. Only football can bring unbridled joy to the masses. Football, as an industry, is, to borrow a line from a famous film, bigger than U.S. Steel. Football is culture, economy, politics. It's a force that shapes national identities. As I have already stated, football is a continuation of politics by other means.

Croatian flags were still waving proudly in the country, two months after the end of the World Cup. It is easy, and tempting, to identify with those who are powerful and successful. And the Croatian football players who won the silver medal at the World Cup are powerful and successful. They are the panacea for all the country's ills. They are our light at the end of the tunnel. They are our pride and joy not only because they reached the final but also because football fans all over the world agree that Croatia was the better team in the match.

Not everybody jumped on the Croatian bandwagon though. Undoubtedly there were many football fans in Argentina and England, and many Russian football fans, whose enthusiasm for the game was dashed by the Croatian national team's victories. "Who are these damn Croats and how dare they embarrass us in front of the world like that?" posted an English fan on his Facebook profile after the semifinal game. His post, brimming with bitterness and shock, encapsulates the English perception of the footballing reality and of the new balance of footballing power in Europe. England is the birthplace of football and English fans believe that the nation is long overdue for a World Cup success. They may be right, they may be wrong, but it is clear that it is palatable to them to have their hopes dashed by Germany, Argentina or Italy, and completely unacceptable and traumatizing to lose to Croatia. This condescending attitude actually perfectly mirrors the political attitude of the powerful European states towards the newly formed countries in the Balkans. Croatia has often been a victim of that attitude and the deals made behind closed doors that perpetuated it. In that sense, many people in Croatia considered the victory of the Croatian national team over England in the semifinals as exacting a just revenge on the perfidious Albion, echoing the Argentinian sentiments from 1986 when God punished the British for defeating the Argentines in the Falklands War by giving a lend of His hand to Maradona.

Reaching the final of the biggest single-event sport competition in the world (200 countries participated in the qualifying stages and 32 at the final tournament) is a huge success and as such has an overwhelming therapeutic effect on Croatian society. The Croatian national team improved the nation's collective self-esteem and injected much needed positive energy into the fabric of society. Without positive energy and high self-esteem there is no economic growth and no social changes for the better. Other countries have spent years investing a lot of money and effort into campaigns to bolster national pride, create a healthier society, change negative aspects of their national mentality and boost economic growth. Croatia, on the other hand, has the best campaign imaginable to achieve everything mentioned above, courtesy of the Croatian national football team.

The climax of the Croatian football fairytale happened on July 16, 2018 – the date unofficially now considered the new holiday of Croatian unity – when 550,000 people greeted the

Croatian national team players upon their return home from Russia. Many Croats traveled to Croatia from all corners of the globe for the occasion. Endless rows of people lining the route the open top bus carrying the players to the city centre took from the airport; thousands more congesting the city centre; the players climbing the stage prepared for them in the city center and signing with the crowd; partying on the streets of the capital long into the night – these images were shown all over the world, leaving everyone who saw them emotionally charged and elated. Only the proud Croats can organize a spectacle like that, wrote many foreign newspapers. It was the largest gathering of Croats after John Paul II's visit to Croatia in 1994 and the most magnificent welcome ever. Zlatko Dalić, Luka Modrić, Danijel Subašić, Mario Mandžukić, Ivan Rakitić, Ante Rebić, Dejan Lovren, Domagoj Vida, Ivan Strinić, Ivan Perišić, Andrej Kramarić, Šime Vrsaljko, Marcelo Brozović, Marko Pjaca, Milan Badelj, Josip Pivarić, Mateo Kovačić, Vedran Ćorluka and others became new national heroes.

Nine million Croats scattered all across the globe stood as one during and after the World Cup. And the spirit of unity, national pride and hope returned to Croatia, exorcising pessimism and toxic tribalism. This new sense of optimism imbuing the nation could create an avalanche of positive changes. It definitely forces all of us to strive for excellence, demand results from our leaders, walk with our heads held high and never again think of ourselves as small and inconsequential in the scheme of things. God helps those who dare dream big – and then nothing is impossible.

The 21st century does not belong to territorially big countries with large populations – concluded the American professor and diplomat Joseph Nye – but to those who posses soft power, that is, the ability to attract and seduce. Croatia, finally, is beginning to use its soft power, even if it may not be fully aware of it.

About the Author

Božo Skoko, PhD, is a professor at the Faculty of Political Science of the University of Zagreb. The areas of his scientific research include: communication, international relations, national identity and image and destination branding. He is a long-time strategic communication consultant and co-founder of *Millenium promocija*, the leading Croatian public relations agency. He is a former journalist and editor at Croatian Radiotelevision (HRT). He is the author of *Kakvi su Hrvati (What Are the Croats Like?), Hrvatski velikani (Croatian Greats), Hrvatska i susjedi: Kako Hrvatsku doživljavaju građani i mediji u Bosni i Hercegovini, Crnoj Gori, Makedoniji, Sloveniji, i Srbiji (Croatia and Its Neighbors - How Croatia Is Perceived in Bosnia and Herzegovina, Montenegro, Macedonia, Slovenia and Serbia), Država kao brend (The State as a Brand), Hrvatska – Identitet, image i promocija (Croatia – Identity, Image, Promotion)* and *Priručnik za razumijevanje odnosa s javnošću (Handbook for Understanding Public Relations)*. He has also written over forty scientific papers on public relations, the media and managing the identity and image of Croatia.

Made in the USA
San Bernardino,
CA